A POPULAR DICTIONARY OF
SPIRITUALISM

13674

NORMAN BLUNSDON

A Popular Dictionary of Spiritualism

★

1961
ARCO PUBLICATIONS
LONDON

FIRST PUBLISHED BY ARCO PUBLICATIONS 1962

PRINTED IN GREAT BRITAIN BY
TAYLOR GARNETT EVANS AND CO. LTD
LONDON AND WATFORD

PREFACE

To meet the challenge of the large number of intelligent people who are investigating the claims of the Spiritualist hypothesis, it has become increasingly necessary to have a common interpretation of the various terms used in Spiritualism and psychical research.

The need for an up-to-date directory covering all the words used in every aspect of psychic philosophy and phenomena has been apparent for many years. Many have thought of compiling such a dictionary, but this is the first time that thought has been translated into action.

It is with great satisfaction, therefore, that we now have this dictionary which can be used as a standard of explanation to satisfy the need of all inquirers. This directory is a credit to the compiler, a monument to his study and diligence, and earns our congratulations.

ERIC W. STUART
President, The Spiritualist Association of Great Britain Ltd.
(Formerly the Marylebone Spiritualist Association).

INTRODUCTION

I n compiling this dictionary it has been my constant aim to simplify terms often puzzling to those unacquainted with Spiritualism and its phenomena, and also to guide those who either wish, or are beginning, to investigate this amazing subject for themselves.

Many words and terms current in Spiritualistic thought and literature require a somewhat wider treatment than that usually given by standard dictionaries. Terms common perhaps to the new science of parapsychology or psychical research, are still a little strange to the average layman inquirer. All those which relate to the subject, I have tried to define in the clearest and most direct language. This has been no easy task, because Spiritualism has no well-defined creed or accepted set of beliefs; opinions differ on many new, and therefore controversial themes in discussion. Spiritualism's outlook is really akin to that of science itself; the need for further knowledge is felt and sought, to add to or modify if necessary, the existing foundations of its beliefs.

Unlike that excellent and monumental work *The Encyclopaedia of Psychic Science* by Dr Nandor Fodor, this work includes many terms more properly relating to the various religions, yoga and theosophy, as I find them of frequent occurrence during discussion among Spiritualists and inquirers. While this may seem to be 'trespassing', it must be remembered that Spiritualists are essentially students; seekers after knowledge from any possible source which may provide further evidence of man's psychic propensities. At the same time I have made the source of these terms clear to avoid the charge of linking them with Spiritualist belief.

Having mentioned Spiritualist belief, I will presently try to

7

state briefly the main outlines upon which I would venture to say there is general agreement. It should be borne in mind, however, that as a religion in its own right, Spiritualism is still in the teething stages; not yet coherent in its entirety perhaps, but groping still towards a fuller understanding of man's place in the universe. For the rapid progress of science in every field has now brought mankind to the brink of a materialistic precipice! Nineteenth-century materialism has had a severe shaking: matter becomes ever more indefinable in concrete terms: people are searching again to discover a new basis for ethical values, in place of old religious creeds which have lost face under the searching ray of science.

We appear to be in danger from stupendous new forces released by nuclear energy techniques. People are beginning to ask: 'Does the scientist know where we are going?' Yet the spate of invention continues—inexorable and mostly incomprehensible to the mind of the average person. New ideologies are gaining ground in huge sections of the earth's population, and are ousting religion as outworn superstition.

The shackles of 2,000 years are being rapidly loosed. Like a young virile giant, a new era is being born with a monstrous power potential—to raise humanity to unimaginable heights of achievement, or to shatter it utterly! Is there anywhere a stable foundation of decency to which one can appeal—a rational base which, while not outraging the mind of an intelligent person, can lend support to the basic contentions of the great moral reformers like Jesus, Mohammed, Gandhi—to love one another, the certainty of God, survival after death?

Belief in Spiritualism, it is claimed, is based upon the demonstrable facts of mediumship, and through this channel, the accumulated evidence for the survival of the personality of each human individual. The knowledge so gained by one's personal experiences gradually builds a logical conviction that man is a spiritual being, and that the earthly trial is only a small part of some vaster existence. A seemingly infinite path of spiritual endeavour and progress unfold themselves, to infuse life with new purpose and a sense of spiritual kinship with God, the First Cause—call it what you will.

Perhaps Spiritualism is unique among religions in having its phenomena verified by some of the greatest scientists of the age. Certain persons it has been established, possess psychic powers, that is: powers which cannot all as yet be explained by any single known hypothesis except that of spirit survival. These people, known as 'mediums' in Spiritualism, can bring convincing personal evidence of survival to the persistent and open-minded inquirer. The first step may thus be taken: death is not extinction. What of the future life?

I would sum up the present Spiritualist theory as follows: by these same means of communication, through the mediumship of a psychic person, one learns of future states of being, and of certain 'laws' of spirit contact. That 'like attracts like', or that it is our wishes and inner desires which are operative forces in the spirit state of existence, and it is these mental qualities which determine our contacts. Here it seems, we have the oft-preached 'love one another' and 'do unto each other' principle, not as an impossible ideal, but shown to be a practical part of the system in which we are placed.

By not loving, we are opposed to the system, it leads to individual isolation and loneliness in future states. Thus the only 'punishment' is self-inflicted. On the other hand, by conforming *in heart* to the main principles (common to most religions), we are actually drawing nearer to those who reciprocate, reflect, and mutually assist mankind's spiritual evolution.

It is characteristic of ancient eastern philosophies to describe this earthly life of ours as illusory, or 'Maya'. In the light of Spiritualism's revelations would it not rather correspond to the Formation School? Where we as the children, may sometimes break the furniture to relieve the tedium of our studies, but where little real harm can be done. The arrangement of the universe would seem to be under wiser guidance than man's, and perhaps our infantile violence is viewed with the tolerance shown by a loving father towards his children. Thus we can be reconciled through reason, to the basic tenets of religious belief.

In this book it is possible to find the confirmatory evidence for the phenomena of Spiritualism, as gathered from many sources by psychical researchers, scientists and eminent people from all walks of life. Anybody can test for themselves the value of survival evidence by sitting with reputable mediums, although it is not recommended that the more spectacular phenomena, materialization, etc., should be sought, as it is comparatively rare and sometimes imitated by unscrupulous persons. However, the testimony for this phenomenon is particularly strong by reason of the many thorough studies of physical phenomena under laboratory conditions by such reputable scientists as Sir William Crookes, Sir Oliver Lodge, Russell Wallace and many others whose careful and precise reports can still be read.

Psychic powers, Extra Sensory Perception and mediumship are *facts*—one may depend on that. It is up to each person to *use* these facts to convince themselves of survival; the first step to understanding, for those with no religious beliefs, heartwarming for those who already have faith but lack knowledge. From there, each may build for himself the sense of certainty of man's 'Divine spark' and the mission of service for humanity which is unceasing.

We are spirits *now*, and by our intentions we are sensed by other spirits both here and in the next stage of existence. All this provides a motive for co-operation and friendly feeling; for the breaking down of national barriers with their shortsighted aims at world supremacy; the realization that death is not to be dreaded, but is the door to further progress; to joyful reunion with kindred spirits who, when free from earthly encumbrances can the more perfectly express their divinity.

In addition to terms and words current in Spiritualist thought, the names of many well-known people connected with the movement, are included, also references in the Reading Guide (page 237) to literature of all kinds which bear at all upon

Spiritualism. Names appear of eminent psychical researchers and some authors, perhaps not eminent in their own right, but believing themselves to be inspired or moved, as were the Biblical prophets. For Spiritualists think that God's revelation is continuous throughout the ages; the message essentially the same but varying according to man's need and level of progress.

I offer this book in the hope that it may to some, prove to be a first stepping-stone, and that it may kindle here and there a desire for further study of this knowledge which I think could enlighten and guide this all too materialistic age.

I acknowledge and pay full tribute to all those who have assisted me, including the many literary sources upon which I have drawn freely, notably: *Encyclopaedia of Psychic Science* by Dr Nandor Fodor (Arthurs Press); *Facts of Psychic Science and Philosophy* by Campbell Holms (Kegan Paul); *Law of Evidence* by J. P. Taylor (Sweet and Maxwell); *Modern Experiments in Telepathy* by Dr S. G. Soal and F. Bateman (Faber and Faber); *Phenomena of Spiritualism* lecturettes (Spiritualists' National Union); *Rock of Truth* by J. Arthur Findlay (Psychic Press); *More Light on the Dead Sea Scrolls* by Millar Burrows (Secker and Warburg).

A POPULAR DICTIONARY
OF SPIRITUALISM

Aberration   A deviation from the normal.

Absent Healing   Healing through the intercession of a healing medium (often but not always assisted by a dedicated group), to spirit doctors on behalf of patients who have no direct contact with the medium. Patients are often unaware that they are being treated, more especially if they are ignorant or known to be hostile to Spiritualism. The aim is to benefit the patient spiritually, mentally and physically if possible, but no promises are given. These healers receive many postal applications for healing, mostly from concerned relatives of sick people.

Academia de Estudo Psychicos 'Cesar Lombroso'   The Cesar Lombroso Academy for Psychical Research founded in São Paulo 1919. Investigated the outstanding mediumship of Mirabelli (q.v.) during 392 sittings, with extraordinary results.

Adare, Lord   Son of the Earl of Dunraven, author and friend of famous medium Daniel Douglas Home (q.v.).

Additor   A modified ouija board (q.v.) with a little hollow box and pointer. The box is supposed to conserve psychic power, as would a cabinet used for materialization phenomena.

Adept   An occult title representative of the highest attainment on this earth by an Initiate, with conscious and complete mastery of psychic powers. Sometimes associated with the Great White Brotherhood who are supposed to exert a guiding influence over mankind. The highest stage of Yoga (q.v.).

Theosophists understand it to be the passing of the fifth stage of initiation.

Adventist   One who believes in the second coming of Jesus the Christ.

Affinities   According to reincarnation theories, one person's destiny may be bound to another's throughout many earth lives. If they are fond of each other, an extremely close bond of affection is said to be formed which transcends death and the possible alternation of sex. These two are then said to be 'affinities'.

Afflatus   Inspiration drawn upon. An aura of divine origin.

'Afid'   Well-known control of Mrs Blanche Cooper (q.v.) English Direct Voice medium, who gave test sittings to Dr S. G. Soal during 1921–22. Her other control was 'Nada'.

Agent   In psychical research, one who acts as the transmitter in telepathic communications.

Agnostic   Scepticism of the unknown. One who denies the possibility of proving or disproving anything beyond material phenomena.

Ahimsa   The Hindu doctrine of non-violence, used as a political expedient by Gandhi.

'Aimee'   Well-known female control of Arthur Colman, English materialization medium. After his death this control was also claimed by F. F. Craddock, another English medium.

Akashic Records   An occult term said to be a cosmic picture gallery and record of every thought, feeling and action since the world began. Often advanced as an explanation of clairvoyant and psychometric perceptions. Somewhat akin to the idea of Cosmic Consciousness (q.v.). Yogis believe that this record can be contacted when in certain psychic states of consciousness. Reference should be made to the Moberley and Jourdain case (q.v.).

Aksakov, Alex N. Pioneer Spiritualist and psychic researcher of Russia; an Imperial Councillor to the Czar. Was greatly influenced by Swedenborg and A. J. Davis. Translated many important works of psychical research (1832–1903).

Alchemy Early chemistry, concerned with the search for the 'philosopher's stone', a substance which, it was believed, would possess the power of converting base elements into gold.

Alleyne, John (Captain Allen Bartlett, 1861–1933) The medium responsible for part of the Glastonbury scripts (q.v.), as a result of which the lost Edgar and Loretto chapels of the abbey were discovered. Frederick Bligh Bond made the necessary excavations and proved the truth of the statements.

Altruism Sacrifice of self for others, a doctrine in keeping with much of Spiritualism's teachings.

American Institute for Scientific Research Founded by Dr Hyslop in New York 1906 to investigate abnormal psychology and psychical research. This last section later became known as the American Society for Psychical Research (independent).

American Psychical Institute and Laboratory Founded by Dr Hereward Carrington, the noted American researcher in New York 1920. Many scientists of international repute were on the advisory council.

American Society for Psychical Research (A.S.P.R.) Founded Boston 1885, dissolved and re-established under Dr Hyslop

(*American Institute q.v.*), still in existence today, its publications are 'Proceedings' and 'Journal'.

Amnesia A gap or loss in one's memory. It often occurs during trance states of mediums, the amount of material forgotten depending upon the depth of trance in each case.

Anaesthesia Loss of the sense of feeling, exhibited sometimes by mediums in the trance state, has often been demonstrated. The extent varies from slight to complete loss of sensation. Anaesthetics have been used to induce clairvoyance, notably nitrous oxide in experiments conducted by Dr N. Jeans, and the use of peyotl and mescalin by certain Amazonian tribes.

Analgesia Loss of feeling, insensibility to pain. *See* **Anaesthesia.**

Andrade, Mme Spanish physical medium, an uneducated peasant, the subject of a long series of experiments by Dr d'Oliveira Feijao, Professor of Surgery at Lisbon University. He became convinced of the reality of psychic phenomena.

Angel Essentially a messenger from a higher realm; easily identifiable with the more noble of the guides and controls known to Spiritualism. In this sense they would be true 'spiritual intermediaries' (Nuttall's) between the hierarchies of spirit and the earth world. When seen clairvoyantly they are usually described as robed and shining, of either sex but devoid of wings.

Animal Magnetism The name given to most psychic phenomena, prior to the advent of modern Spiritualism in 1848. *See* **Mesmerism, Emanations.**

Animals, Survival of Much information concerning animals has been given through mediums. They are capable of psychic faculties similar to man's own and there is much evidence of their survival, although it seems as if this may be conditioned by the amount of affection the animal has received on earth. According to some accounts (F. W. H. Myers through the hand of Miss G. Cummins), the evolutionary scale determines the extent of individualization possible, and therefore an animal low down on the scale is overshadowed by a 'Group Soul' to which its spirit returns on death. It would seem to depend upon how much individual consciousness the animal has achieved during its earth life, for it is this part only which survives.

Animism   The theory that all objects have a natural life and are linked to a separately existing immaterial soul, is supported by evidence from communicating entities and the psychometric faculty. It has been advanced as a counter theory to spirit survival by Alex. Aksakov (q.v.) in his three-point hypothesis ('Animism and Spiritism'), and supposes that the medium's spirit is alone responsible for the phenomena.

Anthropoflux   The researches of E. K. Muller, Engineer of Zurich and Director of Salus Institute for Nervous Disorders, demonstrated the existence of an emanation from the human body which can decrease the resistance in an electrical circuit. These experiments were verified by Professor Farny of the Zurich Polytechnicum, who coined the term. He established that the maximum emission is from the inner surfaces of the left hand fingers. It also appears in the breath. *See* **Emanations.**

Anthropomorphic   The conception of Deity in the form of a man.

Anthroposophy   Man's knowledge. Usually refers to the occult system of philosophy as taught by the Anthroposophical Society founded by Rudolph Steiner. It aims to liberate man from selfishness by the development of his responses to the subtler natural influences. Emphasis is placed on the significance of colour and rhythm.

Apocryphal Of unknown or doubtful authorship.

Apparition A supernormal appearance which suggests the presence of a person living or dead. From extensive research, it would appear to be of most common occurrence when special anxiety and the desire to send an urgent message concurs with physical extremity on the part of the agent. *See* **Ghosts.**

Apports The entry of objects by seeming penetration of matter: one of the most astounding examples of physical phenomena. According to spirit communicators, objects are first 'dematerialized', then reassembled in the seance room. Many witnesses testify to the interesting fact that the articles are often hot on arrival. Flowers, live animals and birds have been apported at various times, but it is a rare phenomenon. The apporting of human beings is termed 'transportation' (q.v., and *see* **Mrs Guppy**). Some of the most wonderful apport cases were received through the mediumship of Mme d'Esperance.

Aquarian Age An astronomical epoch which will be occasioned by the entry of the Vernal equinox into the constellation Aquarius in about A.D. 2740. This is due to the phenomenon of precession, a very slow revolution of the pole of the earth round that of the ecliptic once every 26,000 years, changing the relationships of the signs to the constellations. Therefore approximately 2,000 years are spent by the vernal point in each constellation. As the present epoch is towards the end of constellation Pisces, this is taken by many as showing a special esoteric link with the past 2,000 years of Christianity, and it is said that we are on the brink of a new age which will be characterized by the astrological qualities of the sign Aquarius. This is illogical since it is the constellations which are being traversed by the signs which are the significators.

Arcana That which is hidden. Mysteries and secrets.

18

Ariola, Pepito   Spanish musical prodigy introduced in 1900 to the International Psychic Congress by Professor Richet. Although Pepito was only three and a half, his tiny hands grew as he played the piano enabling him to stretch full octaves.

Aristotle   (384–322 B.C.)   Greek founder of Peripatetic school of philosophy. A pupil of Plato and tutor of Alexander the Great. One of the truly great minds of the past, he wrote treatises on metaphysics, logic, politics, ethics and natural history. He believed in a primordial principle to which 'the gods' were subordinated. Famous teacher of the golden mean, the path between two extremes.

Arithmancy   Divination by the use of numbers.

Ars Geomantica   Or Art of Punctation, a method of divination involving the throwing of grains, dice or coins, known since the thirteenth century, once very popular but considered inferior to its eastern counterpart, the I Ching (q.v.).

Asana   The third stage of Yoga. The assumption of bodily postures to assist the development of certain thoughts. There are eighty-four postures.

Ascendant   Astrologically, the degree of ecliptic longitude rising in the east at any given time. Said to be of special significance for any person or thing which comes into being at that moment.

Ascetic   A hermit. Austere, self-denying or disciplinary.

Aspects   Astrologically, angular distance between celestial bodies as viewed from the earth. Various angles are said to promote harmony or otherwise between planetary principles.

Asports   Apport phenomena in reverse; objects disappear from the seance room and reappear elsewhere.

A.S.P.R. American Society for Psychical Research (q.v.).

Astral, The A common abbreviation for the astral sphere or plane of the spirit world.

Astral Body Among Spiritualists, it is commonly used to denote the etheric body or double (q.v.). Theosophists, however, distinguish astral matter which is said to be invisible, from etheric matter which may be visible. To them, the astral body is the 'desire body'.

Astral Light The light natural to the astral sphere, as perceived by clairvoyant sight. Unlike terrestrial light, it proceeds from bodies themselves, and not from a central illumination source like our sun.

Astral Plane In Spiritualism, often synonymous with the etheric plane (q.v.) but in Theosophy it means the plane occupied by the recent dead and non-human nature spirits or 'elementals'.

Astral Projection A state of separation between the physical and etheric bodies in which the cord is still intact. This occurs more often during sleep and the sleeper is usually unconscious. According to Muldoon, the bodies normally move a little out of coincidence during sleep, in order that the double can recharge itself. When run-down or ill, there is more separation than usual, using this fact, a technique can be acquired to accomplish projection at will consciously, and instances are known where information has been brought back and afterwards verified. This faculty offers an explanation of the seeing at a distance by Indian fakirs and witchdoctors.

Astral Shells An occult idea that the etheric body at death is soon discarded, leaving an inner astral or spirit body which continues. The discarded etheric vehicle, they say, may continue to manifest dimly on earth with a repetitive, mechanical intelligence, held to be responsible for hauntings and some apparitions. There is a little support for this theory in the automatic writings of *Letters from Lancelot* by R.M.T.

Astral Sphere   *See* **Astral Plane.**

'Astor'   A control of automatist Hester Dowden; he was intelligent, plain spoken, saw pictures of the future but was indefinite as to time which, he said, could not be measured in his sphere.

Astrology   The art of character delineation and prediction, based on various interpretational systems applied to astronomical data. Not part of Spiritualism, but communicators sometimes refer to it as worthy of study.

Atheism   A disbelief in any deity. Not compatible with Spiritualism.

Atlantis   A mythical civilization said to have sunk beneath the waves of the Atlantic about 10,000 years ago. Some slight evidence for its existence is claimed, notably Plato's reference to the destruction of a great centre of culture about 9500 B.C.

Atman (with capital A)   Hindu conception of the Great Self, identifiable with Brahma the Creator; yet capable of being split into individual egos, or invisible 'Higher selves' (spelt with small **a**).

Atmosphere   Any peculiar quality detected in surrounding conditions is often described as atmosphere by mediums and psychics. There is evidence that a special atmosphere or aura surrounds all living bodies. *See* **Aura** and **Dr Kilner.**

At-onement   Realization of the essential unity with God, the Great Spirit.

Attraction, Law of More commonly spoken of as 'Like attracts like' (q.v.), on the mental level.

Aubert, George French pianist-medium who claimed to play under control of classical composers. He was investigated in 1906 by the Institut Générale Psychologique in Paris, where he played a Mozart sonata perfectly while blindfolded, and his ears plugged with tubes from two gramophones playing separate music simultaneously.

Auditor A therapist of the Scientology system.

Aura A field of radiation round the human body, sometimes visible as bands of colour to clairvoyant sight. Akin to the 'Aureola' emanations spoken of by medieval saints and mystics. Experimental investigations were made by Dr W. J. Kilner of St Thomas's Hospital, London, which led to his invention of coloured screens with slits to render the aura visible to normal sight. There are three main zones: that closest to the body extending $\frac{1}{4}$ to $\frac{1}{2}$ in., corresponding with the etheric double, next to the inner aura, a band of about three inches, then the outer band extending to a foot or more. Dr Kilner found it varied in colour and brilliance during illness and mental or emotional stimulation, shrinking to nothing at the approach of death. Mediums confirm these findings and can often discern impending changes physical and mental by study of a person's aura.

Automatic Painting and Drawing Artistic expression without the medium's conscious volition, sometimes in complete darkness and at great speed. The results vary much in quality and subject: hieroglyphs, visions (*see* William Blake's work), departed relatives, guides have all been depicted. Remarkable evidence has come through this means, usually termed 'psychic art'.

Automatic Speaking Impulsive speech without conscious volition, either in trance or the waking state. Retention of consciousness is possible but unusual. Some very fine oratory has been given, books and poems of great length have been dictated and published.

Automatic Writing Scripts produced without the control of the conscious self. A very common form of psychic activity, but not always true mediumship. It leaves very much room for self-delusion, therefore great caution should be used in its development. In its highest form, it is an excellent channel for teachings from the spirit world. Usually the hand of the medium is controlled and writes at a furious pace without pause for thought, often in an unfamiliar handwriting. The medium can be conscious and otherwise engaged mentally in reading or conversation while the writing progresses. The scripts sometimes exhibit a knowledge far exceeding that of the medium.

Automatism Functioning of the body, not under control of the conscious self. Can be either subconscious self or a discarnate entity. It embraces automatic speaking, writing, drawing, painting, playing musical instruments, dancing, surgical operations. Sensory automatism would include clairvoyance, clairaudience, crystal gazing.

Automatist Properly the medium or operator in automatism, but is usually meant to describe an automatic writing medium.

Autoscope Any mechanical means whereby communication from unknown sources may reach us. Planchette, ouija board, table, etc.

Autoscopy Coined by Feré to describe a vision of one's own double 'in a morbid state' (external autoscopy). To see one's own internal organs is an example of internal autoscopy.

Auto-suggestion Suggestion applied to oneself.

Avotar Hindu word for a 'descent' or incarnation of a deity in human or animal form.

Awareness An exalted state, an expansion of consciousness in which one becomes aware of higher powers or the presence of protective entities. Meditation is often practised as a means of its attainment.

Bahaism A non-ascetic, modern religion recognized by the United Nations. Originally a branch of Islam in the middle nineteenth century. Mirza Ali Muhammed of Persia in 1844 claimed to be the 'Herald of Islam', proclaiming a 'greater One to come'. From then, it diverged from orthodox Islam. Mirza Husaya Ali (1817–92) a former disciple, claimed to be the prophet foretold, and wrote three books of Bahai scripture They believe in upholding the unity of God and his Prophets, that Divine revelation is continuous, that all mankind should be united, but that a Chosen Mouthpiece only is able to bring it about.

Bailey, Charles Australian apport medium and bootmaker. Was private medium to millionaire Thomas Welton Stanford who made a large collection of apports.

Balfour, Earl of (1848–1930.) Eminent student of psychical research. His sister was the wife of Professor Henry Sidgwick, first president of the S.P.R., and became president himself in 1894. His brother, Rt Hon. Gerald W. Balfour, also held the chair and became Earl after his brother's death. He wrote a most important paper on 'Ear of Dionysius' case of cross-correspondence for S.P.R. in Nov. 1916.

Band, Psychic A peculiar sensation of pressure often felt around the head during phases of mediumistic development.

Other sensations like tickling and cobwebs on the face denote psychic operations by unseen workers. The presence of specific entities are often sensed by the signal touch which is characteristic of that personality. Psychic perfumes and lights are used in the same way. A group of spirit helpers often describe themselves as a 'band'.

Band, Spirit A group of spirit people working with a medium to achieve a definite purpose or phase of mediumistic activity. There is usually a 'doorkeeper' who safeguards the medium's body from the spirit side, the chief guide or control who gives instructions to the leader of the circle and others of the 'band' who are co-operating at the time. A medium may exhibit many forms of mediumship and there is usually a specific entity in charge of each form; a spirit doctor for healing, and so on.

Bangs Sisters The Misses Lizzie and May of Chicago, mediums who specialized in direct writing, drawing and painting ink messages produced in sealed envelopes. They were investigated by Hereward Carrington in 1909 and accused of fraud, but were defended by Admiral Moore. In some of their spirit portraits colours were precipitated on the canvas in eight minutes by daylight.

Baraduc's Biometer Constructed by Baraduc to measure nervous force and unknown vibrations connected with the human body.

Baraduc, Hippolyte French psychic researcher who experimented with thought photography. He claimed to have proved that something misty and vaporous leaves the human body at death. Inventor of the Biometer. He published several books.

Barbanell, Maurice Editor *Two Worlds*. Author of several books on psychic subjects, the last being *This is Spiritualism*,

1959. Minister of the Spiritualists' National Union. Has lectured on Spiritualism all over Britain, in U.S.A., Canada and on the Continent.

Barker, Elsa English automatist, author of *Living Dead Men* series. Her communicator was said to have been David P. Hutch, a Los Angeles magistrate.

Barkel, Mrs Kathleen English trance, healing and physical medium, controlled by 'White Hawk' Chief of the Sioux of 800 years ago. Worked for the M.S.A. (now the Spiritualist Association of Great Britain) and the British College of Psychic Science in London. Healing, direct voice, and apports of beautifully cut stones, were among the phenomena she produced.

Barrett, Sir William Fletcher (1845–1926) Professor at the Royal College of Science, Dublin. Noted psychic researcher. In January 1882 he called a conference at the British National Association of Spiritualists and inaugurated the Society for Psychical Research. He also provided the impetus for the formation of the American Society of Psychical research during his visit there in 1885. His final conclusions summed up in a paper to the S.P.R. (*Proceedings*, Vol. XXXIV, 1924). 'There is evidence for: 1. The existence of a spirit world. 2. For survival after death. 3. For occasional communication with those passed over.' He wrote many books of his experiences.

'Dr Beale' Spirit doctor control of Miss Rose, British healing medium, credited with the cure of many hopeless cases. Her sanctuary was at Hulham House acquired in 1921.

Bedbrook, David A businessman who devoted his spare time to much public work for Spiritualism. Hon. member of the Society for Psychical Research and the Société des Philadelphes, Paris. President of many Spiritualist societies, national and international, clairvoyant and clairaudient medium and lecturer himself, and an accomplished linguist and author.

Benediction Thanks to God for blessings; a short informal prayer given at the end of a Spiritualist service.

Beraud, Martha *See* **Eva C.**

Bergson, Henri (1859–1941) Noted French philosopher, Nobel prizewinner for literature. One of the most prominent thinkers of his time. His philosophic ideas were concerned with relating time to personality; for substituting durational for the non-temporal values of most philosophers since Plato. He believed that the true nature of things could be apprehended by intuition.

Berkeley, George (Bishop) (1685–1753) Eminent Irish philosopher who denied the reality of matter. Existence was not possible, he maintained, which was not either conscious spirit or the ideas of which such spirit is conscious. This synthesis of subject with object asserts the mind alone as the ultimate reality. Nature, by this reasoning, is conscious experience forming the symbols of divine universal intelligence.

Bernstein, Morey American businessman, author and hypnotist who, through the technique of hypnotic regression, claimed to have produced evidence for a former incarnation of his subject as 'Bridey Murphy'. Recordings were made of the actual statements made during the experiments.

Bessinet, Miss Ada (Mrs W. W. Roche) American physical medium tested by Professor Hyslop of the American society for Psychical Research, 1911. After seventy sittings, he expressed the opinion that the medium was responsible herself for the phenomena, but functioning by means of a secondary personality and therefore not morally responsible for fraud.

J. Hewat McKenzie of the British College of Psychic Science also tested her for six months in 1921 and considered the phenomena genuine.

Besterman, Theodore (Born 1904) Lecturer for University of London, officer of the Society for Psychical Research. Author of many important works on psychic research.

Bhagavadgita Part of an Indian epic *Mahabharata*, but later than the original. Hindu sacred writing supposed by Vishnu 'the Preserver', a beneficent god incarnated as Krishna the charioteer, showing devotion to a personal god. It is a compendium of Upanishadic teaching containing the famous doctrine of avotars. Strict Brahmins do not accept it.

Bhakti Hindu emotional practice for the maintenance of a personal relationship with God. Exposition in *Bhagavadgita* (q.v.).

Bhakti Yoga A branch, or one of the seven paths of Yoga. The way of devotion.

Bianchi, Dr P. Benigno Professor of Psychiatry, Naples. Director of Salerno Insane Asylum, Minister of Education. He investigated the phenomena of Eusapia Paladino in 1891. With Professor Falcomer he also sat with Nilda Bonardi and asked for private details of his family life. They were described in such detail that he admitted his scepticism shaken and was after inclined to believe in Spiritualism.

Billet Reading A form of mediumship more common in America than England. It takes the form of a public demonstration; the audience write, on pieces of paper or billets, messages to their departed friends. These are gathered and placed before the blindfolded medium. The heap of folded slips are not only read, but answers are given as well as facts of evidential value to the writers.

Bilocation Being present in two places at once. Histories of the saints abound in this phenomena which in Spiritualism is attributed to the separation and separate appearance simultaneously of the double, or etheric body. *See* **Astral Projection.**

Biological Phenomena The amazingly supernormal growth of plants has been known. Charles Bailey, Australian apport medium, caused marked mango seeds to sprout swiftly and an Indian myrtle to grow to the height of sixteen inches in twenty minutes. There are also cases of arrested decomposition of organic bodies as well as destruction of bacteria under the action of certain mediums. Healing of course is the outstanding example today.

Bio-magnetism Animal magnetism. Mesmerism (q.v.).

Biometer of Baraduc *See* **Baraduc.**

Bird, J. Malcolm Research Officer of the A.S.P.R. 1925–31. Sat with many well-known mediums—John Sloan, Mrs Osborne Leonard, William Hope, Mrs Deane, Evan Powell, Frau Maria Vollhardt, Mrs Margery Crandon. He was convinced of the objectivity of physical phenomena, and wrote several books on the subject.

Birth A spirit entity's assumption of a new outward form; in our world, the physical body. At death the spirit leaves the physical body and remains clothed in the etheric body (q.v.) which corresponds to a birth into a new state of existence. There would appear to be many such births, judging from communications, including the possibility of reincarnation, or being reborn on earth.

Black Box *See* **Delawarr camera.**

'Black Hawk'   Red Indian control of English medium Evan Powell, J.P. (1881–1958); one of the few guides who has succeeded in establishing evidence of his former earth existence by mention of a statue erected to his memory in Illinois, and an autobiography (*The Life of Ma-Ka-Tai-Me-She-Kia-Kiak, or Black Hawk*, dictated by himself, Boston, 1834). An intensive search was made by a book agent who succeeded in verifying the details given. A copy of the book was found and is still to be seen in the museum of the Spiritualist Association of Great Britain, London.

Blake, Mrs Elizabeth   American direct-voice medium, produced unusually powerful voices in broad daylight. David P. Abbott of A.S.P.R. and E. A. Parsons, both expert conjurors, tested her in 1906 and became convinced of the identity of spirit operators.

Blavatsky, Mme Helene Petrova (1831–91)   Russian born, and, with Col. H. S. Olcott, founder of Theosophical Society. She lived a mysterious and adventurous life, was undoubtedly mediumistic, though she was exposed as fraudulent by Dr Hodgson of the S.P.R. in an investigation into the 'mysteries' of the Theosophists' headquarters at Adyar in India. Accomplices confessed to fraud and Dr Hodgson's report reversed the first favourable one issued by the S.P.R. in Dec. 1884. Mme Blavatsky continued undaunted however and later published a monumental work, *The Secret Doctrine*, written it is claimed in a supernormal state and containing the ancient wisdom of the East.

Blue   Colours clairvoyantly perceived have a generally recognized significance. Usually connected with the aura, they were experimentally verified by Dr Kilner of St Thomas's Hospital, London. Pale blue is supposed to be the colour of healing and spirituality. *See* **Colours.**

Boddington, Harry One-time Vice-president of the S.N.U. Active in many societies for developing mediums, and prolific author. He endeavoured to extend Dr Kilner's discovery of the use of dicyanin screens for auric vision development.

Bodhi-Dharma Semi-legendary founder of Zen Buddhism in Japan; a sect which developed a new branch of Mahayana Buddhism.

Bodhisattvas Northern Buddhist conception of High Beings who sacrifice their attainment of Nirvana in order to incarnate as saints, out of compassion for mankind.

Bodies To the inquirer, mention of many 'body' names is apt to be confusing. Spiritualism believes in the etheric body as the double of the physical body, the two being normally coincident throughout earth life; the whole being supported and animated by the spirit (ego or thinking part) which is indestructible and assumes other bodies as suits of clothes appropriate to the plane of existence. Various brands of occultism use the same terms and claim knowledge of distinctions between them in their complicated theories of human development, but these cannot be checked with facts and there is much disagreement over them. The 'double', however, has validity by reason of psychical research and the many spirit communications supporting it, also many personal 'out-of-the-body' experiences (astral projection, q.v.) and the cases in medical records when the patient under anaesthesia sees his own body, and is later able to give circumstantial details of operations at the time.

Boirac, Emil French Rector of Dijon Academy. Studied animal magnetism and exteriorisation of sensitivity. His book: *Our Hidden Forces* was awarded the Emden prize in 1917 by the French Academy of Sciences.

Bolton, Gambier Noted naturalist and keen student of psychical research, experimented for many years on the claims of Spiritualism; later becoming a much sought after lecturer on the subject. Although possessing no psychic gifts of his own, his keen analytical mind made him a respected protagonist.

Bond, Frederick Bligh, F.R.I.B.A. (Revd) (Born 1864) Excavator of the lost chapels of Glastonbury Abbey. Ecclesiastic, archaeologist, architect, editor of *A.S.P.R. Journal.* Author of many books based upon automatic writing in collaboration with John Alleyne (q.v.) and Hester Dowden. Also conducted experiments in thought photography with Mrs Deane. Outlined his conception of immortality in *Journal of A.S.P.R.,* 1929, 'Athanasia'.

Book of the Dead Ancient Egyptian texts 2500 B.C.–A.D. 200, often inscribed on mummy-cases and tombs. They have no particular form, being a collection of chapters. Many versions of them are known. They describe the travails of the human soul after death according to Egyptian theology, and were already old in 3500 B.C. Their Egyptian title 'per em hru' means 'coming forth by day'.

Book Tests Experiments designed to exclude the possibility of telepathy in medium's communications. Usually the spirit communicator in answer to a question, indicates a certain line of a page in a specified book accessible to the sitter and gives the appropriate text which can afterwards be verified. Many successful tests of this kind have been made. It was first performed by Rev. Stainton Moses.

Borderland Library The W. T. Stead, founded by Estelle Stead his daughter in 1914 in continuation of the work of 'Julia's Bureau'.

Boston Society for Psychical Research Founded May 1925 by Dr Walter Franklin Prince, formerly Research Officer of A.S.P.R. It issues Bulletins and books.

Botazzi, Phillipe Professor of Physiology and Director of the Physiological Institute in the University of Naples. Had sittings with Eusapia Paladino in 1907. All the manifestations were controlled by instruments in the presence of Professors De Amicis, Scarpa and Pansini, and convinced Bottazzi of the reality of physical phenomena.

Boursnell, Richard (1822–1909) Medium for spirit photography, discovered by W. T. Stead. Many negatives are preserved at the British College of Psychic Science.

Bozzano, Professor Ernesto (Born 1862) Noted Italian psychic researcher, had many sittings with Eusapia Paladino and became convinced of the truth of Spiritualism. Wrote many books and articles on the subject.

Bradley, H. Dennis English author, developed direct voice mediumship himself after contacts with American medium George Valiantine. At first, a great champion of this medium, he afterwards recanted, and his enthusiasm waned. Later he publicly declared in the daily press that genuine phenomena did occur, and that communication was practicable.

Brahmā Hindu verbal image of the Sacred, the Creator or most High God. Identified also with the Atman or Great Self, differentiated into separate egos.

Brāhmana A member of the noblest Hindu caste.

Brath, Stanley de English psychic researcher. A government engineer then headmaster of a preparatory school at Grinstead for twenty years. Worked at Institut Métapsychique with Dr Geley. Became convinced of the truth of Spiritualism. Author of several books and translator of Dr Geley's works.

Breathing Considered to be worthy of great study in psychic development. Levitation feats are commonly connected with special breathing techniques as also are the feats of Yogis. Dr Hereward Carrington, famous American psychic researcher, made experiments on scales with the popular lifting game whereby the lifters easily lift a person by the fingertips by one co-ordinated breath, and registered an over-all loss of weight amounting to 60 lb. during the experiment. (*Story of Psychic Science*, by Carrington.)

Breezes Cool currents of air combined with a drop of temperature is a well-known phenomena in physical seances, although the reason for it is unknown. Apparitions are notoriously chilly. Margery's control 'Walter' attributed breezes to psychic emanations from the sitter's brains. This view has support of statements by a control of D. D. Home, and observations of the phenomena of Eusapia Paladino whose head emitted a noticeable draught at the site of an old injury. Drops of 20°F have been recorded by Harry Price in tests with Stella C. at the National Laboratory of Psychical Research.

British College of Psychic Science Now dissolved, founded in London in 1920 by J. Hewat McKenzie and his wife for the sustained study of mediumship and for the assistance of researchers. Sir Arthur Conan Doyle was its President for some years until shortly before his death. Many fine mediums were tested there, by reason of the McKenzie's wide travels abroad. Among them were Ada Bessinet, Frau Silbert and Franek Kluski.

British Journal of Psychical Research The official organ of the National Laboratory of Psychical Research, replaced later in 1926 by 'Proceedings' and Bulletins.

British Spiritualists Lyceum Union *See* **Lyceum.**

Brittain, Mrs Annie English trance medium, contemporary of Sir A. Conan Doyle who sent her many clients and kept detailed records of reports.

Britten, Emily Hardinge (1823–1899) English medium, and inspirational speaker of great erudition. Developed in America after acquaintance with American medium Mrs Coan (Ada Heyt). One of the best attested cases of spirit return was given through her mediumship when the mail steamer *Pacific* sank, and one of the crew possessed her in trance and disclosed the tragedy before it was generally known. She was threatened with prosecution, but her story turned out to be true. A great propagandist for Spiritualism, she travelled in many countries. Founded and edited the Spiritualist paper *Two Worlds* and wrote many books.

Broad, Professor C. D., Litt. D., F.B.A. President of S.P.R. 1935–36 and 1959–60, famous philosopher, outspoken in his criticism of science's neglect of psychical research. While admitting the existence of psychic phenomena, he thinks that none of them entails, though a few of them suggest, more than the persistence of a limited portion of an individual's mind after the death of his body.

Brofferio, Professor Angelo Italian scientist who became a Spiritualist by his experiences of the mediumship of Eusapia Paladino.

Brooks, Tom J., M.B.E., M.P., J.P. Known as the 'father' of the Fraudulent Mediums Act 1951 for which he was responsible by dint of great effort over many years. Normanton is his constituency in the West Riding, England; a mining district. He is a convinced Spiritualist and President of a Spiritualist church.

Brown, Dr William, M.D., D.Sc., F.R.C.P. Harley Street specialist, Wilde Reader in Mental Philosophy at Oxford University. Psychic researcher. Was convinced of the genuineness of psychic phenomena through the mediumship of Rudi Schneider.

Buchanan, Professor J. Rhodes (1814–1899) American scientist, Dean of the Faculty and professor in the Eclectic Medical Institute, Covington, Kentucky. Became interested in phrenology which led to his discovery of a psychic faculty of sensitivity to which he gave the name 'psychometry' 1842. He believed that all substances gave emanations which may be sensed and interpreted, and declared that the history of the world was entombed in the present.

Buddha An enlightened and wise person who has attained perfect wisdom. 'The Buddha' refers to Gotama (Prince Sakyamuni) 560–480 B.C., who renounced family and position. After prolonged meditation he formed a practical philosophy of active works by example. His 'Four noble truths' are: the truth of suffering, the cause of suffering, the cessation of suffering, the path to the ending of suffering. Like other great reformers, his work has become obscured by sacerdotalism.

Buddhism The religion based on the teachings of Gotama has today probably 750 million nominal followers. Gotama was a Hindu reactionary of 560 B.C., born into an age of preoccupation with Yoga techniques, and with the oral tradition of the Upanishads and the Vedas as background. He saw the necessity for a personal practical application for the alleviation of suffering and endeavoured to set an example. There are no contemporary writings; the Pali Buddhist canon is the earliest (probably 80 B.C.), in which there are suspected interpolations. Gotama's modifications of Upanishad teachings so far as we know may be summed up as: seeking the Self (Atman), removal of passion, moderation, abandonment of asceticism and the

Hindu caste system. At a council (Patni, 270–240 B.C.) under King Asoka, Buddhism split into two main divisions known today as the northern Mahayana and the southern Hinayana. The latter, at that time a majority, excommunicated the former, but now the position is reversed and Mahayana (Great system) holds sway over most Buddhists. They both tend to monasticism, which is the negative side of Gotama's teaching, though the north is less rigid and employs the idea of Bodhisattvas, reincarnations of Buddha. Today one feels Gotama would have taken up the cudgels for social reform but this idea seems sadly lacking in Buddhist doctrine. The Buddhist 'eightfold path' is: right views, right resolve, right speech, right conduct, right livelihood, right effort, right mindfulness, right concentration.

Bull, Dr Titus American physician, member of American Association for the Advancement of Science, Director of the J. H. Hyslop Foundation for the treatment of obsession. In collaboration with a medium, Mrs Duke, he was able to cure many patients. In 1932 he published a summary of his conclusions over twenty years of research. Similar methods are employed in Spiritualist rescue circles.

Cabbala An occult science of ancient origin (probably Egyptian), by means of which rabbis claim to make mystic sense of the letters and words of the scriptures, utilizing their numerical values.

Cabinet A small space enclosed usually by a curtain, in which most materialization mediums claim to condense the psychic energy necessary for a manifestation. Not all mediums have considered it necessary (*see* **Home** and **Stainton Moses**). Some sit inside, others outside the cabinet.

Caduceus The Wand of Mercury symbol; a rod entwined by a dark and a light serpent for three and a half turns, surmounted by wings. Said to represent the Yogic psychic channels of man's body. It was adopted in early medicine, as a symbol of disease and cure.

Camp Meetings Meetings of mediums held in America regularly during the summer season. Lily Dale, New York, and Lake Pleasant, Massachusetts are the largest. Many mediums travel from abroad to meet there.

Cannon, Alexander, M.D., Ph.D., D.P.M., M.A., Ch.B., F.R.S.M., F.R.S. Author, student of psychiatry and hypnotism. Inventor of Psychograph (q.v.) or thought-reading machine, the Common Hypnoscope, and a highpower 400,000 volt static electrical machine for depossessing.

Carrington, Dr Hereward Noted American psychic researcher and author of many books on psychic research. Was assistant to Professor Hyslop at the A.S.P.R. Made an important investigation of Eusapia Paladino's mediumship in Naples which convinced him of the existence of genuine phenomena, and led to him postulating the Spiritualist hypothesis as the only one rationally to explain all the facts. This view of his was strengthened by his examination of Mrs Eileen Garrett in 1933.

Castelwitch, Countess of Private physical medium tested by Dr d'Oliveira Feijao, Professor of Surgery at Lisbon University (1913–20). Loud noises and telekinetic phenomena including table levitation were produced, of great power.

Catalepsy A state of body rigidity during which the normal functions are suspended. The causes are unknown, it may last for several days. According to some authorities on astral projection, it is a temporary phase of projection while the astral body is within a few feet of the physical body, or within 'cord range'. Catalepsy, usually spontaneous, can be induced by hypnotic practices. Indian fakirs are said to use it sometimes when producing supernormal phenomena.

Causal Body Occult term for a permanent element of man said to reincarnate; composed of 'higher mental matter' and having a sexless human form.

Cayce, Edgar (1877–1945) American healer-medium, born on a farm in Kentucky, of little education. At the age of twenty-one he lost his voice, but regained it temporarily under hypnotic treatment. When speaking under hypnosis, he diagnosed his own trouble and cured himself by post-hypnotic suggestion. This was extended to diagnosis for others with astounding success; in trance, the ignorant Cayce spoke like a professional physician. The patient did not have to be present, providing the name and address were given. Even 'incurables' were cured. His first famous case was that of Aime Deitrich of Hoptonsville, Kentucky, considered a hopeless case but who was saved from a rare brain disease. Her father testified before a notary public on 8 October 1910.

Celestial Heavenly. An adjective commonly used to denote the higher spheres in the Spirit world.

Celestial Magic Asserts that the planets are controlled by spirits who have influence over man.

Census of Hallucination An inquiry conducted by a distinguished committee of the S.P.R. in 1889 to collect substantial data of apparitions. The report was published in 1894. Out of 17,000 people canvassed, 1,684 claimed to have seen apparitions.

Centres, Psychic *See* **Chakras.**

Centurione Scotto, Marquis Carlo Italian nobleman and medium. An M.P. for eleven years. Did much research work. At suggestion of American medium Valiantine, he developed direct voice mediumship very quickly. Other phenomena included levitation, transportation, apports, xenoglossy. The S.P.R. queried his phenomena which caused Sir A. Conan Doyle to resign from the S.P.R., considering it a slur on the reputation of Ernest Bozzano the original investigator.

Chakras Centres of psychic power, according to Hindu and occult ideas, situated in the subtle body which permeates the physical body. There are said to be six main chakras (though authorities differ); they ascend in order from the base of the spine. Normally quiescent, by special disciplines of body (asanas) and mind, it is claimed they can become active and confer psychic powers. Some psychics and mediums claim to see these centres clairvoyantly and the power to discern thereby the psychic and spiritual development of the individual. Certain spirit healers claim to work on the chakras to stimulate healing of the physical body.

Chela Hindu and Yogic term for pupil, that of the master being the 'Guru'. Yoga is normally learned by close association of pupil and master who demands unquestionable obedience.

Chemical Phenomena Have often been recorded in the seance room. Lights which are cold, ozone smells, phosphorescence, fire production seemingly in defiance of normal chemical means.

Chemicographs Guillaume de Fontenay's term for supernormal photographs obtained without a camera.

Child Guides Often encountered in a Spiritualistic inquiry. It seems that they retain the childish mannerisms of their last earth years, irrespective of the time they have spent in the spirit world. Their knowledge and intelligence however are usually adult in accordance with their growing to maturity in spirit life. They often lighten the proceedings with their humour, and endeavour to bring a cheerful atmosphere to their mediums.

Chiromancy   Palmistry. Divination by the lines and forms of the hand.

Christian Science   Founded by Mary Baker Eddy in 1875, it asserts that as God and the mind is the only reality, the power of thought is sufficient to counteract all physical ailments and handicaps as they are 'unreal'. While Spiritualists agree that thoughts are much more potent than generally recognized, they would consider suitable action to be equally necessary and, unlike the Christian Scientist, realize the value of orthodox medical skill in addition to the Divine power of healing.

Christian Spiritualism   Spiritualists who believe, as orthodox Christians do, that Jesus was more than human, and recognize him as a Divine spiritual leader, form a minority group and run their services on more orthodox Christian lines, while retaining the evidence of survival demonstration which is the common feature of Spiritualist services.

Christ Spirit   Although usually associated with Jesus, many Spiritualists believe that the Messianic or Christ spirit has been operative through many other great teachers of spiritual wisdom on earth, and is therefore not the prerogative of Christianity alone.

Circle, Development   A group of people who meet regularly for the purpose of developing any latent psychic abilities they may possess. Some circles sit for one particular type of phenomena, say clairvoyance or trance mediumship, but with most it is general. The time taken for individual development varies: some people attain proficiency readily, others may take five years of regular sitting or even longer. Physical phenomena usually takes very much longer than mental phenomena and the conditions of its operation are much more exacting which explains perhaps its comparative rarity. After a medium has developed in the circle or group to the fullest extent he may

41

venture forth on his own. The circle provides protection from undesirable entities during the tender early stages.

Circle, Home *See* **Home circle**

Circle, Meditation According to Eastern tradition, spiritual knowledge can be gained by the practice of meditation. By sitting quietly in a group and letting the mind play gently upon a given theme, an attunement with higher powers may be achieved, therefore many Spiritualists run circles expressly for this purpose.

Circle, Open A circle which is open to any visitor. This is not favoured in the main by experienced Spiritualists as the attraction of undesirable entities is regulated by the spiritual advancement of the visitors. Too many strangers, it is felt, may breed feelings of suspicion and distrust which hamstring the efforts of the sincere.

Circle, Physical This circle has to rely upon the physical potentialities of its sitters, in so far as the production of sufficient ectoplasm of the right quality is essential for phenomena. Structures have to be built from this elusive substance, the medium during its production is extremely sensitive to actinic light and dark conditions are necessary for its early production. Many circles are formed for this purpose but few succeed as the going is long and arduous. There is also real physical danger for the mediums so employed if ectoplasm is touched without permission from the controls, or if lights should suddenly be switched on. The new enquirer would do well to shun physical circles until more experience and knowledge of Spiritualistic phenomena is attained. The darkness lends itself to fraudulent imitation of phenomena to exploit the unwary.

Circle, Rescue Perhaps the most exacting kind of circle. It needs much love for the unfortunates of humanity, plus self-sacrifice on the part of all members of these circles to operate successfully. The medium has a perilous task and has to rely implicitly upon the power of her own control to eject the undesirable or foolish entity who is allowed a brief period of control of the medium's body. The 'rescued' are usually weak or foolish spirits who are still ignorant of the new conditions and possibilities of progression in the spirit world. By entering the medium's aura they are then able to converse with the circle, state their difficulties and be advised as to their own progress. Much good work is being done unobtrusively by these little dedicated groups.

Clairaudience A faculty of Extra Sensory Perception described as 'hearing' by the medium. It is often blended with clairvoyance in demonstrations of clairvoyance. Mediums with this faculty well developed can often give evidential details of unusual names.

Clairsentience Psychic perception by sensing conditions pertaining to communicating entities and auric emanations, a faculty often blended with clairvoyance and psychometry in mediumship.

Clairvoyance As meant by the Spiritualist: Extra Sensory Perception described as 'seeing' by the medium in which paranormal images are formed in the mind's eye. Generally used to describe any form of spirit communication by a medium in the 'normal'. In psychical research the meaning of clairvoyance is limited to paranormal perception of earthly objects beyond the range of the normal senses. The science of parapsychology defines it: 'An Extra Sensory correspondence between a present mental pattern of A and a past, present or future object or event in the physical world. In order to establish clairvoyance by experiment it is necessary to show that there is no mental pattern correlated to the physical event which belongs to the present, past or some future experience of any person other than A. That is, the event must never at any time be the object of sense-perception'. (Soal and Bateman).

Clairvoyant Painting Paintings inspired by the artist's own clairvoyant visions, often of guides or deceased relatives of the sitter. These last may furnish excellent evidence of survival. Also known as 'Psychic art'.

Clayton, Arthur Known as the Blind Seer, English inspirational speaker and clairvoyant, he wrote several books on Spiritualism.

Coiled Serpent *See* **Kundalini**

Coincidence The casual concurrence. This is held to be the result of chance, if however, by calculation of probabilities, more than chance is required for explanation, psychic research may shed light on the problem. Many experiments in E.S.P. are based on this.

College of Psychic Science Formerly known as the London Spiritualist Alliance. Founded in 1881. Renamed as above in 1955. Not a religious organization, but non-sectarian. Membership of the association does not commit members to any definite belief. Objectives of the College are the investigation, study and classification of psychic phenomena. Their co-ordination of scientific knowledge and their application to the subject of survival and possible communication with the discarnate. H.Q. 16 Queensbury Place, South Kensington, London.

Colley, Thomas, Ven. Archdeacon of Natal and Rector of Stockton. English psychic investigator who once issued a £1,000 challenge to Maskelyne the professional conjuror, to reproduce psychic phenomena. He promoted interest in Hope, the psychic photographer and founded the famous Crewe circle. Died in 1912.

Colman, Arthur   British materialization medium. As many as five fully materialized spirit forms were seen at one time, as described in *There is no Death* by Florence Marryat.

Colours   Much significance is attached to colours perceived in the human aura (q.v.). Gold is spirituality, pale blue and purple —healing, pink—pure love and affection, red is desire and anger, dark red is passion, green—intellectual apprehension, browns and dark muddy hues—illness and disease. Colours are also used by spirit guides and controls as personal symbols, a code by which they may be recognized. Colour therapy is used by some healers, particular hues are said to influence the physical and psychical wellbeing of the patient.

Commonwealth of the S.A.G.B.   A scheme of co-operation between the Spiritualist Association of Great Britain and various Spiritualist bodies and churches, by which interchange of services and facilities for members of all member bodies is secured.

Communication, Spirit   Can be established in many ways. Human beings are the 'instruments' employed although many efforts have been made to construct mechanical apparatus to supplant the medium. Up to now the results are controversial. If they succeed, then spirit communication enters the domain of physics. Mental communication is effected by control of the vocal organs of the medium, by telepathy between spirits on different planes, by visual images, by auditory means or by sensing conditions. Automatism is common. Communication by physical phenomena, when the medium's mind is not employed directly; rappings by code, direct voice, speech by a materialized form. We are told that the purpose of spirit communication is to uplift humanity from materialistic apathy, to an awareness of each person's Divine participation, and responsibility for his inner intentions.

Communicator A personality seeming to be that of a deceased person or other discarnate being.

Communigraph The 'Ashkir-Jobson Communigraph', a small table with a free pendulum beneath, which can make contact with a number of metal plates representing the alphabet. When contact is made, the appropriate letter appears illuminated on the table top. It was claimed that no medium was necessary for its operation.

Community of Sensation A relationship between hypnotizer and subject. The subject reacts to physical sensations experienced by the hypnotist, by this means taste, smell, vision and hearing are known to have been transferred. This phenomena was investigated by Dr Paul Joire. Mediums experience this when sensing conditions of past lives of their spirit contacts, and also the phenomena of psychometry is worth noting in this connection.

Compacts, Death An agreement between two people to endeavour to give evidence of their continued existence after death to the other. In *Phantasms of the Living* by Gurney, Myers and Podmore, twelve cases are recorded where an apparition was seen within twelve hours of death. In some cases much longer times are required, and of course the failures may be due to insufficient sensitivity on the part of the intended receiver. On occasions the apparition has been seen by a third party.

Conan Doyle, Sir Arthur (1858–1930) Doctor and famous author of 'Sherlock Holmes' stories. One of Spiritualism's most earnest champions, he experimented in home circles and as a member of the S.P.R. for more than twenty years before he decided positively for Spiritualism, then he literally gave up his career at its peak to devote himself whole-heartedly to its propagation by lecturing in many countries and writing literature on the subject. He became president of many societies, notably the International Spiritualist Federation, the Marylebone Spiritualist Association (now the Spiritualist Association of Great Britain) and the London Spiritualist Alliance (now the College of Psychic Science). On several occasions since his passing he has given evidence of his continued existence and interest in the cause of Spiritualism. At a Reunion Service at the Albert Hall in 1930 he was seen clairvoyantly by medium Estelle Roberts who gave a message to members of his family which was accepted as evidential by them. Another evidential communication was given to Harry Price through the mediumship of Mrs Garrett.

Conant, Mrs J. H. (1831–1875)   American trance medium who, in collaboration with Luther Colby editor of *Banner of Light* gave free public seances in Boston for seventeen years. Her trance messages were said to be perfectly in character with the communicator, and they were published regularly. She was a healer controlled by 'Dr John Dix Fisher'. In trance she spoke in many tongues, including Indian dialects of which normally she knew nothing.

Concentration   A mental exercise whereby the mind is kept continuously on a focal point, a very difficult exercise to main-tain, but a good preparation for the stilling of the mind's normal activity which prevents psychic impression.

Concord   A system of Spiritualist education for young people sponsored by the S.A.G.B.

Conditions   Very frequently referred to among Spiritualists. Usually descriptive of the immediate environment of the medium and its psychic quality as affecting the ease or otherwise of communication. Sometimes conditions are stipulated by the medium before a seance. While these may seem whimsical or trivial to the investigator, it is best to observe them as far as reasonably possible, as experience has proved that the results are greatly affected by the degree of co-operation accorded by the sitter.

Conjunction Astronomically the apparent meeting of two celestial bodies; astrologically this is held to be the most powerful 'aspect' linking strongly the two principles associated with those bodies.

Conjuring Lodges A hut or tent used by early N. American Indians for mediumistic purposes, probably as a primitive form of cabinet (q.v.).

Conklin, J. B. American medium who specialized in billet-reading. President Lincoln was his patron and Conklin was often a guest at the Presidential mansion.

Consciousness Normal cognition. This appears to be a barrier to supernormal manifestation. By trance it can be removed, then the organism of the medium responds to the spirit controls' manipulation of the subconscious mind, or in the case of physical phenomena, facilitating the extrusion of ectoplasmic substance from the medium's body.

Contact Healing Healing where bodily contact is made between the healer and the patient, either by 'laying on of hands' or by rubbing and manipulation. Spirit healing where contact does not take place is known as 'absent healing' (q.v.). There appears to be little difference in the effectiveness of either form of healing proving that contact is not always necessary. Amazing results have been achieved by both.

Contemplation A mental exercise whereby knowledge is gained by identification with the object contemplated. Widely believed by Eastern philosophers, but not current in the West. Psychometry may provide evidence of its validity.

Control The state of possession of a medium by another personality. The spirit operator in charge of a medium or seance proceedings. They are often called 'guides' when the personality is well known as a regular helper at a series of sittings, or is constantly associated with a particular medium. The control is usually the 'expert' who directs the operation of communication, the medium being the instrument and often described as such by the controls. It should be mentioned that control by the living has been known, often without their knowledge. It may therefore be a function of the subconscious mind in these cases. Among controls, all nationalities are met, though for no clear reason North American Indians seem to preponderate. They make excellent guardians or doorkeepers, helpers for physical manifestations and circle development, often strong healing powers accompany them. Many child controls are also known.

Cook, Miss Florence (1856–1904) Famous materialization medium of Sir William Crookes, responsible for the control 'Katie King'. These were the first materializations known to have been produced under test conditions in a good light. Some flashlight photographs were taken of her and Sir William arm in arm. Katie King could change the colour of her skin and was different in stature and personality from the medium. Sir William Crookes published his report on her mediumship in 1874 bringing a storm of ridicule and sarcasm on his head. In one test by Crookes, the medium was placed in an electric galvanometer circuit (devised by Cromwell Varley his assistant), throughout the seance, yet 'Katie' appeared as usual while the instrument registered no movement.

Cooke, Grace British trance medium, healer and with her husband Ivan Cooke, founder of the White Eagle Lodge.

Cooper, Mrs Blanche English direct voice medium who collaborated in a series of experiments with Dr S. G. Soal, the eminent E.S.P. researcher. One of these provided an instance of control by the living. Soal's friend, Gordon Davis, believed dead but subsequently discovered alive, unknowingly 'communicated' through the direct voice phenomena. All the mannerisms of his speech and voice were produced, and he described boyhood incidents known only to Soal. Mrs Cooper also took part in several interesting book tests (q.v.) in 1923–25.

Co-operative Healing A system of healing discovered by L. Eeman, in which the patient is treated as a valve in a wired circuit connected with the healer. Eeman was not a Spiritualist, but his experiments seem to confirm the existence of the human aura, and the possibility of it flowing along copper conductors arranged in suitable circuits. Concealed switches were used in his experiments to rule out hypnotic suggestion as the cause of his patient's observed reactions.

Copyright By a decision of Mr Justice Eve, London, July 1926, the medium who is the amanuensis for the transmission or production of any written communication made in the presence of sitter or sitters, is adjudged to be the sole author of the script produced, and therefore the sole owner of all copyright values inherent in same (subject to the absence of any special agreement to the contrary); whether such script be addressed to a sitter as recipient or otherwise, or whether it contain matter personal to the sitter.

Cord, Silver The link between the physical and etheric bodies, sustaining the physical body during earth life but severing at death. Often, but not always seen as a silver thread of indefinite extension by projectionists. Opinions differ as to its point of attachment, the majority saying the base of the skull, others the navel. According to Muldoon, when the bodies are within a few feet, the cord acts as a rigid arm which controls the relative movements at the beginning and end of projection, also the bringing together instantaneously should danger threaten the physical body.

Cosmic Consciousness A revelation of knowledge of life and order in the universe. It is realized usually in a moment of ecstasy by certain people and brings moral and intellectual illumination. The conception of a huge 'mind reservoir' which all can share on attainment of certain psychic states.

Coven A regular gathering of witches, usually thirteen in number, including a high priest and six mixed couples.

Crandon, Margery One of the most outstanding American mediums who helped to establish for all time the reality of physical phenomena. Under very strict control, excellent manifestations were obtained in the presence of Dr Gustave Geley and Professor Richet. Harry Price's fraudproof table was levitated in white light twice to a height of eight inches. Chinese scripts were produced in red light when the medium's eyes were closed. Cross correspondence tests were successfully carried out with Dr Henry Hardwicke of Niagara Falls, 450 miles from the seance at Boston. Malcolm Bird picked a sentence which was to be given to Hardwicke in Chinese. A telegram arrived very soon after the sitting with the Chinese message required. Hereward Carrington admitted himself baffled by the extraordinary powers of this medium.

Crawford, Dr N. J., M.B. Painstaking investigator of the famous Goligher circle, vouched for by Sir William Barrett, 1917–20. He formulated laws governing the production of telekinetic phenomena. By the use of scales, he established the fact that the weight of levitated objects was supported by the medium, and that rod-like structures were produced for this purpose from ectoplasmic substance, using ordinary cantilever principles to initiate the desired movements. Attachments to objects were made by the formation of suckers at the ends of the rods which could also be employed for the production of raps or percussive effects by means of their elasticity. That the ectoplasmic flow proceeded from the medium he proved by traces of carmine powder deposited along its course, and at its origin, on the medium's body and clothing.

Craze, George (1871–1946) An exceedingly modest yet indefatigable worker for Spiritualism, who was elected in 1917 to the Council of the Spiritualist Association of Great Britain (then the M.S.A.), as President for many years, he was literally its backbone during the dark and difficult war years, enabling the Association to maintain its services throughout.

Cremation Disposal of a corpse by burning. Some controversy exists concerning the wisdom of this method. By some it is maintained that the dissociation of the etheric or spirit body from its earthly counterpart is not given sufficient time to be completed before cremation, and that corresponding distress is felt by the spirit in passing. There is little evidence for this point of view. Many who have been cremated, have given plentiful evidence of their survival without mention of the matter.

Crespigny, Mrs Philip Champion de Daughter of the Rt. Hon. Sir Astley Cooper-Key, First Sea Lord of the Admiralty. One-time Principal of the British College of Psychic Science and well-known authoress of many novels dealing with psychic subjects.

Crewe Circle Founded by Archdeacon Colley in 1908. Hope, the spirit photographer, belonged to this circle.

Crisis Apparitions In moments of crisis, apparitions would seem to be more likely to manifest than at other times. Many such cases are recorded in *Phantasms of the Living*, Gurney, Myers and Podmore.

Crookes, Sir William (1832–1919) Great physicist of the last century. Upon entering his investigation of Spiritualism (1870), he made a public announcement that scientific methods would 'relegate the worthless residuum of Spiritualism into the unknown limbo of magic and necromancy'. He investigated D. D. Home, assisted by his brother Walter, Sir William Huggins eminent physicist and astronomer ex-president of the Royal Society, and Serjeant Cox a well-known lawyer. A report was submitted in due course to the Royal Society but it was refused when it was found to support the truth of Spiritualistic phenomena. Then his famous investigation of Florence Cook and 'Katie King' (q.v.) seemed too fantastic to be credible to his contemporaries. In spite of the danger to his scientific standing, Crookes stood by his discoveries to the end.

Cross Correspondence Some of the most convincing evidence has been obtained by this method, which rules out the possibility of telepathy or mind reading on the medium's part. By request, a spirit message is split up and the two parts delivered to different mediums simultaneously, but unknown to each other. When subsequently the parts of the message are assembled, the whole makes sense.

Cryptesthesia Coined by Professor Richet to describe a 'sixth sense', perception by means of an unknown mechanism which produces cognition as an end result. His theory was, that it is activated by some mysterious external vibration which he termed 'the vibrations of reality'. It was offered as an alternative explanation to the Spirit hypothesis, to account for the phenomena of Clairvoyance, premonitions, psychometry, dowsing and telepathy. The modern term would be Extra Sensory Perception.

Cryptomnesia Unconscious memory which may be drawn upon in special circumstances. In trance or under hypnosis information may be given which at first sight seems foreign to the individual, but which may be traced to an early impression long since forgotten by the conscious mind.

Crystal Gazing or **scrying** A very old form of divination by gazing at a crystal ball. After an initial cloudiness, scenes and pictures are said to appear if one is so gifted. Although often associated with 'clairvoyants' of the sea-side pier variety, in Spiritualism the crystal is rarely met, and is hardly, if ever, used by Spiritualist mediums. The developed clairvoyant does not require material aids.

Culture Heroes Historical personages whose teachings and adventures are propagated in the myths and legends of their people. They are usually raised by posterity to divine status, or considered to be incarnations of gods.

Cummins, Miss Geraldine Most outstanding Irish automatist medium of modern times. Her extraordinary scripts, excellently constructed and written unconsciously at terrific speed, are worthy of close study by reason of the detailed information concerning little known periods of history, and certain Biblical and historical characters. Much of her detail has been verified by experts of these times. In collaboration with Dr Connell of Ireland, she undertook a series of psychometrical experiments which succeeded in convincing the Doctor that the origin of many patients' troubles was accessible by this means, and could be adduced as evidence for reincarnation and a form of 'Karmic' law.

Curran, Mrs John H. Remarkable medium of St Louis, Mo., responsible for the *Patience Worth* books. Herself untravelled, and of little education, gave a literary output of extremely high quality. The control 'Patience Worth' was male.

Daimôn Name of the famous supernormal guide who advised Socrates when in doubt. There are many modern parallels in clairaudient phenomena as known in Spiritualism.

Dalai Lama The ruler of Lamaism on earth. He is said to be an incarnation of a powerful Bodhisattva, and is traditionally chosen by lamas from the common people's babies; born at an astrologically specified time, they must exhibit the necessary signs of wisdom.

Davenport Brothers (1841–1911) Ira Erastus and William Henry. American mediums of whom outstanding manifestations of physical phenomena were reported. Although they gave many public demonstrations in America, England and France, they were never detected in fraud. No knots could hold them; mysterious hands played tricks with the investigators while the mediums were tied and immobile. In France they demonstrated before the Emperor and Empress Napoleon with a party of forty guests at the palace of St Cloud. They also appeared before the Czar in St Petersburg, and visited Australia.

Davis Case, Gordon Dr S. G. Soal, psychic researcher, received through a medium a communication from a friend, Gordon Davis, who later turned up alive. The description given of Davis' house was incorrect at the time, but was correct a year later.

Davis, Andrew Jackson The Poughkeepsie Seer (1826–1910), famous medium and author of many Spiritualist books which had a great influence on the development of ideas about Spiritualism of his time. Born of uneducated parents in poor circumstances, Davis developed as a clairvoyant and clairaudient, but received no education until the age of sixteen, when he was apprenticed to a shoe-maker. After some experimenting with Mesmerism, he recounted a strange experience in 1844, during the course of which he said he met Galen and Swedenborg and received mental illumination. From that time he began to dictate, while in the trance state, many instructive books, and was able to answer difficult questions correctly. His Hebrew quotations were vouched for by Dr George Busch, Professor of Hebrew at New York University. The publication of his great work: *'The principles of nature, her Divine revelations, and a voice to mankind'*, was an overwhelming success; it ran to thirty-four editions in less than thirty years and made Davis famous. As head of a band of enthusiasts, he published a paper *'Univercoelum'*. Late in life he retired to a small Boston bookshop where he sold books and herbal remedies.

Dead Sea Scrolls Ancient texts, written by a Jewish monastic order whose H.Q. at Qumran dated from end of second century B.C. to A.D. 70. Fragments of these scrolls have been found in caves since 1947. The community is generally identified with the Essenes, although this is not certain. The scrolls consist mostly of manuscripts and commentaries of scriptures of Old Testament, and Rules for the Congregation of Qumran. Of special interest is matter relating to a certain 'teacher of righteousness' antedating Jesus; this teacher was a member of the sect.

Deane, Mrs Ada Emma English spirit photographer, obtained her first extra in June 1920. She gave many sittings at the W. T. Stead Borderland Library. Testimony by the A.S.P.R. 1921 of a remarkable sitting with Dr Allerton Cushman, Director of the National Laboratories of Washington, in which a startling likeness of his daughter appeared on the plate. For three years experiments were made of exposing plates during the Cenotaph ceremony, many extras were obtained and the case received wide publicity. Dr Hereward Carrington tested this medium with success and reported the details in the *Journal of A.S.P.R.*, May 1925.

Death To Spiritualists, death is merely the casting off of the earthly garment—the physical body, leaving the etheric body (or double), a duplicate form still associated with the conscious mind and spirit of the individual, but functioning now in a different sphere. This separation of the etheric from the physical self, has been witnessed at the deathbed many times by people with clairvoyant tendencies. After death, the personality and the character of the individual are not changed, but there is no longer the need to eat, sleep or work for the maintenance of this new body. It feels solid and moves in the same way among seemingly solid surroundings. The mind, however, has a more direct power of action upon the environment and modifies this according to its habitual mode of thought. Thus, a person might find himself dressed in familiar clothes among recognizable surroundings, but finds that a strong creative mental effort is needed to construct further. *See* **Spheres.**

Deathbed Experiences It has often been noted how dying persons frequently look up with the light of recognition in their eyes, and murmur a greeting to an invisible deceased friend or relative. Sometimes a wonderful vision is described, causing an expression of rapture to light the dying features. That this supports survival is shown by the fact that it is *deceased* people who are seen, and that this experience has been known to happen to people who have expressed scepticism of survival all their lives. To the Spiritualist it would seem to be the first realization of the functioning of vision in the etheric body.

Deism Belief in one god as creator, but not revelatory.

Delawarr Camera An invention used for diagnosing illness by taking photographs by supernormal means. It is claimed to operate on an entirely new physical theory, called 'radionics' by its inventor. It is as well to point out that many supernormal photographs have been obtained through mediumship without the necessity for special apparatus.

Delphic Circle   A development circle for mediums was organized under Frederick Thurston, M.A. in London. Mrs Thompson, Alfred Vout Peters and Mrs Laura Finch were developed there.

Delphic Oracle (400 B.C.)   The famous ancient Greek oracle, the prophetess Pythia, who worked under a trance induced by intoxicating fumes, and who, according to Plutarch, used to give advice to the kings of that period.

Delusion   A fallacy, deception, or false belief.

Dematerialisation   The disintegration and disappearance of matter, or a materialized form. At physical seances parts of the medium's body have been known to temporarily disappear. Small objects have also disappeared, if these reappear elsewhere, they are known as asports. *See also*, **Apports, Matter through matter.**

Demiurge   The world builder and maker of Platonic philosophy.

Demonstration   *See* **Public Demonstration**

Denis, Leon (1846–1927)   Was successor to Allan Kardec. French Spiritualist and medium, propagandist and author of many books.

Denton, William   Boston Professor of Geology who checked Dr Buchanan's researches into psychometry (1863).

Dermography   The appearance of writing on the skin, similar to stigmatic writing except that it does not last for very long. Some mediums have given answers to messages in this way (ref. Mrs Seymour and Miss Coggswell of Vermont). It is known that similar marks can be produced in certain cases by hypnotic suggestion.

Dervish A member of a Moslem order. A brother of an association of mystic ascetics.

Descartes, Rene (1596–1650) Famous French rationalist philosopher who starting from the premise 'I think, therefore I am', built up a demonstrable system of philosophy and founded the rationalist school which believes that reason may attain knowledge, owing nothing to sense experience (*a priori* knowledge). Mathematics and logic are good instances of knowledge so gained.

Descendant That degree of the ecliptic which is setting. Opposite the Ascendant.

Desmond, Shaw (1876–1960) Well-known Irish poet and Spiritualist speaker, wrote many psychic books. Was a firm believer in reincarnation, claiming remembrance of some of his former lives.

Determinism The opposite of freewill. Doctrine in which all human action is the result of external influences on the will.

Deva Hindu term for a radiant being, a god.

Devachan Hindu term descriptive of an intermediate state between incarnations. Not to be confused with the spheres of Spiritualism.

Development, Mediumistic *See* **Circle development.**

Devil Traditional personification of evil influences, he has no place in Spiritualism, which teaches that evil is the result of man's ignorance and cruelty, that man alone bears the responsibility for this and has the opportunity to make reparation for wilful evil-doing, both here and in the next stage of existence.

Dharana The sixth stage of Yoga. Mental composure and steadying of the mind.

Dharma   Law of Buddha; a sense of divine duty at a given moment.

Dhyana   The seventh stage of Yoga. Thought fixed on Absolute idea.

Diagnosis, Healing   Some healers find they have developed a power of diagnosis along with their healing ability. This is usually due to the co-operation of a doctor in the spirit world. While spirit healing can do nothing but good, diagnosis may be in error (as also may be its earthly counterpart), therefore responsible healers refrain from pronouncing a diagnosis to the patient unless it is confirmed by medical opinion.

Diakka   A term coined by A. J. Davis for mischievous and ignorant spirits.

Dialectical Society   Founded in London in 1867 'to investigate the phenomena alleged to be Spiritual Manifestations, and to report thereon'. It had a committee of thirty-three members, including Sir Alfred Russell Wallace. Their report was published in 1871 and contained six propositions establishing psychic phenomena with a summary of evidence obtained.

Dianetics   Technique of Scientology for alleged discovery of past lives.

Dicyanin Screens   Devices for making the human aura visible to normal sight, invented by Dr Walter J. Kilner (1847–1920) of St Thomas's Hospital. They work by inducing eye fatigue in the short visible purple range thus making the eye temporarily more sensitive to waves beyond the normally visible. Two small dicyanin screens can be made into spectacles, they are then commonly referred to as 'Kilner goggles'.

Dingwall, Dr Eric John, M.A., D.Sc., Ph.D. Was Director of Department of Psychical Phenomena A.S.P.R. 1921–22. Research Officer of S.P.R. 1922–27. Author of several books on phenomena and psychic research.

Direct Drawing and Painting Psychic drawing and painting where the hand of the medium is not used; the materials combining directly to produce an artistic result. These are sometimes found to bear a striking resemblance to existing works of art. Mediums known for this phenomena: David Duguid, Mrs E. J. French and the Bangs sisters.

Direct Voice The phenomena of a voice proceeding from an artificial larynx, made from ectoplasmic material extracted from the medium and sitters. A very striking phenomena, as the voices often sound identical in intonation with that of the deceased person represented. The perfection of this form of mediumship depends on many factors: the communicating spirit is said to need much experience in manipulating the larynx, which he has to operate by moulding it to his own vocal organs. Often the 'voicebox' is attached to a megaphone or trumpet which moves around the room apparently unaided, but really actuated by rods of the ectoplasm. Sittings usually take place in dim light although results have been obtained in good daylight. Proof of the validity of this phenomena was obtained in the Margery seances by B. K. Thorogood who constructed a soundproof box containing a microphone connected to a loudspeaker in another room. Under these stringent conditions, the independence of the voice was proved.

Direct Voice Telephone An instrument devised by J. B. McIndoe to enable the Direct Voice phenomena to be heard in daylight. A sensitive telephone transmitter was placed on the medium's larynx under a highly buttoned, high collared coat, the sitters were connected to the transmitter by a telephone receiver. Experiments with this apparatus on medium Andrew McCreadie were successfully carried out.

Direct Writing Psychography. Writing produced without visible contact with the medium, though synchronized movements of the hands have been known to accompany it (Eusapia Paladino). Partly materialized hands have also produced written messages. Writing has been obtained in a sealed metal box through Mrs Everitt's mediumship and a control 'Sambor'. In 1931 writing was produced on wax tablets enclosed in boxes by Mme Ignath of Oslo. A familiar form of this phenomena is known as 'slate writing' where writing appears between a pair of sealed slates face to face. This last method is open to question because of the many cases of fraud known in its production.

Disassociation Term used in psychic research for an independent activity of a part of the mind which behaves in some way like a separate individual.

Discarnate Not incarnate. Not possessing a body of flesh. Usually descriptive of a spirit person who has died in the earthly sense.

Divination Wilful exploration of the future or the discovery of hidden things by various practices. Most common are: astrology, dowsing, dreams, cards, crystal-gazing, numerology, palmistry, omens. It does not form a part of the practice of Spiritualism, although spontaneous prophecy is occasionally given.

Divining Rod A V-shaped rod of various springy materials, traditionally a twig of hazel. When the dowser holds it in a state of tension the apex will move when a source of water, or some specified hidden objective is traversed. According to J. Cecil Maby (*Physics of the Divining Rod*) there would appear to be a variation of muscle tone somehow influenced by the hidden sources, of which the twig becomes a sensitive indicator.

Dixon Smith, Lt. Col. Spiritualist author who proposed a theoretical extension of known physics, based on the quantum theory, to account for the interpenetration of spirit spheres of existence with the earthly state.

'Doctor' A control of Rev. Stainton Moses, claimed to be Athenodorus, stoic philosophical instructor of Tiberius. He was recognized as the supervisor and guide of Stainton Moses for twenty-one years, and author of the two books of Spirit teachings delivered through S.M.

Doorkeeper The personal spirit control of a medium, said to be responsible for the maintenance of the physical body during the production of mediumistic phenomena. North American Indians and Zulus are commonly met with in this capacity, presumably for their qualities of steadfastness and reliability. They work in close co-operation with a band of spirits who are combined for any specific purpose connected with phenomena.

Doppelgänger German term for the astral body.

Doten, Miss Lizzie (1828–1908) Noted American medium, inspirational speaker and poet. Claimed the influence of the late Edgar Allen Poe, in production of a poem 'Resurrexi' very characteristic of his style.

Double Also known as etheric body. Interpenetrating counterpart of the physical body and linked to it by an extensible cord. Normally coincidental, but capable of detachment under certain conditions, spontaneous or induced. Tests have been made by various researchers, notably Col. Rochas, Dr Durville by hypnosis methods. Dr Malta and Zaalberg. Van Zelst weighed the double and pronounced it to be $2\frac{1}{4}$ oz. This weight agrees with experiments conducted by weighing dying persons by Dr Duncan McDougall of Haverhill, Mass. There is also photographic evidence for the existence of the double by Rochas, Durville, Delanne, Aksakov, and Dr Ochorowicz.

Dowden, Hester (Mrs Hester Travers-Smith, 1868–1949) Automatist from Dublin, Ireland. Although convinced of survival she never called herself a Spiritualist, maintaining that she was all her life a psychic investigator. Was associated with Sir William Barrett and the S.P.R. Her control 'Johannes' was a great exponent of the 'Law of Affinities'. At the first sitting with Sir William, a ouija board was used but later discarded for a glass-topped table three feet by two feet with letters in haphazard order. The medium operated blindfolded, with her hand on a heart-shaped pointer mounted on felt pads. With this device, words were spelt out at the rate of 2,000 per hour. Some automatic writing was also produced; among communications received were facsimiles of Oscar Wilde's script and signature, Ellen Terry and Fanny Stirling.

Dowding, Air Chief Marshal, Lord, G.C.B., G.C.V.O., C.M.G. Former head of the Technical Department of the Air Ministry, 1930–36, Commander-in-Chief of Fighter Command during the Battle of Britain in 1940. A fearless champion of the truth as he sees it. An avowed Spiritualist and a pioneer for the cause of animal welfare. Lecturer and author of several books on Spiritualism, including *Many Mansions* and *Lychgate*.

Dowsing Water divining by rod, twig or pendulum. Also known as rhabdomancy, radiesthesia. Nowadays dowsing techniques are applied to many fields: healing, the finding of missing objects or people, mineral prospecting, sexing of chicks, diagnosis by analysis of blood or sputum spots. Not regarded as mediumistic phenomena.

Drapery, Spirit Spirit robes, the simple flowing garments worn by spirit people in their own sphere is usually so described. If they wish to give evidence of survival they have to remember their former appearance, and convey somehow an image to the medium which can be recognized, this would have to include the appropriate dress. Spirits when first released from the physical body at death, tend to retain replicas of the clothes they have been accustomed to wear, as they are conditioned by the mental habit. Later, they discard these for the more comfortable and graceful 'spirit robe'. The drapery observed at materialization phenomena is ectoplasmic in substance and is said to be drawn from the actual clothing of the medium. It is used to cover and protect unformed parts of the figure and to satisfy the requisites of modesty. On occasions, pieces have been submitted for analysis which is necessarily brief, as it disintegrates rapidly into the air. It is interesting to note that the clothes of materialization mediums are reputed to be subject to heavy wear during seances, particularly in the lining of the underarms.

Dreams Experiences during the sleeping state are common enough, and are normally dismissed as fancy. There are some however, which offer interesting evidence of the existence of supernormal faculties, and these present many problems to the psychic investigator. Spiritualists maintain the possibility of visits during the sleep state, by the double to the spirit spheres where contact is made with departed friends and relatives. Unfortunately, disjointed memories are mostly all that are retained until passing the gate of death oneself, when complete memory returns. Many cases are known where difficult problems have been solved in or by a dream. Some spirit communicators have stated that they need to be in a dream state themselves in order to communicate. An interesting feature of J. W. Dunne's philosophy of Serialism, is the possible foreshadowing of the future in dreams, as testified by his own experiments.

Dream Allegory According to Freudian psychology, dreams are allegorical, they 'dress up' our less admissible desires to the waking consciousness thereby providing a safety-valve for emotions which are suppressed by the conventions of our society.

Dream Body *See* **Astral body** and **Projection.**

Dream Communications Come usually as warnings to the individual, and are vivid enough in their impression to influence actions subsequently taken. This could well be a form of temporary clairvoyance or clairaudience on the part of the dreamer.

Dream Prophecies Are repetitive and often accompanied by sweating and trembling on awakening. They usually consist of some kind of pre-vision in detail of some imminent disaster. Many authenticated cases have been recorded.

Dreaming True The possession of control and consciousness whilst in the dream state. This occasionally occurs spontaneously with some, but according to Dr Hereward Carrington it can be acquired with practice.

Dreisch, Dr Hans Prominent German psychic investigator and Professor of Philosophy at University of Leipzig. President of S.P.R. 1926–27. Became convinced of the actuality of psychic phenomena. Tested physical medium Willi Schneider in 1922. Author of several books on psychical research.

Dualism Doctrine of opposing forces of good and evil.

Dual Personality Usually advanced as an alternative to spirit control, by psychologists. There are many well-known pathological cases of dual personality, where the one body appears to be the battle-ground for conflicting personalities. Superficially this resembles mediumship, but closer acquaintance with mediums reveals not a conflict, but a close co-operation of personalities under a definite control and mutual agreement. The bringing to light of knowledge unknown to the medium cannot be explained by any system of 'subconscious personalities'.

Duguid, David (1832–1907) A non-professional medium of Glasgow who often produced direct drawing and painting in complete darkness. Telekinetic phenomena and direct voice, fire immunity, spirit photography were also recorded of his mediumship. Among his controls were claimed Jacob Ruisdale and J. van Steen. He dictated a book said to be the history of 'Hafed', a warrior prince of Persia and contemporary of Jesus and the Magi.

Duncan, Helen Materialization medium of Dundee. There was much controversy over her phenomena. The S.P.R. branded her as a fraud in 1931 and her husband confessed. In Edinburgh, 1932, she was exposed again. In view of the many responsible people who vouched for the genuineness of her phenomena, it appears that she may have stooped to fraud when the genuine phenomena would not come.

Dunne, J. W. Originator of a philosophic conception of the nature of time, the universe, and the veridical nature of dreams. He wrote several books on his theory of Serialism, in which he takes the view of man's consciousness following a prescribed path through events; the 'travelling now' he calls it. This accounts for possible pre-vision by a widening of the perceptive field of attention during sleep.

Du Prel, Baron Carl (1839–1899) German philosopher and psychic researcher. Tested mediums Eglinton and Eusapia Paladino and became convinced of the existence of transcendental beings and human survival.

Dweller on the Threshold An occult term for the 'doorkeeper' (q.v.).

Dynamistograph Two Dutch physicists, Dr J. L. W. Matla and Dr G. J. Zaalberg Van Zelst of the Hague, under spirit guidance constructed a complicated instrument for direct communication without a medium. The device was placed in a sealed room; through a small window in the wall a dial could be observed on which selected letters would appear. Long intelligent communications were received by this means.

'Ear of Dionysius' Case   A remarkable case of cross-correspondence attributed to the discarnate minds of Professors Verrall and Butcher. A paper on this case was presented to the S.P.R. by its president the Earl of Balfour in 1916.

Earthbound   Descriptive of spirits who are still operating close to earth conditions by reason of old attachments, habits or ignorance of their state. The habitual attitude of mind is said to be the strongest factor in determining the future state of a person after death. Self-centredness bars progress, because the individual voluntarily shuts himself off from helpful contacts. Earthbound spirits are sometimes held to be responsible for hauntings. They can certainly exert a bad influence over like-minded people still on earth by gratification of their earthy desires by proxy, which they cannot satisfy in their new state. Rescue circles help to enlighten such misguided and ignorant spirits.

Earth Plane   All that pertains to the ordinary earth life, as distinct from the spirit world.

Ecstasy   A rapturous state, common to mystics and saints of all religions, during which the centre of perception changes from the material into the spiritual world. The faculties are often exalted and supernormal feats have been achieved while in this state. Akin to the Yoga state of 'Samadhi' and of trance-like states reached by the process of meditative practices.

Ectenic Force   A term for Psychic Force (q.v.), coined by Professor Thury.

Ectoplasm   A subtle living matter present in the physical body, primarily invisible but capable of assuming vaporous liquid or solid states and properties. It is extruded usually in the dark from the pores and the various orifices of the body, and is slightly luminous, the more so when condensed. The temperature of the room is usually lowered when ectoplasm is produced; it possesses a characteristic smell and is cold to the touch. This substance is held to be responsible for the production of all phenomena classed as 'physical', and is the substance out of which materialized forms are built by the spirit operators. In addition they build elastic or rigid rods to produce movement in objects (telekinesis), raps and noises; artificial 'voiceboxes' for the phenomena of the direct and independent voice. The levitation of tables and heavy objects is accomplished by building extensible columns under them. Hands have materialized, dipped themselves into molten wax and then dissolved, leaving perfect moulds behind that are impossible of duplication by ordinary means (*see* **Kluski**). Solid balls of cold light are familiar manifestations in physical phenomena. Ectoplasm has been photographed on many occasions and appears opaque white by infra-red flashlight which is the usual method employed. Sudden exposure to white light is of great physical danger to the medium when the ectoplasm is being used, due it seems to its swift elastic recoil as it returns to its source. In movement it can be swift or slow, it can build a perfect representation of a living human body with pulse warmth and muscular movement. Dr Dombrowski of the Polish S.P.R. had a sample analysed in 1916 and to quote a summary of the bacteriological report: 'The substance is albuminoid matter accompanied by fatty matter and cells found in the human organism. Starch and sugar, discoverable by Fehling's test, are absent.'

Eddy Brothers   Horatio and William, American materialization mediums investigated by Col. Olcott. Later regarded as of doubtful authenticity by Podmore.

Eddy, Mary Baker   American founder of the Christian Science movement in 1866. She elaborated her system after receiving healing from Dr Quimby of 'New Thought' movement.

Edinburgh Psychic College   Founded 1932 by Mrs Ethel Miller to investigate psychic phenomena and to assist in spreading knowledge concerning it.

Edmonds, John Worth ('Judge Edmonds' 1816–1874)   Early American champion of Spiritualism who published his experiences in the *New York Courier* as early as 1 August 1853. Later he himself developed mediumship and exerted a great influence on the early growth of American Spiritualism.

Edwards, Harry   Famous Spiritualist healer of England, tireless worker for spirit healing. Has demonstrated many times its power in public meetings and deals with an enormous weekly postbag of several thousand letters, mainly requests for absent healing treatment which is freely given. He is President of the National Federation of Spiritual Healers and has challenged the medical authorities on his test cases of healed 'incurables'. Was a close friend of Welsh medium Jack Webber, and sat in the circle which produced outstanding physical phenomena, much of which was recorded by infra-red photography. In all his work Edwards is assisted by George and Olive Burton.

Eglinton, William   English physical medium, over whose slate-writing phenomena a great controversy raged between the S.P.R. and the Spiritualists. Many weighty testimonies to his genuineness were furnished including those of Aksakov, Sir Alfred Russell Wallace and Professor Richet. Archdeacon Colley once exposed him, but the Council of the British National Association of Spiritualists dismissed the charge on the grounds that no direct evidence could be obtained from the accusers. Among his most startling feats was recorded that of his own transportation on 16 March 1878 through a ceiling to the floor above (*The Spiritualist*, 22 March 1878).

Ego The self-consciousness of the individual. The soul.

Eidolon Word coined by Professor Daumer, meaning 'shape' for ectoplasmic forms which he maintained were neither bodies nor souls.

Eidos, The World of The fourth sphere, level of consciousness, or the Plane of Colour, as described in an alleged communication from F. W. H. Myers, through the hand of Miss Geraldine Cummins.

Elberfeld Horses The potential mathematical genius of horses was discovered by William von Osten in 1891. The work was continued after his death by Herr Krall of Elberfeld, who taught four horses mathematics, including the extraction of square and cubic roots and the ability to spell. They gave answers by blows of their hooves. This was attested by at least 14 famous scientists of the time, but no explanation was ever discovered. Spiritualists might incline to a belief in the possibility of a horse being controlled as a medium.

Electrical Phenomena Have been observed in the seance room. Dr Ochorowicz discovered the fact that a medium could decrease considerably the electrical resistance of her body, confirming experiments by E. K. Müller of Zurich. Dr Kilner found the human aura completely dispersed under a negative charge. Some marks found on sealed photographic plates, after contact with a medium's fingers suggest radioactivity.

Electronic Communication The goal of many enthusiastic, electrically minded Spiritualists. Some machines have been constructed, mostly consisting of tuned circuits of various kinds, and claims have been made to the effect that mediumistic development can be assisted by their use, but little satisfactory evidence for this has yet appeared. An early attempt at mechanical communication was the Dynamistograph (q.v.).

Elemental Occult term for a 'nature spirit' said to possess little intelligence by human standards, but great power in its natural element (meaning the primitive elements of fire, air, earth, water). The word is also used occasionally to denote a discarnate entity of low intelligence.

Elementary Occult term for an astral 'shell' which is supposed to account for hauntings and poltergeist phenomena. The theory is that after death this shell gradually disintegrates, the 'wicked' ones lasting the longest. Not accepted by Spiritualism.

Elliot, The Rev. G. Maurice (Born 1883) An active worker for bringing psychic phenomena to the notice of the church. Supporter of Mme St Clair Stobart in her projected Federation of Churches. He was Secretary to the Churches Fellowship for Psychical Study, and a member of the Archbishop's Commission on Divine Healing. He urged the churches to carry out Jesus's injunction to 'heal the sick'. Noted author of many works on theological, historical and psychic subjects.

Elongation A peculiar phenomenon associated with some physical mediums, in which the body of the medium is altered considerably in stature. D. D. Home exhibited this phenomena on several occasions, once by at least fifty people. His maximum 'growth' was recorded as eleven inches. Home's own explanation was that the hipbone and the short ribs separated to a greater than normal extent. Legs and arms are reported to have lengthened and shortened independently. Other mediums who produced this phenomena were: Florence Cook, Frank Herne, J. J. Morse, Eusapia Paladino and Mrs Thompson. Spanish musical prodigy Pepito Ariola at three and a half years could stretch only five notes, yet sounded full octaves during performances (q.v.).

Emanations Radiations of many kinds are now known to science. Those which are as yet unknown, may be responsible for many of the problems of psychical research. In particular, the faculties of psychometry, dowsing and radiesthesia, may well be due to the interpretation of some emission from various objects and minerals. Baron Reichenbach in 1840 discovered that certain people could see light from magnets in complete darkness; his testimony was confirmed by experiments of the S.P.R. There have been positive tests demonstrating the radio-activity of living matter. Frau Silbert during experiments with Dr Joseph Bieniedal in 1930, produced fluorescence in a glass of uranium salt solution, by holding it in her hand; in the dark it was visible to a distance of ten yeards. The physical phenomena of Spiritualism are made possible by an emanation from the human body, called ectoplasm (q.v.).

Empiric Founded on experience and, or, observation, not theory.

Empiricists One of the two great divisions of opinion in early philosophy, represented by Locke, Berkeley and Hume, as opposed to the 'rationalist' school. They held that knowledge is ultimately derived from the experience reached through the senses; which means that nothing exists which is not known.

Engram Term of Scientology for a painful mental image, occasioned by suffering in a past incarnation.

Entering the Silence A short quiet period, often observed in Spiritualist Church services, as a brief time for meditation or attunement to spiritual influences. Meditation services and circles are held for longer periods for the same purpose.

Entity A discarnate personality. An individual.

Epiphenomenalism The materialistic idea that consciousness is a by-product, and arises from physical neural processes.

Epistemology That part of philosophy which studies the origins, methods and validity of knowledge.

Epworth Phenomena Psychic tappings at Epworth vicarage in 1716, the home of the Rev. Samuel Wesley, father of John Wesley. The medium concerned was probably Hetty Wesley, one of his daughters, and the spirit was known as 'Old Jeffrey'.

Equinox The point where the sun appears to cross the celestial equator; this occurs twice every year, when day and night are of equal length all the world over. The basis of our calendar measurement.

Eschatology Those sections of theology and philosophy which deal with the end of physical forms and future states of being.

Esoteric That which is not accessible except by initiation. Unfortunately 'esoteric' cults tend to form around any medium who has a strong control with an impressive flow of oratory. In true Spiritualism however, there is little wisdom required on our part which is hidden or difficult to acquire. Discrimination and common sense should be used when assessing communications. The teachings of true missionaries from the other world proclaim the same truths in essence, although couched in terms suitable for their time and age. We do not need initiation to understand; the teachers are unanimous—Service to God through humanity. Tolerance and kindliness to all.

E.S.P. Extra Sensory Perception (q.v.).

D'Esperance, Mme Elizabeth (1855–1919) A non-professional medium who exhibited the whole range of mediumistic phenomena. Many attempts to discover fraud were unsuccessful but damaged the medium's health. In order that she herself might be seen at the same time as the materialized figures, she sat usually outside the cabinet. An interesting feature is her own account of the curious 'community of sensation' she experienced with the materialized form. If, for instance, the form was embraced, she felt this in her own person. It was with this medium that Aksakov witnessed the famous case of partial dematerialization of the medium from the waist downwards. Wonderful apport phenomena included the production of an exotic Indian plant (Ixoro Crocota) 22 in. high, with a stem filling the neck of a bottle containing the roots. This was presented to William Oxley, who kept it for three months. On another occasion, a great Golden Lily, seven feet high, was apported before Professors Boutlerof, Fiedlev, Aksakov and others.

Essenes An early Jewish sect of high ideals, located in the Dead Sea region, contemporary with the time of Jesus, who it is thought by many may have belonged to the Essenes and imbibed their teachings. They may have originated from Buddhism, as they can be traced back from Judea to Egypt, then to Indian sources; especially as the life of Jesus forms a parallel in many respects to that of Gotama. In practice the Essenes were monastic, self-sacrificing and versed in the art of healing. With the finding of the Qumran Dead Sea Scrolls, much more knowledge of those times is coming to light. Some think it significant that Jesus while rebuking Scribes and Pharisees, never criticized the Essenes.

Ether Hypothetical all-pervading, fluidic substance, which fills the universe and is responsible for the transmission of light and heat. We are told that the material of the spirit spheres permeates that of earth; the word appears to have been adopted by Spiritualism to describe these finer substances.

Etheric body A counterpart of the physical body which lives on after death. Also known as the spirit body, double or perispirit by Spiritualists. Although made of material it is considerably lighter. It is purported to weigh $2\frac{1}{2}$ oz. approximately, by results of experiments conducted in weighing dying persons. Normally invisible, it is occasionally seen by clairvoyants. During earth life it is linked to the physical body by a cord; when this is severed, death of the physical body takes place.

Etheric Double *See* **Etheric body.**

Etheric Plane, or sphere That part of the spirit world adjacent to the earth. The landing place of all, in passing through the gates of death, and gravitating to the various groups according to their spiritual development. This is the plane most often contacted for evidence of survival by mediums. The surroundings are said by its inhabitants to resemble the earth, but are more amenable by means of constructive thought acting directly upon them.

Etheric Senses These, so we learn by communication, correspond closely with our earthly senses, and function similarly, but there would appear to be important extensions of sense, difficult for us to comprehend, plus telepathy as a normal means of communication. Their senses, like ours, function only on their own sphere, the next higher remaining invisible.

Ethics, Philosophy of So far as Spiritualism is concerned, its ethics are of the Objectivist kind, seeking the four values of moral goodness, truth, beauty and happiness. They would assert that these values represent eternal reality.

E.T.P. Extra Temporal Perception (q.v.).

Euthanasia The practice of a voluntary or intentional painless termination of life for incurables. By the standards of Spiritualism any taking of human life is misguided, as Spiritualists take the view that earthly life is a training ground for an indestructible spirit being; therefore to hasten the transition would effect

76

no useful purpose. On the other hand, a doctor who mercifully terminated a life of pain would not necessarily be accused of unspiritual action, as the motive is considered to be the most important indicator of individual spiritual attainment; therefore if the doctor was actuated purely by humane motives, for him it would be a spiritual act.

Eva C. Also known as Martha Beraud, Mme Waespé; a French materialization medium who provided some of the best attested evidence of this phenomena. Tested by Professor Richet, then Baron Schrenck-Notzing, who employed detectives to check on her private life. A series of experiments was held with the Baron and Mme Bisson, emetics were administered to test for regurgitation with negative result: 225 good photographs were obtained of phenomena during these sittings. Another important series was held in Dr Geley's laboratory under the most stringent conditions during 1917–18, and phenomena were witnessed in all by 150 people, many of whom were noted scientists.

Evangelist   A writer of one of the four Christian gospels. An authorized preacher of the gospels.

Evans, W. H.   English trance and inspirational medium, exponent of A. J. Davis's work *Harmonial Philosophy*. Did much public work and edited a London monthly *Beyond*. Also author of many books on Spiritualism.

Everitt, Mrs Thomas (1825–1915)   The first non-professional British medium to produce the direct voice in England, noted for the loudness of the voices. She also attained extraordinary speeds in direct writing. Sir William Crookes and Serjeant Cox both sat with her on more than one occasion and she convinced some of the keenest minds of her day. Her services for Spiritualism were given freely until her passing.

Evidence, Law of There are many arguments about what constitutes 'evidence', so here is an excerpt from Taylor's *Law of Evidence*: 'None but mathematical proof is susceptible of that high degree of evidence called demonstration, which excludes all possibility of error. In the investigation of matters of fact, such evidence cannot be obtained, and the most that can be said is that there is no reasonable doubt concerning them. The true question, therefore, in trials of fact is not whether it is possible that the testimony may be false, but whether there is sufficient probability of its truth; that is, whether the facts are proved by competent and satisfactory evidence. By *competent evidence* is meant that which the law requires as the fit and appropriate proof in the particular case ... By *satisfactory evidence*, which is sometimes called *sufficient* evidence, is intended that amount of which ordinarily satisfies an unprejudiced mind beyond reasonable doubt. The circumstances which will amount to this degree of proof can never be previously defined. The only legal test of which they are susceptible is their sufficiency to satisfy the mind and conscience of an ordinary man, and so to convince him that he would venture to act upon that conviction in matters of important personal interest.'

The above definition of legal proof makes it clear that the common man is capable of proving for himself.

Evil Spirits We hear more of these from theology than Spiritualism. As the 'spirits' are human, albeit in a different sphere, it follows that they are no more evil than we. Indeed, many of them have advanced spiritually in tolerance and understanding. From the Spiritualist's law of 'like attracting like', it is obvious that a person predisposed to cruelty and intolerance will attract spirits who are earthbound by the same kind of ignorance, whereas one who desires peace and kindliness, can only attract those in the next sphere who are willing to assist. To call spirits 'evil', is mainly the result of fear of the unknown. In most cases they could with more truth be called ignorant—misguided—stupid, but rarely evil. Testimony from many Spiritualist rescue circles would amply confirm this.

Evolution, Theory of Now generally accepted by science as a fact, that higher forms of life are derived from earlier and simpler forms.

Evolution, Spiritual The gradual unfoldment of spiritual understanding on this earth and the succeeding progress in the spirit spheres.

Existentialism A modern pessimistic philosophy, emphasizing the view that human existence is of utter insignificance and value. It possibly originated through the Danish philosopher Kierkegaard (1813–1855).

Existents Branch of philosophy which deals with categories of 'being' or the different forms which reality can assume. A division of existents postulated by Professor Whitehead: '1. The true and real things which endure. 2. The true and real things which occur. 3. The abstract things which recur. 4. The Laws of Nature.'

Exorcism The act of expelling evil spirits by Divine appeal; often practised in the early churches, but to a much lesser degree now. The services of Spiritualist mediums are sometimes resorted to when conventional means fail. By their psychic perception they can usually detect the nature of the possessing spirit (not necessarily 'evil'), and can enlighten its understanding and persuade it to cease from troubling the victim, and seek the path of love and truth. This treatment is routine to the rescue circles of Spiritualism, where the possessing entity is persuaded to leave the victim for the body of the medium, whereby the controls of the medium have some power to restrain its activities, and enable the circle to address and reason with the spirit.

Exoteric Not secret, opposite to esoteric.

Exteriorization of Motricity Action of a medium's motor force outside the bounds of his body. Sympathetic movements of mediums which coincide with telekinetic phenomena. In support of a theory to explain telekinesis, many instruments have been constructed to demonstrate the existence of a repulsive and attractive force generated from each side of the body. (*See* **Biometer of Baraduc.**) Movements were said to be produced when the forces were not balanced. The modern view is, that ectoplasm is the moving agent.

Exteriorization of Sensation, and sensitivity Sensory perception of the medium outside the bounds of his body, discovered by Dr Paul Joire in 1892. Sensations exteriorized in the double were observed during studies of hypnology and psychical phenomena. Mme d'Esperance, materialization medium, experienced the physical sensations of materialized forms, in her own body.

Exteriorization of Substance *See* **Ectoplasm, Emanations.**

Externalized Impression An impression perceived as though coming from without, but which has really originated from within the mind.

Extra Descriptive of the supernormal appearance of a face or figure on sensitive photographic material.

Extra Sensory Perception (E.S.P.) Scientific term for perception without use of the recognized sense channels. Many thousands of experiments have been conducted by Professor J. B. Rhine of Duke University, N. Carolina, which give sound statistical evidence of the existence of a telepathic function in some individuals, not dependent upon the known physical laws relating to radiation and time lag in signal reception.

These facts are often advanced as an 'explanation' of medium-ship, but a brief study will soon show important differences. The medium's function is to give evidence of survival, not telepathy. The information given is often unknown to the sitter at the time, and in the absence of a 'transmitter', the E.S.P. explanation does not suffice. (Unless we allow the sender to be in the spirit world!) A scientific definition gives: 'A partial or complete correspondence (a) between the mental patterns of two persons A and B which is not to be accounted for by normal sense perception, or by inferences drawn by sense-perception or chance-coincidence *or* (b) between a mental pattern of a person A and an object or event in the physical world which is not to be accounted for by normal sense-perception or by inferences drawn from sense-perception or by chance coincidence. In neither (a) nor (b) need the corres-pondence be between contemporaneous patterns or between a mental pattern and a physical object which are contempor-aneous.' (*Modern Experiments in Telepathy*, by Soal and Bate-man.)

Extra Temporal Perception (E.T.P.), E.S.P. Through time, as well as distance in space.

Extrovert Descriptive of a sociable, impulsive, sympathetic character, whose interest is outside of the self. Opposite of introvert.

Eyeless Sight A faculty for seeing from the skin, said to be a property of the etheric body.

Facsimile Writing Some impressive reproductions of famous people's writing, even their signatures, have been written by automatists. Notable cases are those of Oscar Wilde through Hester Dowden, and the Blanche Abercromby case, in Stainton Moses' mediumship.

Fairies   Evidence for the existence of the little folk, comes mainly from photographs. Sir A. Conan Doyle wrote of Miss Elsie Wright, of sixteen years, daughter of a mechanic who with her ten-year-old cousin claimed to have seen fairies since 1915, and on being given a box camera, took some clear photographs of them in bright sunlight. Opinions of authorities were, that the photographs could have been produced by studio work but there was no evidence of this. Only a few Spiritualists subscribe to the belief. An alternative view is that clairvoyant perception may sometimes see spirit forms in miniature. It is possible too, that thought can produce photographic effects.

Faith   Belief in what one cannot see (St Augustine). Belief without proof, not expected in Spiritualism where proof is offered.

Faith Healing   Healing which is said to be effected by the patient's faith in Divine power. Distinct from the term Spirit healing, in which the patient often has no faith. Sometimes an animal is treated and cured, which rules out faith as the necessary factor. The healing at Lourdes provides best attested cases of faith-healing.

Fakirs   Members of a Moslem mendicant sect, who possess or claim to possess psychic powers. They often practise self-mortification and suffer self-inflicted wounds. Although much of what we hear is probably legend, some do achieve remarkable powers. Burial alive in a self-induced catalepsy has often been demonstrated, also control over heart-beats and all body functions, swift healing of cuts, stoppage of the blood flow, insensibility to pain. Some of their 'miracles' have been attributed to mass hypnosis.

Familiar   A term much used in medieval witchcraft to denote a spirit attendant of a witch. Sometimes identified with the witches cat. Socrates and Joan of Arc also claimed spirits which advised them in emergencies.

Famous Returns   Many of the illustrious are alleged to have returned, but it is very difficult to prove their claims; the more so when we hear of the possibility of impersonation by spirits who possess histrionic powers and wish to shine in a little reflected glory. F. W. H. Myers, founder of the S.P.R., famous literary man of great learning, is purported to have written much through the hand of Miss Geraldine Cummins. This script has been approved as being perfect in character of expression and idiom. Oscar Wilde is alleged to have written through Hester Dowden and signed his name. It is easier perhaps for the average person to give evidence after death, as there are only a few who know very much about him, and there is little incentive for deception.

Fatalism   Doctrine of complete determinism by divine power.

'Feda'   Famous control of Mrs Osborne Leonard, English medium. 'Feda' was said to have been married to one of the medium's ancestors in India, and to have died at the age of thirteen years in 1900.

Feminine Principle   Matter, wisdom and form, have been considered feminine by polytheistic religions. Occultists interpret this as passive, negative and receptive qualities of cosmic order.

Findlay, J. Arthur, O.B.E., J.P.   Perhaps the best known modern writer of Spiritualist literature. Lecturer and researcher, founder of the Glasgow S.P.R. in 1920. Co-founder of Psychic Press Ltd, the Proprietors of *Psychic News*. Devoted five years of study to the direct voice mediumship of John C. Sloan. A prolific author, his best known work *On the Edge of the Etheric* ran to thirty impressions in its first year, and has reached its fifty-ninth impression since, and has been translated into nineteen foreign languages.

Finite   Limited, having an end or termination.

Fire Immunity   There are many famous cases in history: St Francis of Paula, St Catherine of Siena, St Francis of Assisi. Clovis, the Cansard leader in the rise of the Huguenots against Louis XIV in the presence of 600 men stood in a pyre until it burnt out; he was unscathed. The Fire Ordeal of medieval times though cruel, may have been the result of this phenomena being connected with saintly persons. D. D. Home demonstrated the handling of hot coals many times, and was able to transmit immunity to other persons or flowers, by the touch of his hand. Lord Adare and Sir William Crookes were witnesses of these feats. Other mediums said to have exhibited this wonder were: J. J. Morse, David Duguid, Dr Hooper, American medium Mrs Suydam, John Hopcroft of Glasgow, Mme de Crespigny and Mrs Annie Hunter. A control of Stainton Moses said it was due to a protective aura thrown around the object.

First Cause   Synonymous with Deity. Origin of the universe, the beginning of all things.

Flammarion, Camille (1842–1925)   Famed French astronomer, past-president of S.P.R. who experimented with psychic phenomena and himself developed automatism. He readily accepted the independent existence of the soul from the body, also the existence of faculties unknown to science, but not survival as a proved fact. He delivered the funeral oration at the death of Allan Kardec, where he declared that, 'Spiritualism is not a religion, but a science of which we as yet scarcely know the a.b.c.' Tests with mediums include those with Mme Girardin in Victor Hugo's home in Jersey, Mlle Huet, and Eusapia Paladino. Towards the end of his life he admitted: 'telepathy exists just as much between the dead and the living, as between the living.'

Flower Clairsentience   This form of mediumship requires a flower from the sitter. By holding it, the medium can contact and interpret various personal psychic associations.

Fluid Motor   Invention of Count de Tromelin to demonstrate the power of emanations from the hands. A balanced paper cylinder would revolve by this power.

Flying Saucers   Technically described as U.F.O's, or unidentified flying objects. There is general agreement about the saucer shape with three spherical supports beneath. Sound evidence can be found for the existence of these unheralded objects, but there is much dubious literature pandering to sensational tastes. Spiritualism holds no definite views on the subject.

Fodor, Dr Nandor, Ll.D.   Psycho-analyst of Budapest. Research Officer of I.I.P.R., Hon. member Hungarian Metaphysical Society, Budapest, and S.P.R. Assistant editor of *Light* 1933–35, lecturer and author of several books, including *Encyclopaedia of Psychic Science*.

Fortune Telling Act (Vagrancy Act)   Now repealed since the introduction of the Fraudulent Medium's Act 1951. Previously, mediums were liable to punishment, but now have a legal status, and are free to practise their gifts for the benefit of humanity.

Four Noble Truths   *See* **Buddhism.**

Fourth Dimension   A mathematical welding of space and time, as a framework for all natural phenomena. It is now generally accepted by scientists as a working hypothesis; it grew from Einstein's Relativity concept, and has now superseded the old idea of an all-pervading 'ether' for which no demonstrable evidence could be found. It is interesting to note that parapsychology experiments seem to deny the validity of ordinary 'time' concepts, and that Spiritualist communications often mention peculiar difficulties in the way of our understanding of spirit 'time'.

Fox, George (1624–1690) Founder of the Society of Friends (Quakers). At the age of nineteen he received a Divine command and forsook all family ties to preach against formalism in religion.

Fox Sisters Kate Margaret and Leah (the last-named also known as Mrs Fish, Mrs Brown or Mrs Underhill). Leah Fox wrote a book *The Missing Link* describing the historic phenomena. They are usually acclaimed as the founders of modern Spiritualism. In 1848, raps were heard in their home in Hydesville, America, and through the establishment of a code, intelligible messages were received from a deceased person.

Fraud Is confined almost entirely to private demonstrations of physical mediumship. (Direct voice, movement of objects and materialization.) The production of ectoplasm is necessary for this kind of phenomena, and as white light is said to be inhibitive and painful to the medium during the process, most of the manifestations have to take place in almost complete darkness. This makes it fairly easy for unscrupulous persons to fake phenomena in the presence of sensation seekers and gullible inquirers. It is quite obvious that the ordinary person visiting an unknown place under the dark conditions imposed, has no sure means of satisying himself whether the phenomena are genuine or not. Unless an investigation is made by a committee of experienced researchers under strictly controlled conditions, the possibility of fraud must be reckoned with. To the inquirer Spiritualists would say—leave physical phenomena alone; its existence has been demonstrated to qualified scientific inquirers many times, and it is on their testimony that we should accept it. If one needs proof of survival, mental mediumship is by far the safest and, to the thinking person, the most convincing. The best mediums for this work are vouched for by several respectable societies, and one may be sure of honesty throughout.

Fraudulent Mediums Act Became law in 1951, mainly through the unflagging efforts of Tom Brooks, M.B.E., M.P., for Normanton, West Riding, England. It replaced the Vagrancy Act, now repealed, under which mediums had been liable to prosecution. As a result genuine mediums now have legal status.

Freethinkers Rationalists. Persons not bound by religious beliefs or dogmas. Agnostics. Usually antagonistic to Spiritualism.

Friends, Society of (Quakers) Non-formalist religious society founded about 1666 by George Fox of Leicester, England. The name of 'Shakers' or 'Quakers' was originally a derisive epithet bestowed because of slight trembling movements noticed before a Friend became inspired to speak. Similar trembling is sometimes seen when a trance medium goes under control.

Gatty, Oliver, M.A., B.Sc. Oxon. Psychic researcher who undertook with Mr Besterman, investigations of Rudi Schneider for the S.P.R. in 1934.

Geley, Dr Gustave (1868–1924) Distinguished French psychic researcher. Director of the Institut Métapsychique Internationale. Many supernormal manifestations were produced in his fraud-proof laboratory. He suffered much opposition and prejudice from his former medical colleagues. Some of the best wax moulds were produced under his direction, through the mediumship of Kluski. Author of several works on psychical research including *From the Unconscious to the Conscious*. He accepted as true, survival, reincarnation and communication.

Gestic Magic Black magic in which assistance by evil spirits is said to be invoked.

Ghost   Apparition or supernormal appearance of a deceased person to the living. A popular term often associated with Spiritualism but in fact hardly mentioned by Spiritualists.

Ghost Club   Founded in London in 1862 for the investigation of current psychic phenomena. Many distinguished men were members when it was revived in 1881 by Sir William Barrett, F.R.S., and later in 1938 by Harry Price, when membership became open to both sexes. Its present object is to discuss and examine current psychic topics.

Gibbes, Miss E., F.R.G.S.   Member of S.P.R., colleague and publisher for Miss Geraldine Cummins, the noted automatist. Writer of several articles on experimental psychic work.

Glastonbury Scripts   A famous series of automatic communications covering a period 1918–27, published in nine booklets. In this case of cross-correspondence several widely separated mediums were involved at different times: John Alleyne, Hester Dowden, two American mediums, Bligh Bond, a lady from Winchester, and Margery Crandon. The communications were edited by Frederick Bligh Bond, and concerned unknown portions of Glastonbury Abbey and its history. Through the information obtained, the lost Edgar and Loretto chapels and the Norman wall of Herlewin's chapel were discovered by excavation.

Glossolalia   Speaking in pseudo tongues. *See* **Xenoglossy.**

Glottologues   Mediums who are enabled to speak in unknown tongues. *See* **Xenoglossy.**

Gnani Yoga   The yoga path to the Absolute, by the attainment of wisdom.

Gnostics Members of an early Christian church sect, professing special knowledge of an Oriental esoteric nature, and claiming divinity for Jesus in opposition to the Arians, another sect who did not.

God A conception of the supreme Being. Often referred to in Spiritualism as 'The Great Spirit', 'Great White Spirit', or 'Supreme Spirit'. There is little difference between the conception of God by Christians and that of Spiritualists. Though of the latter it might be said to partake more of a pantheistic form: that of life manifesting in all things. Also the Divine mode of working would seem to be by delegation, through successive heirarchies of evolved spirits before reaching the earth sphere. As most Spiritualists were brought up on orthodox lines, they tend to retain orthodox abstract conceptions, welding these into the new fabric of Spiritualism's main foundation—the facts of communication and survival.

Goodness Kindness, the easing of pain, and the bringing of happiness to others.

Goligher Circle Comprising the family of mediums with whom Dr W. J. Crawford successfully conducted many detailed experiments on ectoplasmic structures from 1919–20. There were six: Mr Goligher, four daughters, a son and a son-in-law. The seances were held in either their home or Dr Crawford's, by dim red light.

Gordon Davis Case *See* **Cooper, Blanche.**

Gotama Gautama *See* **Buddha, Buddhism.**

Gow, David Editor of *Light* for many years, journalist and prolific writer who became convinced of Spiritualism, throwing up a lucrative career to propagate the tenets of what he believed to be the world's future religion.

89

Greater World, The   Christian Spiritualist League, was founded in Britain in 1931; their first President was Alfred Morris.
A world-wide organization, their teachings are based on those
of 'Zodiac', a control of Miss Winifred Moyes, trance medium
and first editor of *Greater World*. The teachings claim to
be purely Christian. 'Zodiac' is said to have been the scribe
mentioned in Mark XII, 28–35. Their headquarters since 1932
are 3 Lansdowne Road, London, W.11.

Great White Brotherhood   *See* **White Brotherhood.**

Green   Green light perceived in the human aura, is generally
held to be indicative of intellectual activity.

Grey   Patches in the human aura are noticed at the site of
incipient physical disorder.

Group Soul   An interesting and original explanation of soul
relationship, by which many souls are linked by a group in a
scale of spiritual evolution. In its complete outline (as purported to have come from F. W. H. Myers in *Road to Immortality* by Geraldine Cummins), it involves the concept of
reincarnation, each soul leaving an earth pattern or 'karma' for
a new soul of his group to be born into.

Guardian Angel   A guiding spirit, control or guide, more
particularly the personal control who is charged with the wellbeing of the medium, often known as the 'doorkeeper'.

Guide   Spiritualist term for a beneficent control who acts in a
protective or instructive capacity. Distinct from discarnate
friends and relatives, they are said to be advanced spirits who
voluntarily return with a sense of a mission to fulfil. Many
different nationalities seem to be represented with North
American Indians predominating. Some of these give typical
Indian names by which they were known on earth, others say

they are only mediums or mouthpieces for even higher entities. Their capabilities and temperaments vary widely, and discrimination must be used with regard to their teachings.

Guppy, Mrs Samuel   British medium discovered by Dr Alfred Russell Wallace in his sister's house. She had remarkable powers for telekinesis and apports were produced in large quantities, plants and flowers particularly. Her chief claim to fame was her alleged transportation from her home at Highbury to 61 Lambs Conduit Street, London, three miles away! She was never known to have made any financial gain from her mediumistic gifts.

Gurdjieff, George Ivanovitch (Died 1949)   Greek mystic, wrote a cosmological epic based on a legend of Beelzebub banished to the solar system. He was the inspirer of Ouspensky who developed his teachings in the West, and together they formed a Gurdjieff trust in London.

Gurney, Edmond (1847–1888)   Outstanding English psychic researcher. First Hon. Secretary of the S.P.R. Classical scholar, musician and student of medicine. Was first intrigued by the subject of thought-transference and memory. He was the actual writer of the famous work *Phantasms of the Living* in collaboration with Myers and Podmore. After his death, Sir Oliver Lodge obtained remarkable evidence from him through the mediumship of Mrs Piper, American medium.

Guru   Hindu for tutor, usually applied to a teacher of Yoga.

Hades   Commonly known as the 'infernal regions', 'purgatory' and similar after-death states. From communications from F. W. H. Myers there would appear to be intermediate states between each sphere or plane, where the soul reviews its past experiences and chooses to go either up or down the ladder of consciousness. There is, he says, no punishment except by the

91

soul's own spiritual discomfort. Hades, in this communication, is classed as the Intermediate Plane, or the second level of consciousness.

'Hafed, Prince of Persia' *See* **Duguid.**

Halo A circle of light often depicted around a saintly person's head. A nimbus. May have some connexion with the aura as seen by clairvoyants.

Halls of Learning Places for instruction in the spirit spheres. Sometimes said to be visited by earth people during sleep-state.

Hallucination Perception which can be recognized as lacking any objective basis. Not to be confused with illusion. Hallucinations may be induced by suggestion in a hypnotized subject.

Hamilton, Dr Glen American medical practitioner, and President of Winnipeg S.P.R. Had his own laboratory in which groups of stereoscopic cameras were trained on physical phenomena. His circle consisted of four medical men, a civil and an electrical engineer. Among non-professional mediums tested were Elizabeth M., Mary M., and Mercedes. He was responsible for many good photographs of levitation, telekinesis, materializations. His critical analysis of trance states is a valuable work for psychic researchers.

Hatha Yoga Yoga pathway by means of physical culture and health discipline.

Hauntings Regular supernormal disturbances commonly attributed to spirits of the dead. The manifestations usually include: strange noises, objects moved, strange lights, chilliness, nasty smells and phantoms of various degrees of solidity. Little or no intelligence is displayed. One who suffers a violent death would appear to be the primary cause of haunting, not attributable to remorse, as it is the sufferer who haunts, never the murderer. Mrs Sidgwick, author of S.P.R.'s report on haunting, wrote that she could not avoid accepting provisionally the conclusion, that there were, in a sense, haunted houses.

Haxby English materialization medium, vouched for by Dr Alfred Russell Wallace 1870, who conducted comparative measuring tests, proving a discrepancy between the medium's body and that of the materialized form.

Healing, Faith *See* **Faith Healing.**

Healing, Magnetic First named by Mesmer, who combined hypnotic passes with metallo-therapy (the 'Baquet'). Mesmerism was superseded by Braid's exposition of the power of suggestion, or what is known today as hypnotism, used by doctors in medical treatment. Spiritualists believe that doctors passed to spirit, are mainly responsible for healing through the channel of healing mediums, yet contact healing may be due, at least in part, to some personal quality of the healer himself. Gordon Turner, well-known healer, claims to have produced effects on sealed photographic material by placing it between his fingers and a patient during a healing session.

Healing, Spirit Healing by spiritualist healers is claimed to be primarily due to the power of doctors in the spirit world who are able to co-operate with them, following intercession for a particular patient. There are two main methods: Contact healing, where physical contact takes place between healer and patient, and Absent healing in which case the patient may have been interceded for by a friend, and may be completely ignorant that he is being treated. The results of the latter method are surprisingly as good as the contact variety. Spiritualists are inclined to consider that healing by any means is helped by spirit doctors, and that most medical men are probably spiritual healers though unaware of it. Some orthodox churches practise healing by the traditional 'laying on of hands', equivalent to the Spiritualist's contact healing.

Heaven   Traditionally the location of Deity. Today, it is more often defined as a blissful mental state. Spirit communications mention several successive spheres of life beyond the earth, and speak of a continuous, apparently boundless evolution into more ideal states that would seem to approach the idea of heavenly bliss and possibly absorption into the Great Spirit from which we come. As we are told that the Great Spirit permeates all matter, there cannot be any one location we could name as Heaven, but a comprehensive consciousness of the entire universe might produce the nearest concept possible of such an ultimate state. Many great teachers have maintained that 'the kingdom of Heaven is within'.

Hedonism   Philosophical doctrine that pleasure is the chief objective or good, in man.

Hegel, Georg Wilhelm Friedrich (1770–1831)   German idealist philosopher who attempted to represent reality as a development of Absolute Mind ('The Idea'). It was a process of Nature becoming Mind and vice versa; we could only really know ourselves, by learning at many levels. His ideas were later developed by Karl Marx.

Heindel, Max   Author of many books of Rosicrucian philosophy and astrology. He conducted a healing clinic for thirty years based on astrological diagnosis and psychic treatment.

Helios, The World of, or the **Plane of Flame**   The fifth level of consciousness according to F. W. H. Myers's communication. He gave seven planes in all.

Hell   A supposed region of eternal punishment for the wicked after death. According to the Spiritualist's teaching of 'like attracting like', it is the grouping of the unevolved and distorted minds. Every soul at all stages can choose to progress spiritually. Once a soul reviews its present state with remorse and discomfiture, and desires a betterment, it gravitates to another home in the 'Many Mansions'. *See* **Hades.**

Helper, Spirit   Term for a discarnate entity, not necessarily possessed of superior knowledge, but who is eager to assist a subject in a humble way. Maybe also an entity under the direction of a superior guiding spirit or band. Helpers are usually of more recent passing, sometimes deceased relatives and friends, as distinct from guides who have a greater experience and an understanding of spiritual matters garnered from higher spheres.

Hermes   Greek god of flocks, travellers and heavenly messengers; identified with Mercury by the Romans, and Hermanubis and Thoth by the Egyptians. Was once worshipped as the revealer of divine wisdom.

Hermetic Philosophy   Properly, the writings of Hermes Trismegistus, supposed author of ancient sacred writings studied by the Egyptians, but often used today to describe occult teachings generally.

Hettinger, Dr John   Writer on telepathy and E.S.P., who became convinced by his studies and experiments of the reality of survival. He once made a detailed investigation of psychometry at King's College, University of London.

Hierarchy of Spirit   A term often used by controls of trance mediums. It is descriptive of the integration between the different spirit planes of existence; Divine inspiration not passing direct, but by means of a system of delegation; a chain of communication through the spheres to the medium on the earth plane. The higher spheres are said to be conscious and observant of the lower adjacent sphere, which they are able to influence and impress, but knowledge of the higher can only be revealed through the mediumship of spirits at the lower level.

Hierophant A priest instructor for initiatory ceremonies and ritual. No necessity for these in Spiritualism.

Higher Self An Eastern esoteric concept of a super consciousness attainable by meditation practices. *See* **Atman.** It bears a similarity to the idea of cosmic consciousness.

Hill, J. Arthur Hon. Associate of S.P.R., well-known author of many books on religion, psychology, psychical research and Spiritualism.

Hinayana The Southern Buddhist doctrine; an 'inner' Buddhist creed supposed for the intelligent minority, also called 'little system', Mahayana, 'great system' being the doctrine for the masses. Hinayana is mainly a technique for absorption into the Absolute, has no belief in Buddha as a continuant and disclaims the notion of Buddhist saints or Bodhisattvas.

Hinduism The main religion of India practised by about 216 million people. The foundation of all existence is said to be Brāhma, the verbal image of the Deity who encompasses all things. There is also the doctrine of the Atman or Higher Self; a concept of a united self yet divided into many egos. This Great Self is later identified with Brāhma. The personal reaction is to discard the earthly experience as an unreal perception, as being worthy of only a misperceived 'little self', therefore meditation must centre on the Great Self to conquer the little self. The sacred writings of the earliest periods are the Rig Veda, in ten books of 1,028 hymns dating 1500–1000 B.C. and later the Upanishads, Gita and Bhakti contemporary with the ideas of reincarnation and the corresponding development of the philosophy and teachings of Yoga 500–100 B.C.

Hodgson, Dr Richard (1855–1905) One of the keenest and most critical investigators of the early days of the S.P.R.

Australian born, he studied law at Cambridge. It was he who exposed Mme Blavatsky when he was sent to India to investigate phenomena alleged to have occurred at the H.Q. of the Theosophical Society there. He was very sceptical of all physical phenomena for the major part of his life, but changed gradually and completely after intensive investigation of Mrs Piper's mediumship over fifteen years as Secretary of the A.S.P.R. During his last years he developed mediumship himself.

Holy Grail, The Much sought-for sacred vessel of innumerable symbolic myths and legends.

Home Circle The kernel of the Spiritualist movement. A dedicated group of about seven friends, meeting regularly but unobtrusively in a room of an ordinary home, rejecting all feelings of jealousy and animosity, united in their belief that spirit helpers are ready to uplift them and stimulate their efforts to serve humanity or to develop their psychic powers for the same ends. No formal ceremonies, 'mysteries', creeds or hymns are required. There is usually, but not always, a developed medium present, who can sense the appropriate conditions generated, besides forming a mouthpiece for the control. One member is nominated 'leader', somebody of experience who is in charge of the proceedings. The subsequent course of action for the circle is given by the chief control or guide who issues instructions and teaching from time to time. Some home circles, already developed, sit for specific purposes: absent healing, individual psychic development, direct voice, or the gaining of inner wisdom by meditation.

Home, Daniel Dunglas (1833–1886) Scottish physical medium, perhaps the most outstanding in the history of Spiritualism. Confronted with his startling powers, many eminent hardheaded critics melted overnight! He appeared before Lord

Brougham, Sir David Brewster, Thackeray, Robert Browning, Lord Lytton, Mr and Mrs Trollope, Napoleon III, King of Bavaria, King of Naples, the German Emperor and the Queen of Holland. His marriage to Mlle Alexandrina de Kroll, sister-in-law to Count Koucheleff-Besborodska, was attended by Count Alexis Tolstoy. His phenomena were attested by Lord Adare and Sir William Crookes among many others, and included levitation, fire immunity to an astounding degree, strange music from nowhere, and elongation of the body. Crookes maintained that over several years of close acquaintance with Home, he never once detected anything suggesting trickery.

Hope, William (1863–1933) A carpenter of Crewe who became famous as a spirit photographer medium. The centre of much controversy and accusation of fraud, he was nevertheless able to convince many of the leading investigators that he possessed genuine powers. It is in his favour that he never commercialized his gift, charging only his carpenter's rate (4s 6d per dozen prints). Supported by Archdeacon Colley, Sir W. Barrett and Sir W. Crookes, doubted by Harry Price and Sir Oliver Lodge.

Horoscope A symbolic map of the heavens at a particular moment, drawn by an astrologer from astronomical data, for the purpose of interpreting an alleged correlation between the positions of the celestial bodies and earthly tendencies at that time. The chart is based upon the circle of the ecliptic and the zodiac signs, upon which are inserted the planets, sun and moon, the whole being quartered by the horizon and meridian of the observer. A further hypothetical division into twelve segments shows the 'houses'. While not accepted generally by Spiritualists, astrological terms are sometimes used by mediums or their controls.

House Astrological term, *see above.*

Hugo, Victor (1802–1885)   The great novelist was convinced of the truth of Spiritualism. He wrote of French Spiritualists: 'To avoid phenomena, to make them bankrupt of the attention to which they have a right, is to make bankrupt truth itself.' When he died he left an unpublished MS on Spiritualism to Paul Meurice. During his exile many circles were held which he attended. The medium was Charles Hugo.

Hulme, A. J. Howard   Authority on Egyptology (Hons. Cert. Oxford University), distinguished author, lecturer and translator of words of 'Lady Nona' who spoke ancient Egyptian in the Rosemary case. Also compiled Egypt-Esperanto Dictionary.

Human Personality   Spiritualism, by revealing man's enormous potentialities as a spirit, increases the complexity of human personality. From the F. W. H. Myers communications, it would appear that the earthly individual is only part of a larger entity—the Group Soul—which he will join at a later date, having formed by his reactions, an earthly pattern for a new successor of the group to follow. The exact relationships of all these 'facets' of a large human personality are fraught with interest; they promise a working hypothesis which might solve many problems. Our 'guides' may be other facets or parts of the same soul group; the popular idea of reincarnation may be a crude glimpse of this far more complex process; the homing instinct of animals and birds; the community life of insects, may all be understood by participation in a group intelligence controlling its lesser parts. By the phenomena of astral projection, the exteriorization of sensation in materialized figures and hypnotic experiments, we can see that the human senses are not confined to the physical body, it is conceivable that at a later stage of development, they may all be incorporated in some greater being, where all these facets of experience which we call persons, may be united for the benefit of the whole.

Hume, David (1711–1776)   Scottish empiricist philosopher. As a sceptic he developed the conclusions of John Locke. Agreed with Locke and Berkeley on the unreality of abstract ideas, but did not accept a divine order. He put forward the theory that one's accumulation of knowledge depended upon one's trust in instincts.

Husk, Cecil   Formerly an operatic singer, he became a professional physical medium. His speciality was the passage of matter through matter. In his presence, iron rings were often threaded on apparently impossible places. One ring on his arm, he wore till he died. It had previously been marked by the S.P.R. who wished to chloroform him to test whether it was removable, but Husk would not co-operate.

Hydesville Phenomena   Hydesville, said to be the birth-place of modern Spiritualism, is a small hamlet in New York State, and is where the Fox sisters first discovered and demonstrated their mediumship in 1848.

Hylozoism   A doctrine that life is a property of matter: all things being alive.

Hymns   Songs of praise and worship, used in services of both orthodox and Spiritualist churches. Hymns used in the latter are derived from orthodox sources, some words being altered to conform to Spiritualist beliefs. Among Spiritualists, there is a feeling that new hymns should be written, although a strong minority are in favour of eliminating them entirely.

Hyperaesthesia   Extreme acuteness of the normal senses, often noticed with hysterics and hypnotized subjects. Sometimes advanced as an alternative explanation, to the spirit hypothesis. If the knowledge obtained was already known to the sitter, there are slight grounds for this theory, although it is difficult to determine the kind of clues the sitter could have given. This theory is difficult to maintain when it is considered that the medium often has the eyes closed and takes little notice of the sitter. If the knowledge obtained is unknown to the sitter, hyperaesthesia as an explanation is useless.

Hyperamnesia Extension of the memory powers, a quickening of the mind's sensitivity. Has been noticed in hypnotized subjects.

Hyperborean *See* **Root Race.**

Hypothesis An assumption to explain a fact, or assumed for purposes of argument, though not necessarily true.

Hypnotic Regression Hypnotic technique whereby the subject is able to recall evidential details of events far back in his personal history. Its interest for Spiritualists and psychic researchers, lies in the apparent success of some hypnotists who claim to have regressed the memory to events before birth. The substantiation of these events is advanced as evidence for the theory of reincarnation.

Hypnotism The modern development of Mesmerism. An artificially induced kind of sleep state, the peculiarity of which is the 'rapport' which can exist between the hypnotist and the subject. A suggestion may be obeyed to a supernormal degree; it may even be delayed to the normal waking state before it takes effect quite independently of the subject's own consciousness. The hypnotic trance can be self-induced in order to attain greater self-confidence or mastery over pain. The mediumistic trance seems to be self-induced, though it may be due to spirit hypnotists. The main difference is the absence of suggestibility in the medium; the person longed for, does not always communicate in accordance with the 'suggestion' of the sitter. Medium's controls exhibit a distinct and consistent personality, far surpassing any hypnotized subject's efforts of dramatization.

Hyslop, Professor James Hervey (1854–1920) Distinguished American psychic researcher, Professor of Logic and Ethics at Columbia University, New York. He became convinced of personal survival through the mediumship of Mrs Piper, and regarded survival as scientifically proved. Also, he made an intensive study of multiple personality and supported the view that it was due to spirit possession. By his will, he founded an Institute for the treatment of such cases by mediums.

I.C. Imum Coeli, an astrological 'angle' of importance, corresponding to the point where the meridian of the observer, at any given time, cuts the lowest point of the ecliptic.

I Ching The Chinese *Book of Changes*, the experimental basis of classical Chinese philosophy, in which a grasp of the total situation at any given moment is said to be obtained. It deals with the interplay of dual cosmic principles, the Yin and the Yang. The psychic and physical worlds are held to be the dual expression of a living reality. The method consists of dividing forty-nine yarrow stalks into two random heaps, and counting them by threes and fives, or in throwing three coins six times, each line of a hexagram being determined by the value of heads and tails. Thus each of sixty-four mutations is held to correspond to a psychic situation. There is a similar western method known as Ars Geomantica or Art of Punctation.

Identity Proof Before evidence of survival can be accepted, the communicator has to prove his identity to the satisfaction of the inquirer. This may not be successful at the first sitting, but this is not surprising if one considers the difficulties from the communicator's point of view. He has to remember something specific of his earthly life, yet not commonly known, by which he may be recognized. In transmitting his evidence through the medium he may be successful, but the sitter may not know of the matter mentioned, or its verification may not be possible. Reproduction of personal mannerisms alone are

102

useless if the communicator is well known. The result is that they are driven to family nicknames and personal trivialities which sceptics seize upon as being 'unspiritual' or ridiculous. Yet the fact that the matter conveyed is trivial, may provide the very best evidence of identity. To add to the obstacles, we have to contend with the possibility of impersonation by spirits. This is far more likely to be the case when a famous character is alleged to be communicating, and such claims should be regarded with extreme caution. The best evidence of identity comes usually from a deceased member of one's own family, where intimate knowledge makes impersonation almost impossible. Each inquirer has to decide this matter for himself, in such cases the opinion of any 'expert' is not good enough. *See* **Evidence, Law of.**

Ideomorphs Moulds obtained supernormally.

Ideoplasm A term for ectoplasm with the additional implication that it is capable of being moulded into any desired shape.

Ignath, Mrs Lujza Linczegh (Born 1891) Hungarian medium, unique in claiming a 'pure' spirit control 'Nona', who said she had never been incarnated. Before an audience of 100 people she once produced direct writing on selected parts of the hall. Direct writing was also obtained on wax tablets enclosed in a box, during an experimental sitting with Dr Jorgen Bull, a chemist of Oslo, for the Norwegian S.P.R. Miniature heads were materialized in drinking glasses filled with water. Photographs were taken of these forms, which she said were produced by her thought.

Ignis Fatuus Peculiar lights which appear in cemeteries or marshy places. Although generally ascribed to natural causes, some sensitives claim to see lights where sudden death has occurred.

Illusion Perception with an objective base, but which is falsely interpreted. (*See* **hallucination**). The work of expert conjurors could be correctly described as illusory.

Illusion, Plane of According to an alleged communication of F. W. H. Myers, the third level of the seven planes of human consciousness. Also called by him 'the immediate world after death'. Here, the mind's creative powers are sufficient to formulate appropriate environs according to the habit of thought of each individual spirit. Thus they are enabled to follow an objective life similar to that of earth, only on a more ambitious scale, as the struggle and effort of earthly life is absent. The care of the body—the greatest limiting earthly factor—is no longer the primary consideration, as it is said to be nourished directly from cosmic sources.

Immanence In theology, the indwelling of Deity with the world. (Equivalent to pantheism.)

Immortality Of concern to Spiritualists who believe in it, but not within the province of psychic research. Spiritualist ideas on immortality are derived from the many spirit communications, where no mention of a finite individual existence has yet been made.

Immunity from Fire *See* **Fire Immunity.**

'Imperator' Chief control of Rev. Stainton Moses, who, with a spirit band, came as missionaries in an endeavour to uplift humanity. This control once admitted to being Malachias the prophet. His communications did not come direct, but through the agency of another spirit named 'Rector'. Many instances are known where this same 'Imperator' is alleged to have communicated through later mediums, notably, Mrs Piper, Mrs Minnie M. Soule (Mrs Chenoweth), Dr Hodgson, and Gwendolyn Kelly Hack, automatist.

Impersonation The imitation by one spirit, of another's person and character. This can happen in mediumship, and is due to the fact that discarnates were once incarnate and sometimes retain a liking for mischievous pranks. It is therefore suspicious if a control is pompous and claims to be an important person. The best controls are known for their humility and appeal to one's finer feelings, rather than the making of an impression, in the worldly sense. Controls should be treated as rational human beings, and extravagant claims should be well tested before credence is given to them. Another kind of impersonation occurs when the medium takes on temporarily past conditions of the communicator. Physical symptoms such as lameness, or shortness of breath may be simulated, and can be very evidential to the sitter.

Impression Descriptive of the process by which entities can influence the mind of a mediumistic person. The actual method may be telepathic or hypnotic; the impression may be visual, tactual or perhaps a sudden urge to a certain course of action. An intensification of impression would amount to control.

Imum Coeli *See* **I.C.**

Imprints, Psychic *See* **Moulds.**

Incarnate Clothed in flesh, a spirit animating an earthly body. The individual earthly state of being.

Independent Voice A term for physical voice phenomena, independent of apparatus. A form of Direct voice (q.v.), but produced without a trumpet or megaphone.

Indradason, Indride Icelandic medium, the subject of many tests by the Psychic Experimental Society of Reykjavik 1904–1909. Automatic writing, trance speaking, levitation, telekinesis, direct voice and materialization were developed.

105

The direct voice and levitation took place in the presence of sixty-seven sitters. Heraldur Nielsson, Professor of Theology at Reykjavik University, believed in the genuineness of the phenomena.

Ineffable Name Traditionally, a name for God which must not be spoken.

Infant Prodigies *See* **Prodigies.**

Infinite Boundless, without end or limit. 'The Infinite', God, Deity, or the Great Spirit.

Influence Mediums often refer to spirit influences, usually meaning impression or clairsentience. The term has been applied to objects belonging to the sitter, which seem to assist the medium to contact the ideas of communicators. This process is often confused with psychometry.

Influenced Writing Writing, the substance of which is affected by remote suggestion from another mind.

Ingeborg, Mrs Norwegian trance medium, daughter of Judge Ludwig Dahl who gave impressive evidence for survival.

Initiate One admitted to knowledge of occult mysteries by systematic psychic development.

Inner Light Term used by the Society of Friends for the human capacity for spiritual experience of God.

Insanity It has been said that mediumship is a threat to sanity. In a statistical investigation by Dr Eugen Crowell, based on reports from 42 institutions, out of a total of 32,313 male patients, 215 were clergymen. The total number of male and female Spiritualists was 45.

Inspiration From a study of mediumship it becomes clear that certain information is received from unknown sources. This is an act of drawing-in mentally which parallels the physical concept of the drawing-in of breath. It has become customary to apply this word to cases where a person is merely encouraged by some other person or object on the physical level. Thus we say that an artist is 'inspired' by a scene, or that the mass of people are 'inspired' by a leader. Yet the Spiritualist idea of a mental indrawing from higher sources, is justified by the results of inspirational speaking, writing and drawing, often of a high standard, which mediums often perform without training or natural ability in that field.

Inspirational Speaking Impromptu addresses by mediums in various degrees of trance, the contents of which frequently surpass their own capabilities. Many good mediums of this kind are known: Mrs Richmond, Emily Hardinge Britten, Thomas Lake Harris, J. J. Morse, Mrs Meurig Morris, Estelle Roberts, Winifred Moyes, Horace Hambling, to mention a few.

Inspirational Writing and Drawing Akin to automatism, but without the hand itself being controlled. The writer or artist consciously records a series of mental impressions super-normally received.

Instinct An unreasoned prompting to take necessary action in order to preserve existence and propagation. A possible explanation is offered by the Group Soul theory (q.v.).

Institut Géneral Psychologique Founded in Paris 1904 for psychical research. It did conduct a memorable investigation of the phenomena of Eusapia Paladino 1905–08, but has now ceased to function.

Institut Métapsychique International Founded 1918 in Paris by Jean Meyer. First directed by Dr Gustave Geley, whose committee contained among other distinguished people, Professor Richet, Camille Flammarion, Sir Oliver Lodge and Ernest Bozzano. A later director was Dr Eugene Osty. Many eminent men of science and literature were invited to the seances. Eva C., and Rudi Schneider were among the famous mediums tested.

Instrument A term often used by a control when referring to the medium. Although this would suppose a completely mechanical transmission, this is not so, as the medium's mind and vocabulary have to be employed by the spirit operators, therefore the habitual mental associations of the medium are apt to present themselves in addition to the transmitted material.

Intellect That part of the mind which 'knows'.

Intelligence That practical capacity of the mind to overcome problems.

Interlocked Rings Experiment A famous case where two rings of different woods were prepared by Sir Oliver Lodge, and, at his request, were interlocked by the mediumship of Margery Crandon of Boston, U.S.A. Photographs of them were taken and the rings placed in a museum, but at some subsequent date, they were found parted again. (Characteristic of matter through matter experiments.)

International Spiritualist Federation, The Founded in 1923, revived in London 1948. It aims to strengthen Spiritualism as a world movement, and to foster international relationships by affiliating properly constituted bodies with a Spiritualistic or psychic basis, accepting (a) personal survival, and (b) communication with the spirit world. Also to co-operate in the study of psychic phenomena from scientific, philosophical, moral and religious aspects. Its membership is open to approved societies, groups and individuals.

Interpenetration of Matter *See* **Matter through matter.**

Introspection Observation of one's own mental processes.

Introvert Descriptive of a self-centred character, which turns inwards upon itself.

Intuition Instant knowledge obtained without reasoning. How far impression may be responsible, it is difficult to say.

Invocation A preliminary prayer, usually spoken at the beginning of a religious service. It is given at most Spiritualist churches.

I.S.F. The International Spiritualist Federation (q.v.).

Islam One of the world's great religions, founded in A.D. 622 by Mohammed. Soon after the age of forty he became a prophet through hearing voices urging him to proclaim the name of the Lord. Islam is the worship of Allāh the Deity, not of Mohammed the prophet. The duty of man to Allāh is complete submission. Their sacred writing is the Qur'ān, and contains the utterances (suras) of Mohammed when inspired. It is interesting to Spiritualists to note that the founding was due to mediumship or clairaudience on the part of Mohammed.

Jack the Ripper Case According to the *Daily Express* of 9 March 1931, the criminal in this famous case was traced by a Spiritualist medium, Robert James Lees, who, by walking in trance, led the police to the murderer's house.

Jainism A unique minority religion of India; an offshoot of Hinduism and contemporary with Buddhism, founded by a Hindu ascetic Vardhamana who was born about 569 B.C. Like Buddhism, it rejects the caste system. The chief character-

109

istic is the emphasis on the principle of 'Ahimsa' (non-violence) to extreme limits. They even filter the atmosphere before breathing lest microscopic life should be destroyed. The standards of morality and literacy are exceptionally high. Criminals are unknown among them. The Absolute is regarded as a corporate personality composed of perfected souls, none of whom is supreme. Generally the idea of one supreme Deity is not accepted; rather it is believed there is a plurality of deities who are subject to the law of transmigration as are human beings. Release from the round of Karma by asceticism is their main object.

James, William (1842–1910) Professor of Psychology at Harvard University. Founder member of the A.S.P.R. and president of S.P.R. 1894–95. He was responsible for the introduction of Mrs Piper to the S.P.R., and had contact with her mediumship for many years. He was a firm believer in the reality of psychic phenomena, but never accepted the spirit hypothesis as proven.

Jeans, Dr Norman Experimented on himself with various anaesthetics and discovered that under the influence of nitrous oxide (laughing gas), he was able to witness events at distant places.

Jeanne D'Arc (1411–1431) The Maid of Orleans and her Voices are well known. Although an illiterate peasant, she was able to convince the Dauphin of her divine appointment. Also a clairvoyant and an inspirational speaker, she would have been classed as a medium today.

Jehovah (Y H V A) Has been translated as 'rain-cloud'—the spirit control of Moses and special guardian of the Jews. He was said to have been jealous of the attentions given to the polytheistic cults of his time.

Jehovah's Witnesses   A religious sect whose doctrine is based upon a literal reading of the Bible. They believe that God's kingdom will come on this earth, and that the wicked will be destroyed.

Jesuit   Member of the Society of Jesus, founded by Ignatius Loyola in 1534.

Jesus of Nazareth   The majority opinion of Spiritualists could be summed up as follows: Jesus was an outstanding Jewish medium born about 4 B.C. of Jewish parents. He probably studied the principles of the Essenes in addition to the Old Testament at some time during the early years of his life of which little is known for certain. As a healer and a preacher, he gained a great following but his outspoken criticisms of the narrow ways of orthodox creeds angered the authorities, who saw in his popularity a threat to their power, so they had him arrested and put him to death. It is possible that he materialized after, to some of his followers. Jesus was a Jew throughout his life, and so far as we know, never claimed to have founded a religion. The New Testament teachings are valuable in essence, but are not in any sense original documents. The words used are not translations of the actual words that Jesus used: these were never recorded. Therefore Jesus was a great teacher from whom we can learn; inspired as so many others have been from the higher spheres of spirit life. Revelation continues today as it has always done—through mediums.

Joire, Dr Paul   Professor of Psycho-Physiological Institute of France, and president of Societé Universalle d'Etudes Psychiques. Noted for extensive studies of psychical research and hypnotism.

Jung, Professor C. G.   One of the leading pioneers of psychology who has made a special study of symbolism and methods of divination, particularly the 'I Ching' and astrology, in connexion with his theory of Synchronicity. This theory challenges the causal principle, and he tries to correlate 'meaningful coincidences' or runs on the unusual, with a discernible acausal connecting principle as a special class of natural events, which form another category with space, time, and causality.

Ka Ancient Egyptian equivalent for the double or etheric body. Represented in their drawings as a birdlike duplicate of the deceased. It was supposed to have lived in the tomb, its life depending on the buried provisions, and it presumably haunted any neglectful relatives. The soul was called the 'Ba', which left both bodies at death.

Kabbala *See* **Cabbala.**

Kahn, Ludwig German clairvoyant medium who appeared before Institut Métapsychique in Paris 1925 and 1926. Before a distinguished gathering of scientists, he read successfully the contents of eleven mixed paper pellets.

Kama Rupa Hindu term for an 'astral shell' or eidolon, said to persist after the death of the physical body, but gradually disintegrating unless its existence is prolonged by feeding on the vitality of those on earth who would wish to preserve it. Not recognized in Spiritualism.

Kant, Immanuel (1724–1804) Renowned German philosopher who advanced on the Empiricist–Rationalist dilemma, and was responsible for a new Objective theory of ethics. In this, he allowed determinism in man to a large extent, but drew attention to the conflict between what a man desires and what he feels is his duty. To Kant, the sense of 'ought' or duty, came from a world of reality outside of the Nature represented by our senses; the unknowable world, yet realized by what he called the 'practical reason' (almost synonymous with intuition), the 'theoretical reason' was governed entirely by the world we build for ourselves. Spiritualists would be tempted to identify Kant's 'unknowable world' with the spirit world, where those things he called 'good in themselves' are eternal realities.

Kardec, Allen (1804–1869) (Hippolyte Leon Denizard Rivail) His famous *Book of the Spirits* (*Le Livre des Esprits*) has become a classic among French and South American Spiritualists. It has been suggested that the work was based on trance communications through Mlle Celina Bequet. The book emphasizes a doctrine of reincarnation which is not accepted by all Spiritualists. Kardec and his original followers used the term 'Spiritist' to describe themselves. It was Professor Pierart who used the word 'Spiritualist' as rejecting the dogmatic assumption of reincarnation theory.

Karma The Hindu Law of Action. It is bound up with the traditional religious views of the Hindus regarding the inexorability of reincarnation either higher or lower in the animal human scale. The only release according to them, is by a process of ascetic withdrawal from the world of passion, the techniques of Yoga.

Karma Yoga Yoga pathway of consecrated unselfish action.

Keys of the Tarot Twenty-two cards (Major arcana) of the Tarot pack.

Kilner, Dr Walter J. (1847–1920) Of St Thomas's Hospital, London. Noted for his experimental work on the human aura. By means of dicyanin dye screens, he was the first to demonstrate objectively the existence of the aura. The eyes are first sensitized by looking through the screen, then, by gazing at a naked figure in a dim light against a black backcloth, three distinct bands of radiation become visible to some people not otherwise sensitive. He found that illness affected the size and colours of the radiations, and that the aura shrivels at the approach of death and ultimately vanishes. Kilner's experiments were controlled and confirmed by Dr O'Donnell of the Chicago Mercy Hospital, and also by Dr Drysdale Anderson in West Africa.

Kilnerscreen-goggles Popular name given to screens made in the form of spectacles, based on Dr Kilner's discovery.

'King, John' A well-known spirit control who has manifested through many physical mediums. He claimed to be Henry Owen Morgan, a buccaneer who was knighted by Charles II, and was appointed Governor of Jamaica from 1673–80. His first recorded appearance was with the Davenport brothers in 1850, and stayed with them throughout. Other mediums who claimed his influence were: Mrs Marshall, Mrs Guppy, Miss Georgina Houghton, Mrs Firman, Williams, Mrs Wriedt, Eglinton, Husk, the Holmeses, Mme Blavatsky, and Eusapia Paladino. He also appeared in Dr Glen Hamilton's circle in 1930.

'King, Katie' Beautiful spirit control of Miss Florence Cook, claimed to be the daughter of 'John King' (*see above*). She appeared many times in Sir William Crookes' investigations, during which he photographed her forty times. Crookes was completely sure of her independence of the medium, and risked his scientific reputation by making known his findings. The tests were exhaustive and conducted in his own home. Dr Glen Hamilton also reported the appearance of a beautiful spirit form claiming to be Katie King; though he admitted points of similarity between his photographs and those of Crookes, he would not commit himself as to the truth of her statement.

Kluski, Franek Polish poet, writer and physical medium through whose powers plaster casts of spirit hands and feet were obtained in the fraudproof laboratory of Dr Gustave

Geley. A unique feature of his materialization seances was the production of animal forms.

Knot Tying Experiments   *See* **Matter through matter.**

Knowledge, Theory of   That branch of philosophy which deals with the possibility of our knowing the exterior world, as distinct from the knowledge contributed by our own minds.

Koan   A paradox or insoluble problem suitable for meditating upon in the practice of Zen Buddhism. It works on the principle that a sudden impasse or jolt to the intellect, can bring insight.

Koji-Ki   Oldest known Japanese historical document covering the period from the time of creation to A.D. 628 (compiled A.D. 712).

Kosmon Bible, 'Oahspe'   An astounding work of automatic typewriting, produced by J. B. Newbrough (q.v.).

Krishna   Meaning Christ 'the anointed one'. It was customary to pour oil on sacrificial beasts before burning them as offerings, and the anointing came to be associated with sacrifice, and the idea of the 'Saviour God' who sacrificed himself.

Kundalini   According to Yoga teaching, a hidden psychic force which lies coiled at the base of the spine (the semen), dormant until roused by the various Yoga disciplines and techniques. As it rises to the psychic centres or chakras, it activates them and brings into operation psychic powers appropriate to the centres affected. Often referred to in occult works as the 'coiled serpent'.

Lama   Tibetan or Mongolian priest of esoteric Buddhism, favouring elaborate ritual, and worship by formal and repetitive prayers.

Lang, Andrew (1843–1912)   Philosopher, poet, scholar, president of S.P.R. in 1911. Author of many books on anthropology, mythology, ghosts and history. Also a student of dowsing and crystal gazing. Once he made a study of Joan of Arc from the point of view of psychical research.

Law of Evidence   *See* **Evidence.**

Laws of Nature   Contrary to what may be generally supposed, Spiritualists do not believe in miracles. All phenomena proceeds according to natural laws, the seemingly miraculous being supernormal, but not supernatural. Some natural laws are as yet undiscovered, and therefore their working would seem to produce unnatural effects. The levitation of a table for instance, is not in defiance of natural law, it is merely supported on the top of an invisible pillar, through which its weight is transmitted to the floor beneath. This has been demonstrated by means of scales in the seance room. (Goligher circle.)

Laya Yoga   Yoga pathway of divine union through the etheric plane.

Laying on of Hands   Healing practice, performed by Jesus and once very common, now gradually gaining favour in some churches again. Equivalent to the Spiritualist's 'contact healing' (q.v.).

Leader, Circle   It is usually advisable to nominate a leader for a circle, apart from the medium. This person should be experienced in Spiritualism, level-headed and trusted by the other members. The leader is responsible for the conducting of the circle procedure and arrangements generally, and should be competent to deal with any emergency.

Leaf, Horace Contemporary English clairvoyant, psychometrist, healer, lecturer and author. His interest in Spiritualism and psychical research was aroused in 1904. In 1922 he was invited by Sir Arthur Conan Doyle to follow in his footsteps through Australasia to raise a Trust Fund to send mediums to these far-flung parts of the Dominions. Has acted as official representative in many parts of the world, and is probably the most widely travelled Spiritualist missionary. Has lectured on mediumship at several learned institutions, including the State Hospital, Copenhagen; John Hopkins University; Dartmouth College, New Hampshire; Swarthmore College, Pennsylvania; Oxford and Cambridge Universities.

Lees, Robert James English clairvoyant medium and author. Was received at the palace by Queen Victoria several times. He was also a medium for spirit healing, with an amazing ability for diagnosis; some remarkable instantaneous cures were achieved. Was reported to have been the means of tracing the criminal in the famous Jack the Ripper case. (*Daily Express*, 9 March 1931.)

Legerdemain Deception by dexterity of the hands, practised by conjurors and illusionists. Many of the world's finest exponents have admitted themselves baffled when confronted by psychic phenomena.

Leibnitz, Gottfried Wilhelm (1646–1716) Famous German philosopher who believed in restoring balance and the conciliation of extremes. Once he tried to unite the Protestant and Catholic faiths. Of particular interest is his 'Monad' system; a dynamic conception of reality which replaced the older 'substance' theories. A monad was a non-physical 'centre of force', a living 'atom' in the structure of reality. An infinite number of monads existed in hierarchies extending to God. They all possessed potentialities of perception and movement which became self-consciousness and will. The goal of man was

117

therefore the intellectual love of God. There are many ideas in this philosophy which form parallels with Spiritualist teachings: the monads could be equated with discarnate spirit entities, evolving into the spirit hierarchies, and underlying the physical manifestation of the earth world.

Lemuria *See* **Root race.**

Leonard, Gladys Osborne Well-known British trance medium who sat with Hewat Mackenzie, founder of the British College for Psychic Science, responsible for arranging her first sittings with Sir Oliver Lodge. It was through Mrs Leonard's mediumship that Raymond Lodge, Sir Oliver's son, first communicated. During 1918 she gave seventy-three sittings at S.P.R. and her trustworthiness was never in question. Evidential tests in cross-correspondence were conducted by Rev. C. Drayton Thomas, in which his deceased father co-operated.

Levitation A surprising amount of historical evidence from early days exists concerning the supernormal rising of chairs, tables, human bodies and heavy objects, into the air. The saints are reputed to have risen often when praying, or in a state of meditation or rapture, usually at the altar. Levitation was once considered to be a sign of possession, and liable to be followed by charges of witchcraft. In modern times we have several accounts of mediums' levitation: Henry C. Gordon in 1851 and 1852 at Dr Gray's house in New York. Then the famous D. D. Home (q.v.), of whom levitation was reported over one hundred times on good authority. Sir William Crookes himself tested Home on many occasions. The most famous eye-witness account was that of Home's levitation on 13 December 1868, at Ashley House, Victoria Street, London. Before Lord Adare, the Master of Lindsay and Charles Wynne (Lord Adare's cousin), Home floated from a third storey window and returned through a window of another room. Other well-known mediums reported to have levitated are: Stainton

Moses, Mrs Guppy, Zuccarini, Eglinton, Williams, Herne, Eusapia Paladino (her phenomena were attested by Lombroso, Chiaia, Ochorowicz, Col. Rochas, Perro, Morselli and de Albertis), Willy Schneider, Maria Vollhardt, Mirabelli, Webber and Powell. Explanation of this feat is speculative: Crawford's cantilevers and rods seem too cumbersome and were restricted to about seven feet in range. Yogis claim that suitable breathing techniques practised over long periods can reduce the body weight sufficient to float in air. Ecclesiastics believe the rapture state to be necessary. We do not know.

Life Generally considered to be a characteristic of animals, plant and bacteria only, but science is discovering even more minute forms which seem to hover on the borderline between living and inert matter. The virus can exhibit both phases, should we deny it life? Even 'inert' matter seems rather busy about its own affairs, in states of constant movement and change we are told. It may well be that the dividing line between the living and the non-living is artificial; merely the measure of our ignorance of forms of life only less apparent to our restricted observational powers. This view is more in accordance with accounts we receive from spirit communications about life.

Light Those mediums who produce physical phenomena usually require a very dim light or complete darkness to manifest satisfactorily. This is unfortunate for the researcher, as dark conditions increase the possibility of fraud. Experience has shown that sudden light admitted during a physical seance, can cause severe shock to the medium's body—bruise and weals, haemorrhages have been known to occur as the result of careless treatment in this way. Some experiments suggest that the shock is caused more by the light falling upon the medium, than on the ectoplasmic formations. It was found that if the medium was shielded from the light the emanations could be photographed by flashlight. Sir William Crookes considered the rays at the extreme end of the spectrum the most troublesome; Moonlight he found ideal. Dr Geley used biological light with success. It should be noted that a few mediums on occasion have demonstrated good physical phenomena in bright daylight. (Eusapia Paladino, D. D. Home, Stainton Moses.)

Lights, The   Old astrological terms for the sun and the moon.

Lights, Spirit or Psychic   *See* **Luminous phenomena.**

Like Attracts Like   An important 'law' of spirit contact. It would seem to depend upon the respective qualities of individual auras. The outer auric fields of the human body, are generated by the mind and the emotions. If two persons, incarnate or discarnate have similar tastes and desires, their auras it is said, will blend, and they will be able to approach or even mingle their rays, resulting in a degree of mental rapport. If violently dissimilar, there is automatic repulsion. Between a medium and his control, there is a very close blend of personalities, developed over many years, which enables the control to enter the auric field sufficiently to gain control of the medium's faculties through manipulation of the subconscious mind. This can also explain possession or obsession by undesirable entities.

Lily Dale   Central country headquarters of American Spiritualists, in the State of New York.

Limbo   Traditionally, the border of the next world where fools and sinners were restrained.

Lincoln, Abraham   Former President of U.S.A., was well acquainted with Spiritualism; his decision to free the slaves was perhaps the result of spirit messages through J. B. Conklin, Nettie Colburn and Dr Farnsworth.

Lindsay, the Master of Later the Earl of Crawford and Balcarres. Known chiefly in Spiritualism by his association with Lord Adare and D. D. Home. Before the Dialectical Society he testified to Home's powers, including the famous levitation.

Link, The An international association of Spiritualist home circles founded in 1931 by Noah Zerdin. Its object was to make available useful information on psychic matters to assist the circle's operation.

Locke, John (1632–1704) Great English philosopher of the Empiricist school. He attempted to analyse human understanding from a completely 'common-sense' standpoint. All knowledge, in his view, was a relationship between ideas, and was acquired solely from without—through the channels of the senses. Thus the object of perception consisted of primary qualities giving rise to secondary qualities in our minds. As this idea led to the dilemma of the impossibility of investigating substance itself, or 'essence', he outlawed its study by asserting that it was outside of the province of philosophy, as also was metaphysics.

Lodge, Sir Oliver, F.R.C.S., D.Sc., Ll.D., M.A. (1851–1940) The great British physicist, who thoroughly investigated the phenomena of Spiritualism, and became a fearless champion of survival in the teeth of much scientific opposition. Memorable are his investigations, conducted in Professor Richet's house, of the phenomena of Eusapia Paladino. The return of his son Raymond (q.v.), first delivered through Mrs Piper in 1915, then by cross-correspondence through several mediums including Mrs Osborne Leonard and Alfred Vout Peters, constitutes one of the best attested cases of proved spirit identity. Raymond's return was heralded by a cryptic message from the spirit of F. W. H. Myers in co-operation with the deceased Dr Hodgson. Sir Oliver wrote several books on Spiritualism.

Logical Positivism   A modern materialist philosophical theory, which aims to eliminate metaphysics. It applies a 'Principle of Verifiability' to divide statements into two categories: (a) those capable of verification, (b) tautologies. Statements which fall into neither group are dismissed as 'emotive nonsense'. This doctrine implies a negation of every spiritual truth ever propounded by the great teachers of mankind.

Logos   The Divine word, as representative of the Deity incarnate. Not consistent with Spiritualist religion.

Lombroso, Cesar (1836–1909)   Italian psychiatrist and criminal anthropologist. He sat with Eusapia Paladino on many occasions, and gradually became convinced, not only of survival, but the truth of the spirit hypothesis. His open declarations carried great weight among his scientific contemporaries, and induced some of them to investigate psychic phenomena. Spiritualist author.

London Dialectical Society   *See* **Dialectical Society.**

London Spiritualist Alliance   A Spiritualist society first formed from the British National Association of Spiritualists 1884, it was incorporated in 1896. The London headquarters are now known as the College of Psychic Science.

Lord's Prayer, The   One of the oldest Jewish prayers, which probably originated in Babylon, according to a tablet discovered in 1882. The Jews repeated it in Chaldaic, having learnt it in Babylon during their captivity.

Lost Spirits   Refers to those discarnate entities who are isolated by the results of their self-centredness. The remedy lies in their own hands, by cultivating a sympathetic interest outside of themselves, or by accepting help from a rescue circle (q.v.).

Lotus Seat The crosslegged meditation posture of Yoga, designed to still the body and assist the psychic 'circulation' or the rising of the Kundalini to the various chakras or psychic centres.

Lotus Sutra A classical Buddhist document, a prominent feature of Northern Buddhism (Mahayana), famous in the Far East, in which a transcendant Gotama preaches on a mountain peak the doctrine of a Cosmic Buddha 'in which all things consist', to a gathering of disciples accompanied by various miraculous signs and wonders. (Reminiscent of the Cosmic Christ of the Epistle to the Ephesians.) This teaching put forward the idea of repeated saintly incarnations of Gotama (Bodhisattva) as a Buddha-spirit, Dharmakaya or Vairocana. Nirvana in this scheme, is represented as a celestial home of social pleasures.

Lourdes French resort, famed for its miraculous cures. In 1858 the Virgin Mary was supposed to have appeared to Bernadette Soubiros an invalid child, in a grotto. There is no supporting evidence for the apparition, but some cures are certainly reported on good authority. Spiritualists would maintain that the healing was the result of spirit co-operation, not necessarily due to the faith of the patients. *See* **Healing.**

Lower Astral Common term for that part of the spirit sphere nearest earth. The level of ghosts, apparitions and poltergeist activities.

Loyola, Ignatius (1491–1556) Spanish founder of the Society of Jesus (Jesuits). He was invested by the Pope with absolute authority over his followers, to propagate the conversion of heathen and sinners. Loyola believed himself inspired direct from heaven. He was canonized 1672.

L.S.A. *See* **London Spiritualist Alliance.**

Lucidity A collective term for the faculties by means of which supernormal knowledge may be acquired. It includes the phenomena of clairvoyance, clairaudience, psychometry and premonitions.

Luminous Body Pythagoras' term for the astral body.

Luminous Phenomena Associated with physical mediumship. It would appear to have a chemical origin, the substances used being derived from the organism of the medium, and, according to Dr Gustave Geley, it is akin to the cold light emitted by various luminous insects. These lights vary in brilliance and size, sometimes coloured, they appear as semi-solid objects which float about the room. Slight smells of phosphorus have been recorded as accompanying the phenomena. It is also interesting to note the many accounts of lights appearing at religious revivals and about the persons of saints in ecstasy.

Lycanthropy An ancient and primitive belief that a human being can be transformed into an animal. Animal materialization has been known in psychic research, but it is a rare phenomenon; nevertheless its existence may have provided the seeds of a superstition which has had wide acceptance in the past.

Lynn, T. English apport medium, the subject of an investigation by Hewat McKenzie and Major Mowbray 1928–29. They photographed the ectoplasmic structures proceeding from the solar plexus region of the medium.

Lytton, Bulwer (1803–1873) Famous novelist. Once wrote *A Strange Story*, in which the character of Margrave is a portrayal of D. D. Home, the medium, and Lytton's friend of ten years standing.

Magi A learned class of the ancient Medes and Persians who studied and practised magic. 'The Magi', the three 'wise men' of one of the scripture stories concerning the birth of Jesus. The Magians were priests of religious settlements from Mesopotamia and its surrounds, and existed up to the Christian epoch. They believed in an old nature religion of Iran, which preceded Zoroastrianism.

Magic The art of the supernatural. Practised by most primitive peoples. Sympathetic magic—whereby an article is identified with a person, and treated as such. White magic—magic undertaken for beneficent purposes. Black magic—magic with evil intention. It should be noted that psychic phenomena is supernormal; i.e., it works in accordance with natural laws and therefore should not be classed as supernatural.

Magicians Professional modern illusionists, employ legerdemain and expensive stage settings for their tricks. The supernormal phenomena of mediumship cannot be reproduced in this way, and this fact has been acknowledged by many of the great masters of illusion: Robert Houdin, Bosco, Hamilton, M. Rhys, Professor Jacobs, Samuel Bellachini, Harry Kellar, Professor Hoffman, J. N. Maskelyne, Harry Houdini, Will Goldston, Ottoka Fischer, Harry Rigoletto—all great magicians who have testified to the genuineness of mediumistic phenomena.

Magnetic Healing *See* **Healing.**

Magnetic Phenomena Is known in mediumship. Henry Slade and Mlle Tomczyk both mediums, could influence compass needles. Slade also magnetized knitting needles in experiments conducted by Professor Zöllner.

Magnetometer Instrument of Abbé Fortin. A paper indicator suspended by a silk thread in a glass cylinder was deflected by the presence of a hand, over a dial of 360 degrees. A similar instrument has been used for study of terrestrial magnetism and dowsing.

Magus A control of Rev. Stainton Moses, deliverer of occult teachings, claimed to have lived 4,000 years ago as a member of an ancient African brotherhood. He never disclosed his real name.

Mahabharata Great Indian Sanscrit epic poem of unknown authorship, elaborated over a period from 500 B.C.–A.D. 400 consisting of 200,000 lines, and including as a digression from the main theme, the Bhagavad-Gita. The other great poem is the Ramayana. They both express the Hindu idea that the high god Vishnu was incarnated for humanity's benefit, in Mahabharata, in the person of a charioteer, Krishna, in the Ramayana as Ram or Rama, a hero king.

Mahatma Sanscrit for 'Great Soul'. Applied by occultists to Adepts, Masters and Elders.

Mahayana The larger or Northern division of Buddhist doctrine. Its message is addressed more to the laity, and differs from Hinayana (the 'little system'), in the belief of the incarnation of a Buddha spirit in a series of Buddha saints; secondly, the idea that the human soul passes through a succession of heavens and hells before attaining a final beatitude. *See* **Lotus Sutra.**

Mahdi A future Messiah of Islam.

Man The entire human race. Nearly all communications received through mediumship are from discarnate humans, only one or two have claimed to be 'pure spirit'. Occasional claims of communications originating from other planets are very doubtful.

Mana A Maori term for supernatural forces of nature or magical powers.

Manichaeism A Gnostic religion which flourished in A.D. 400, founded by Mani, a Persian, in an attempt to combine traditional eastern asceticism and Zoroastrian principles with Christianity.

Mantra A Vedic hymn of period 1500–800 B.C. A form of prayer common in eastern religion which is supposed to increase psychic power by its constant repetition.

Mantra Yoga Yoga pathway of divine union and realization by prayer.

Manu Sanscrit for a human archetype. Occult term for Master or Elder.

Many Mansions The many spheres of spirit existence.

Margery Mediumship *See* **Crandon.**

Marryat, Florence (1837–1899) English authoress, daughter of Captain Marryat. She knew most of the famous mediums of 1870–80 in England and America. Wrote several books on Spiritualism and possessed mediumistic gifts herself.

Marshall, Mrs Mary (1842–1884) English professional medium who provided Sir William Crookes and Dr Alfred Russell Wallace with their first introduction to mediumistic phenomena. Raps and table levitations were her main manifestations; later slate-writing developed.

Marylebone Spiritualist Association *See* **Spiritualist Association of Great Britain.**

127

Mass Hypnosis A theory often advanced to explain extra-ordinary feats by fakirs, as due to the hypnotizing of the entire audience, thereby reducing the feat to an illusion.

Master An Adept; occult title for an 'Initiate' who has reached the highest degree of occult attainment possible in this world. These people are supposed to have conquered human limitations and are said to be responsible for spiritual admini-stration in the world. They usually inhabit remote fastnesses and control the world's progress by deep meditation and influence over their distant pupils. This doctrine does not conform to Spiritualism.

Material Pertaining to matter, as distinct from 'spiritual'. Mediums often refer in this way to 'material conditions', mean-ing the ordinary circumstances of earthly life.

Materialization A form of physical mediumship whereby the visible production of temporary ectoplasmic forms in various stages of solidity and completeness, may be observed. The ectoplasm is a substance, normally invisible, which flows from a physical medium, augmented to some extent by the sitters. It is first seen as a slightly luminous vapour or fluid which apparently organizes itself into some recognizable form. According to Spiritualist belief, experienced discarnate opera-tors can mould this living material to their own former like-ness, or utilize it to produce lever-like structures for telekinetic phenomena, levitation of tables, raps, etc. Although incredible maybe to the layman, this phenomena has been thoroughly investigated many times under laboratory conditions by several eminent scientists, who have vouched for the genuineness of the phenomena. A warning is necessary here, for the benefit of inexperienced, would-be researchers: this form of mediumship is rare, and unless encountered under strictly controlled conditions by a competent body of experienced workers, is always suspect by reason of the conditions of darkness, usually laid down by private physical circles. For the purpose of gaining evidence of survival, mental mediumship provides the safest and surest path for the ordinary investigator.

Materialism A philosophy which refers all known phenomena to a material origin, and is completely exclusive of spiritual interests.

Matter An aspect of the energy in the universe detectable by the physical senses. The orderly nature of the solar system, and the phenomena of materialization, show in a remarkable way the amenability of matter to an organizing impetus from unknown sources. That Will-o-the-wisp, the ultimate particle, is still being chased by physicists, and as its bulk decreases it becomes more intangible in the process. To date, the 'fundamental particles' possess, we are told, continuous movement, not always predictable, and exhibit preferences for certain combinations. While this may not be organic life by scientific standards, it is a far cry from the popular idea of inert lifeless substance. Many great philosophers have realized the futility of apprehending matter directly; its so-called attributes are our own interpretations of our sense data, true perhaps by analogy only, to the 'real' world. When one hears from spirit communicators of similar environs in the spirit world, but not subject to the senses as on earth, one wonders if they do not indeed inhabit the 'real' world which must exist beyond our senses. The unchangeable values of goodness, truth, beauty, justice, the 'good in themselves' of the philosopher, known directly independently of the senses, may yet prove to be the driving forces of the universe—that which gives rise to 'matter'.

Matter Through Matter This curious phenomena has been produced in the seance room on several occasions. Knots have appeared in endless cords (Professor Zöllner); sewn-up clothing has been removed from mediums and replaced intact. Two rings of dissimilar woods prepared by Sir Oliver Lodge himself, were

E

linked together. The production of apports, the removal or introduction of a variety of objects from sealed or locked containers was successfully achieved in most carefully conducted experiments with Margery Crandon of Boston, 1932, reported by William H. Dutton in Journal of A.S.P.R. August–September, 1932.

Maxwell, Dr Joseph   Psychical investigator, Attorney General at Bordeaux Court of Appeal. Author of several books on divination. To equip himself for an analytical study of mediumship, he undertook a six years course of study for a medical degree, after which he was fortunate enough to contact a medium, M. Meurice, who produced telekinetic phenomena in good light, and also Mme Aguilana. He was with Col. Rochas in the study of Eusapia Paladino's mediumship. One of his interesting discoveries was that mediums possessed the common physical characteristic of spots in the irises of the eyes. His conclusions were, that phenomena were genuine, but attributed the intelligence to the forming of a collective intelligence of the sitters.

Māyā   The entire phenomena of the physical world, considered to be illusory by orthodox Hindus. Its influence can be traced to the interpretation of the Upanishads known as the Mayavada Vedanta by Sankara.

M.C.   Medium Coeli (q.v.).

McKenzie, J. Hewat (1870–1929)   Founder and Hon. President for nine years of the British College of Psychic Science, psychic researcher, lecturer and author. His wife was closely associated in all his interests. They both visited many countries and sat with many of the best mediums, including M. Kluski and Frau Silbert. They made a particular study of Mrs Osborne Leonard and Mrs Eileen Garrett.

Medicine Man Former priest-magician, specialist in healing and ceremonial magic of the North American Indian.

Meditation A mental discipline whereby the mind has to dwell upon a given theme, employed for the purpose of gaining insight into the inner nature and meaning of the universe. Much used by eastern ascetics, Yogis, monks and Spiritualist development circles.

Medium A subject who, under certain conditions, can be the means of relaying information from deceased persons to the living. The physical state of mediumship is not pathological as it leads to an expansion and development of original powers, and is distinct from hysterical states or epilepsy which degenerate the mentality.

Medium Coeli Astrological term for the intersection of the observer's meridian with the ecliptic, an angle considered to be of prime importance in the horoscope. Also known as the 'Midheaven'.

Mediumistic Development *See* **Circle, development.**

Mellon, Mrs J. B. (née Annie Fairlamb) British materialization medium gave sittings under stringent test conditions, to Professor Henry Sidgwick and F. W. H. Myers of S.P.R. at Cambridge in 1875. Although excellent results were obtained no report was published. In 1877, Alderman T. Barkas of Newcastle obtained wax moulds impregnated with a magenta dye which he had secretly introduced into the paraffin wax before the sitting.

Memory That faculty of the mind which can retain and recall ideas and impressions. Under hypnosis, this faculty may exhibit supernormal powers, to the extent of recalling minute details from early childhood. There are even claims of memory extending to previous incarnations on earth (see hypnotic regression). Certain Yoga practices are said to similarly extend the conscious memory. On passing to the spirit world, we are told that our memories become complete, though if attempts at communication are made, by entering earth conditions the memory becomes again impaired.

Memory, Cosmic An idea similar to that of the Akashic records (q.v.), a 'pool of memory' which may be tapped by individuals during certain trance states. *See also* **Cosmic Consciousness.**

Memphite Drama The oldest metaphysical treatise known, showing the existence of a mature mode of thought in Egypt, already ancient by 2500 B.C. In it, the world of nature is held to be the product of divine intelligence. The copy is incised on a black stone, and may be seen in the British Museum.

Mental Body Occult term for that part of a human personality which is composed of 'mental matter'. It is concerned with thought processes, abstract in a higher mental body, and concrete in a lower. Said to possess a life and consciousness of its own.

Mental Healing Spirit healing has been known to give easement for every kind of illness. Mental troubles may be treated with success either with or without the actual presence of the healer, absent healing can be just as effective by the guides and spirit doctors restoring the mental balance of the patient through the spirit body.

Mental Mediumship The powers of clairvoyance, clairaudience, trance speaking and psychometry are usually so classified as distinct from physical mediumship. It is believed that the spirit control operates the medium's subconscious mind as an instrument of expression.

Mental Radio   A term for telepathy, used by Upton Sinclair in his experiments.

Mentiferous   Conveying or transferring mind or thought; telepathic.

Mescalin   A drug prepared from a Mexican cactus plant, used by local tribes to induce trance and clairvoyant states. According to Aldous Huxley who experimented upon himself, the sense of time recedes, and a heightened awareness of colour and form is experienced under its influence.

Mesmerism   Early form of hypnotism, discovered and used by German physician Mesmer 1815. His method employed hand passes which were thought to convey a vital essence or fluid, which dominated the patient's will. It was also called 'animal magnetism'. Mesmer had success in his healing methods, but upset the orthodox medical opinion of his day and was branded as an impostor. Hypnotism is now used by the medical profession.

Messages, Spirit   *See* **Communications.**

Messiah   Hebrew synonym for Christ or 'the Anointed One'. The Hindu form is Krishna. Probably originated from the practice of pouring oil over the sacrificial animals used as burnt offerings in bygone times, the word becoming symbolic of divine saviour-gods.

Metagnome   A word for 'medium' coined by Boirac for psychical research, and defined: 'a person from whom supernormal phenomena originate, or in express relation to whom these phenomena occur; he is thus essential for psychic research.' The reason for its adoption was to eliminate the Spiritualistic associations of the word 'medium'.

Metagraphology Psychometry from handwriting. Raphael Schermann and Otto Reimann, a bank clerk of Prague, were two notable metagraphologists.

Metaphysics That branch of philosophy which seeks to determine the nature of things which exist—the true nature of that which underlies the familiar world.

Metapsychics A term proposed by Professor Richet, President of S.P.R. 1905, for a science dealing with mechanical or psychological phenomena due to forces which seem to be intelligent, or to unknown powers latent in human intelligence. It was divided into two classes: objective and subjective. The word Parapsychic (Boirac), was adopted in Germany and has proved the more popular term today.

Metapsychic Institute *See* **Institut Métapsychique.**

Metempsychosis Classical theory of reincarnation as man or animal. Occultists would qualify it as human to human only.

Metetherial Term coined by F. W. H. Myers: beyond the ether, the transcendental spiritual world.

Methodists Church of England Protestant body, founded by John and Charles Wesley; administered on Presbyterian and congregational lines.

Meyer, Jean Founder of Maison des Spirites, Paris, which aimed to promote the works of Allan Kardec. Also founder of Métapsychique Internationale for psychic research, recognized by the French government in 1919.

Microcosm and Macrocosm The concept of man as a small universe, a replica of macrocosm—the great universe.

Midheaven   *See* **Medium Coeli.**

Millesimo Castle   Situated in the Italian province of Savona. Owned by Marquis Carlo Centurione Scotto. It was the setting for many important psychic investigations from 1927 onwards. *See* **Centurione.**

Mimpathy   A sharing of feeling, but not necessarily sympathy. A community of sensation.

Mind   The thinking faculty, often termed the soul, spirit or ego; the stream of consciousness that makes personality and continues after death. Psychology divides mind into the conscious or supraliminal, and the subconscious or subliminal (below the threshold of consciousness). Faced with the facts of mediumship and control, one realizes how distinct is the mind from the physical brain, when the same body is seen to be dominated in turn by different personalities. The well-known Spiritualist author J. Arthur Findlay says in his book *The Rock of Truth* 'mind itself is a plastic substance composed of extremely rapid vibrations of an all-permeating ether. When in contact with physical matter it becomes moulded into images of it (thought). After death when in contact with etheric matter which is finer, mind can mould it more easily and directly. The more connected and varied the images, the more intelligent the individualized mind. The Universal Mind is the thinking substance of the universe and is always seeking expression. Mind is said to be in every kind of matter varying only in degree. When it reaches a level of creative strength, it gathers etheric matter and can enter physical matter and promote its growth.'

Mind Cure   First developed by Phineas Quimby, an American, (1802–1866) and a mesmerist who believed that all disease was a delusion of the mind. One of his patients was Mary Baker Eddy, the founder of Christian Science, who afterwards elaborated his teachings.

135

Mind Reading   Often casually advanced as an explanation of clairvoyance. If mind reading was a recognized ability, there might be some grounds for truth in this, providing we include 'reading' of the memory and the subconscious as well. Often, however, information given is not in the mind of the sitter, but has to be verified later. The only recognized form of thought transference that has been proved in any sense, is telepathy or Extra Sensory Perception. Note that the results of these experiments are quite different from the detailed clairvoyant message, one symbol only from a possible five, being transferred by a sender to a recipient; the results are only significant by statistics proving a degree of accuracy above chance level over many thousands of guesses. The medium does not reciprocate the thoughts, wishes or desires of the sitter, the communicator is often someone quite unexpected.

Minor Arcana   The fifty-six suit cards of the Tarot.

Miracles   Effects or events which are supernatural. Spiritualists do not believe in the supernatural, but have ample evidence of the supernormal which does not contravene natural laws.

Mirabelli, Carlo (Born 1889)   South American medium of Italian parents, of whom most extraordinary stories reached England and America. Most of his phenomena were reputed to have taken place in daylight. His powers were first observed by psychiatrists who had him under observation. An arbitration board investigated Mirabelli's phenomena, headed by Dr Ganymede de Sousa, President of the republic with eighteen men of high repute; their report was favourable. In 1919 he was tested at the Acadamia de Estudos Psychicos 'Cesar Lombroso', where he gave 392 sittings in daylight or bright illumination, attended by 555 people. A report of this was published in 1926 and many marvels were recounted. Dr E. J. Dingwall, after a review of the findings, professed himself unable to come to any decision. Professor Hans Dreisch of

S.P.R., who made a personal investigation at São Paulo in 1928 was not impressed.

Mithraism   A religious cult of fertility, which originated in Iran, Persia, about 400 B.C. Later it became very popular with the Roman legions who carried it with their conquests as far as Britain. The Mithraic cult centred around a saviour sun-god hero Mithras, who lived and died for the sins of the world. They had no priests as a professional class although a man could pass through many grades in its service; they believed that the world's events represented a chain of divine action. The official adoption of Christianity absorbed the cult, along with much of its ritual and doctrine.

Mohammed   The founder prophet of Islam (q.v.).

Monad   In Greek philosophy, one or a unit. Leibnitz used the world to name the metaphysical entities which he believed to be the non-physical 'atoms of nature' (*see* **Leibnitz**). Among occultists it is used to denote the indestructible divine spark of an individual carried through successive reincarnations.

Monck, Rev. Francis Ward   English clergyman who gave up his work for mediumship. As a well-known healer he toured extensively, and was called 'Dr Monck'. By his materialization phenomena, Dr Alfred Russell Wallace, Rev. Stainton Moses, Edward T. Bennett of S.P.R., and Judge Dailey of America were convinced of his powers. Although once accused of fraud and sentenced to three months imprisonment, Archdeacon Colley never doubted him.

Monism   Philosophical systems which uphold the fundamental unity of the universe, as opposed to dualism.

Monition   A supernormal warning: the revelation of some past or present event, by other than the normal senses (Richet).

Monotheism   The doctrine that there is only one God.

Mormonism (Church of Jesus Christ of Latterday Saints)   A religion of modern times founded by Joseph Smith in 1830, after receiving a revelation concerning a portion of the lost ten Jewish tribes, who after fighting among themselves were supposed to have landed in America. The name was taken from an alleged fifth century A.D. scripture, telling of a prophet Mormon and his son Moroni who hid the records which were engraved on gold plates. Smith formed a self-supporting community at Utah, Salt Lake City, with their own laws and regulations. Polygamy was instituted in an effort to stimulate their numbers at first, but has now been discontinued.

Morris, Mrs Meurig   Born 1899   British trance medium whose control 'Power' was an outstanding and forceful orator. Some supernormal occurrences took place during attempts to record 'Power's' voice by the Columbia Gramophone Co., and also in the studios of the British Movietone Co. In 1932 Mrs Morris took exception to a poster displayed by the *Daily Mail* reading: 'Trance medium found out', and sued them. Justice McCardie's summary was dramatically interrupted by an address of 'Power'. Judgement was in favour of the defendants on the plea of fair comment, adding that no allegations of fraud or dishonesty had been proved.

Morse, J. J. (1848–1919)   Outstanding British trance medium. In the opinion of the late W. T. Stead, the 'Bishop of Spiritualism'. Morse had very little education, yet when in trance he was able to converse with eminent philosophers on abstruse subjects. He also possessed powers of physical mediumship, demonstrating the fire immunity and elongation phenomena. As editor of several Spiritualist papers and author, he was active throughout in propagating Spiritualism.

Morselli, Enrico (1852–1929) Professor of Psychiatry at Genoa, formerly at Turin. A complete sceptic of psychic phenomena until he sat with Eusapia Paladino which convinced him of its truth. Later, he propounded an important psycho-dynamic theory of materialization phenomena.

Morris Pratt Institute, of Wisconsin. An institution of learning established under the auspices of Spiritualism. Founded by Morris Pratt, an American Spiritualist who made a great fortune from the finding of valuable mineral deposits disclosed to him by his Red Indian guide. The building and land was deeded to seven well-known Spiritualists as trustees.

Moses, Rev. Stainton (1839–1892) A great name in Spiritualism. A minister of the Church of England, Oxford M.A., author, and later editor of *Light*. From his original distrust of Spiritualism, he was forced by the outcome of his own mediumship to accept it. His psychic powers were amazing, powerful and varied: levitation, telekinesis, automatic writing, apports, psychic lights, musical sounds, scents, and many other manifestations. He never worked for money and his habitual sitters were few; they were: Dr and Mrs Speer and Mr F. W. Percival. Occasional sitters were, Serjeant Cox, W. H. Harrison, Dr Thompson, Mrs Garratt, Miss Birkett and Sir William Crookes. The identity of the controls was kept secret until recent times. They comprised a band of spirits forty-nine strong, whose missionary effort was directed to the upliftment of the human race. From 1884 until his passing Moses was the president of the London Spiritualist Alliance in London, now changed to the College of Psychic Science. Under the pen-name of M.A. Oxon he wrote *Spirit Teachings*, often referred to as the 'Bible' of Spiritualism.

Motor Automatism Phenomena classified by F. W. H. Myers as 'active' (similar to the 'muscular automatism' of Maxwell), meaning movement of the medium's head, tongue or limbs, by an inner motor impulse beyond the conscious will. He listed these as:

1. Strong impulse to action without reason.
2. Table tilting, ouija, planchette.
3. Supernormal musical and histrionic execution, contagious dancing.
4. Automatic drawing and painting.
5. Automatic writing.
6. Automatic speech.
7. Telekinetic movements. (*See* **Phenomena of Spiritualism.**)

Motricity, Exteriorized   *See* **Exteriorization of motricity.**

Moulds, Psychic Paraffin wax moulds obtained by the materialized form dipping its hands into molten wax, and then dissolving to leave a thin 'glove' behind. It is impossible to produce duplicates of these by normal means. Other moulds have been made by impression of the form in various yielding substances—clay, plasticine, etc. Dr Geley obtained excellent gloves through the agency of the Polish medium Kluski, under extreme test conditions. The gloves which are on view at the Institut Metapsychique in Paris are only one sixteenth of an inch thick, the fingers are bent and the wrists are a tight fit. Among other mediums who have successfully accomplished this phenomena are, Eusapia Paladino, Kathleen Goligher, Frau Silbert, Mrs Albert Blanchard, Mme d'Esperance, Mary M. Hardy, Margery Crandon, Slade. Moulds provide some of the best evidence for the reality of materialization.

Movement of Objects Is known to psychic research as telekinesis, meaning movement without contact; parakinesis is movement with contact insufficient to explain it. Both are common phenomena of physical seances, ranging from slight movements or vibrations, to levitation of heavy furniture and people. Musical instruments have been played by invisible hands, and complicated apparatus has been manipulated in a manner which shows intelligent operation. It is established that most movement occurs through the agency of a living physical substance extruded by the medium, named ectoplasm, which is capable of assuming any organized structure. This substance has been photographed many times.

Moyes, Miss Winifred Her control 'Zodiac', was responsible for the teachings upon which the Greater World Christian Spiritualist League was founded. He claimed to have been a teacher in the time of Jesus. The movement has a small network of churches over England. Their acceptance of Jesus as sole leader, separates them from the larger proportion of Spiritualists.

M.S.A. The Marylebone Spiritualist Association, now known as the Spiritualist Association of Great Britain.

Multiple Personality *See* **Personality.**

Mummification An unusual form of mediumship, by which a perishable object may be preserved by passes or contact with the medium's hands. Bacteria of various types have been destroyed by this method. Dr L. Clarac and Dr B. Llaguet of Bordeaux conducted a seven-year investigation with Mme X, and published a report in 1912 proving the existence of a fluid emanation which prevented decomposition of plants and animals. Similar phenomena were produced by Joanny Gaillard of Lyons in 1928. Heinrich Nusslein, a German medium, also had this power, and could preserve cut flowers for many days.

Murphy, Dr Gardner Of Columbia University, Hodgson Fellow in Psychical Research at Harvard 1922–25. Author of works on psychical research. He initiated the first experiments in telepathy by wireless, in Chicago and Newark.

Murray, Professor Gilbert, Ll.D., Litt. D. (1866–1958)   Regius Professor of Greek, Oxford University, President S.P.R. 1915–16. A psychical researcher famous for his work on thought transference, a faculty which he possessed to a marked degree. Was in agreement with William James on the concept of consciousness as a stream with a 'bright centre and dim edges' as an hypothesis for the working of telepathy and clairvoyance.

Muscular Automatism   Classification by Maxwell, similar to 'Motor automatism' of Myers (q.v.).

1. *Simple*. Typtology, alphabetic systems.
2. *Graphic*. Automatic writing, drawing, painting.
3. *Phonetic*. Trance speaking.
4. *Mixed*. Incarnations.

Music   There are many instances in history of strange music heard by people during religious revivals. We hear of it again at deathbeds (*see* **Phantasms of the Living**). With mediums, it is rare without instruments, the exceptions being D. D. Home, Stainton Moses, and Mary Jobson. Cases are known where instruments of various kinds have been played supernormally during seances. George Aubert, and M. de Boyonare were controlled by expert musicians and enabled to play instruments, a feat of which they would not normally be capable.

Music of the Spheres   Pythagoras' purely speculative mathematical relationship between the frequencies of the diatonic scale intervals, and the orbital distances of the planets (then unknown).

Myers, Frederick William Henry (1843–1901)   Pioneer of psychical research, held the post of Inspector of Schools for thirty years at Cambridge. Philosopher, scholar and poet. Fellow founder of S.P.R. in 1882, was president in 1900. His main work was *Human Personality and its survival of Bodily*

Death, an exhaustive study of the human mind and its powers. He drew in detail a vast picture of the subliminal self, which he affirmed was the real ego, of which the ordinary consciousness was only a small part. The book covers almost all of the field of psychic phenomena, and relates it in an orderly system. The Rev. Stainton Moses was his friend, and he was also a guest of Professor Richet, Sir Oliver Lodge and Dr Ochorowitz, in the famous experiments with Eusapia Paladino. Other mediums he tested included Mme d'Esperance, Mrs Everitt, Duguid, Mrs Thompson. After his death, proofs of his continued identity were communicated through Mrs Piper by cross-correspondence. Sir Oliver Lodge received independent evidence through Mrs Leonard from Myers that he was communicating through Miss Geraldine Cummins the automatist.

Mysticism   Transcendental knowledge of God by contemplation. The belief that spiritual truth may be attained by direct apprehension, apart from the intellect or normal senses.

National Federation of Spiritual Healers   A Federation of healers founded in 1954 by an amalgamation of county and regional healers Associations. The purpose of the Federation is to serve the public good through the practice and teaching of healing and to speak for healers on a National level on matters relating to healing. It is a non-sectarian organization.

National Laboratory of Psychical Research   Established by Harry Price in London 1925, to investigate every phase of psychic phenomena. Many works have been published of their findings, from time to time.

National Spiritualist Association of Churches   Chief American Spiritualist organization who claim that Spiritualism, as representative of the N.S.A.C., is to teach and proclaim three aspects: the Science, Philosophy and Religion of modern Spiritualism, expressed in the 'Declaration of Principles' and in the adopted 'Definitions' as well as objects of organization. 'Science', because it investigates, analyses and classifies facts and manifestations demonstrated from the spirit side of life. 'Philosophy' because it studies the laws of Nature both on the seen and unseen side of life and bases conclusions upon present observed facts. It accepts statements of observed facts of past ages and conclusions drawn therefrom when sustained by reason and by results observed from facts of the present day. 'Religion' because it strives to understand and to comply with physical and spiritual laws of Nature—*which are the laws of God!*

Natural Philosophy Departments of scientific study, now known as physics.

Naturalist Theory of Ethics Philosophical term for the assumption that the 'natural world' including our minds and emotions, is the only order of reality, thus reducing ethics to psychology. Moral judgements by this view, would be due to concealed fears or mental complexes.

Nature Spirits Non-human spirits, rarely mentioned by spirit communicators. A few psychic people claim to have seen them, and even photographs are shown as evidence of the 'little folk'. They are generally supposed to be helpfully disposed towards humanity. Primitive peoples and occultists believe in powerful 'elemental' spirits, said to control natural forces.

Necromancy Divination by the pretended conjuring up of the dead. A form of black magic. Spiritualists would deny the possibility of 'conjuring up'. It is the so-called dead, who try to communicate; the living have no compulsive powers over them.

N.F.S.H. The National Federation of Spiritual Healers (q.v.).

Negative and Positive   Are words employed very loosely among Spiritualists. They are used mainly as descriptive of personal reactions; positive meaning extroverted, and negative introverted. There is a vague attempt by the less informed, to ally these terms with electric potential, for instance the theory that men should alternate with women to form a sequence of 'positive and negative' in a circle is apt to be confusing, but there are some who would apply these terms to every form of duality discoverable in the universe.

Negative Hallucination   Failure to perceive objects presented to the senses.

Neophyte   A candidate for initiation.

Neo-Platonism   A philosophical religion, first formulated by Plotinus in the third century A.D. Really derived from Indian sources, though claiming Plato's doctrines. It was based on mysticism and had much in common with Upanishadic Hinduism. Its basic ideas were later adopted by hermits in general, exerting a great influence over medieval monastics.

Nerve Aura   Term coined by Dr J. Rhodes Buchanan 1814–99, discoverer of the psychometric faculty, to describe the emanation of the human body which could be perceived by sensitives.

Neumann, Therese (Born 1898) A Bavarian peasant, whose stigmata and visions have aroused world-wide notice. In 1922 owing to a throat abscess she abstained from solid food. Since Christmas 1926 her only sustenance is said to have been a little water. Her stigmata are situated on the left side, hands and legs, and bleed profusely on Fridays. Linguists have vouched for her speech in Aramaic as authentic. She seems to have experienced in her own body the whole drama of the crucifixion.

Neurypnology Term first used by Braid, for what is now called hypnotism.

Newbrough, Dr John Ballou (1828–1891) New York medium for clairvoyance, automatic writing and painting. His main work was the astounding production of '*Oahspe, the Kosmon Bible in the words of Jehovah and his angel ambassadors*'. This was the result of manual automatism on a typewriter. It took fifty weeks, working half an hour before sunrise every morning according to his own account.

New Motor An extraordinary venture by J. M. Spear (1804–87), American Spiritualist preacher who built at Lymn, Mass., a motor intended to be self-generative, at a cost of 2,000 dollars. It did not work and was removed to Randolph, where it was destroyed by superstitious villagers.

Newspaper Tests Experiments devised by spirit communicators to eliminate the possibility of telepathy. Their method was to give names and dates to be published in certain columns of a newspaper yet to be printed. This information was at once posted to S.P.R. Astonishing results were obtained in this way through the mediumship of Mrs Osborne Leonard.

Nichols, Miss Agnes *See* **Mrs Guppy.**

Nictalopes Persons possessing the rare faculty of being able to see in the dark.

Nielsen, Einar Danish materialization medium, the subject of experiments by Baron Schrenck Notzing. Also gave several sittings in 1924 to S.P.R. of Iceland. Remarkable levitations and telekinesis were also produced. Was accused of fraud.

Nimbus *See* **Halo.**

Nirvana   Oriental idea of the extinction of individuality without loss of consciousness.

Niyama   Second stage of Yoga. Withdrawal from the world, purification of the mind and the attainment of contentment.

'Nona'   Control of the Rosemary mediumship (q.v.).

Normal   The usual clairvoyant demonstration is an example of a medium functioning 'in the normal', i.e., not in a state of trance. The messages so received could be described as 'normal communications'.

Nortontaylor, William   New Zealand medium for materialization, direct voice, trance, healer and lecturer, former Principal of Christchurch Psychical Research Institute.

Nostradame, Michael de (1503–1566)   Famous French physician and astrologer. Councillor to Kings Henry II and Charles IX. In 1555 he published ten 'centuries' of a hundred verses or 'quatrains', all coded in a medley of languages, but crowded with amazing predictions, still in the process of fulfilment.

Nous   Occult term denoting the first emanation from the Godhead.

N.S.A.C.   National Spiritualist Association of Churches (q.v.)

Numerology   A study of the occult powers of numbers.

'Oahspe'   Kosmon Bible, automatically typed by J. B. Newbrough (q.v.).

Oaten, Ernest   Noted worker for Spiritualism, was editor of a Spiritualist newspaper from 1919–36. Was President of the Spiritualists National Union for five years, and of the International Spiritualist Federation for six years. Popular lecturer, writer and authority on every phase of psychical phenomena.

Objective Phenomena   That phenomena which has external reality, and which may be perceived by others present in the same way. (As distinguished from subjective phenomena.)

Objective Theory of Ethics   Philosophical theory recognizing the existence of moral qualities in their own right; if so, it follows that correct ethical judgements are possible. This is in accordance with Spiritualism whose ethics are based on rightness of motive.

Obsession   The state of a mind besieged. Medically, it refers to a fixed idea which threatens the mental balance. In Spiritualism it refers to the invasion of the living by a discarnate spirit or spirits, tending to complete possession for the purpose of selfish gratification. Trance mediumship operates on the same principle but is the result of co-operation between an intelligent spirit and the medium. Consideration and respect is shown on both sides and the medium's normal self is only in temporary abeyance during control. The obsessing spirits are usually ignorant or earth-bound, not necessarily evil—any harm they cause may be unintentional. The best treatment is to reason with the entity; to point out the futility and damage of their actions and the possibilities of their own sphere and progression. Some mediums have specialized in this valuable work, and have restored many patients to normality.

Occult Hierarchy   *See* **White Brotherhood.**

Occultism   Theories and practices concerned with the attainment of secret powers of mind and spirit. There are many systems, some very old, others a blend of the ancient with modern psychic practice. Occultists generally maintain that essential wisdom was known to a greater extent among the ancient civilizations of the East, than it is today, and many of them study old writings in the attempt to find hidden indications of this knowledge. Spiritualism is concerned more with service to God through humanity than the personal attainment of secret powers.

Ochorowitz, Dr Julien (1850–1918) Eminent psychical researcher, lecturer in psychology at the University of Lemberg, Co-director of the Institut Générâl Psychologique of Paris from 1907. Eusapia Paladino was his guest in Warsaw 1893–94. Of the genuineness of psychic phenomena he was convinced, attributing it to the action of a fluidic double working independently of the body, but he did not accept the spirit hypothesis. It was he who discovered Mlle Tomczyk, a physical medium who produced phenomena in daylight, for his photographs of this he gained an award of 1,000 francs from the Comité d'Etude de Photographie Transcendental. One notable example of his work was the photograph of an etheric hand imprinted on a rolled film enclosed in a bottle, others included pictures of objects suspended in air, as if attached to the medium's fingers by invisible threads.

Od,—Odic Force Meaning an all-penetrating force discovered by Baron Reichenbach. According to his findings: the mouth, hands, forehead and occiput emitted the strongest emanations. They diminished with hunger and at sunset, and increased after a meal. He claimed that this peculiar force also exists in the rays of the sun and moon, and can be conducted to great distances by all solid or liquid substances, bodies being charged and discharged by contact or proximity. *See* **Emanations**.

Oesterreich, Dr Konstantin Professor of Philosophy at University of Tübingen, and authority on religious psychology. As the result of a challenge by Baron Schrenck Notzing, Dr Oesterreich examined the whole evidence in the Eva C. case, and further investigated the phenomena of Frau Silbert and Willi Schneider, after which he publicly declared his belief in the reality of materialization and telekinesis.

Olcott, Col. Henry Steel with **Mme Blavatsky** Joint founders of the Theosophical Society. On behalf of an American newspaper, Olcott made several investigations of physical mediumship, notably the Eddy brothers, Holmes and Mrs Elizabeth Compton, which established him as a psychic researcher. He met Mme Blavatsky at Chittenden during his investigations, and showed amazing energy in lecturing and organizing, finally establishing a headquarters for Theosophy at Adyar in India. Fraudulent accusations against Mme Blavatsky by Dr Hodgson of S.P.R. showed Col. Olcott in an unfavourable light, for which he has been criticized severely.

Old Soul Term for a soul who has incarnated many times on this earth, and has presumably gained much wisdom in the process. Not all Spiritualists would agree with this possibility. *See* **Reincarnation.**

'Olga' Control of Rudi Schneider.

Om Sanskrit word credited with magical powers by its utterance.

Om Mani Padme Hum Well-known mantra of lamaism, a prayer said to be particularly efficacious by its repetition.

Omnipotent The Almighty. All powerful, as applied to Deity.

Omniscient Knowing all, as applied to Deity.

Ontology (Aristotle) Science dealing with the fundamental essence of things. Metaphysics.

Open Circle *See* **Circle, open.**

Opposition Astronomically, when one celestial body is exactly on the opposite side of the ecliptic circle to another. Astrologically the two principles would be in a state of high tension.

Orthos A spirit term descriptive of the spirit world, coined by the spirit of Betty Buck in a complete spirit philosophy which was communicated in trance.

Ossowiecki, Stephan An outstanding Polish medium who could read sealed envelopes, see auras and move objects without contact. Was investigated by Professor Richet, Dr Gustave Geley and many others. At the International Psychic Congress, Warsaw 1923, he read successfully the contents of a note sent by S.P.R., wrapped in several coloured folds of paper and sealed by Dr Dingwall in an envelope. For this he was acclaimed by the Congress.

Osty, Dr Eugen French physician, Director of Institut Métapsychique Internationale, successor to Dr Gustave Geley. He was the first to employ infra-red and ultra-violet techniques in the study of Rudi Schneider's mediumship. He wrote several very important books on psychical research.

Ouija Board (French 'oui' and German 'ja') A small wooden board with a pointer, placed under the medium's hand, and resting on a polished surface which shows letters of the alphabet. Under control, messages are spelt out by the hand's movements. A similar appliance is known to have been used in Pythagoras' time (540 B.C.).

Ouspensky, P. D. Born 1878 Russian mathematical student of Moscow University, and disciple of Gurdjieff. He formulated a fourth dimensional philosophy as a bridge between Western rationalism and Eastern mysticism, and wrote several interesting books on the subject.

Overself The Great Self. Atman, the ancient Hindu conception of the Great Self, differentiated into individual lesser selves in a state of Maya or illusion. Hence the search for the Higher Self which knows the reality of the eternal state of being, by means of ascetic practices, borrowed and elaborated in recent times by some Western philosophers and writers.

Overshadowing   The controlling of a medium by a discarnate spirit. More often used when the control amounts to only a slight impression. Also used to describe rudimentary trans-figuration.

Oversoul   A term very loosely applied to concepts of Brahma, the Absolute, group-soul, higher self, etc. Not definitive.

Owen, Robert (1771–1858)   Famous English Socialist and humanitarian. He became a Spiritualist when he was eighty-three after a sitting with American medium Mrs Hayden. His formal profession was published in the Regional Quarterly Review.

Pacifist   Non-aggressive. One who practises non-violence.

Painting, Psychic   *See* **Automatic painting, Clairvoyant painting, Direct painting.**

Palmistry, or Chiromancy   Divination by means of the lines and configurations of the hands. Not a mediumistic faculty.

Paladino, Eusapia (1854–1918)   Famous Italian physical medium, discovered by Signor Damiani through the agency of a control 'John King' (q.v.), who claimed Eusapia as his reincarnated daughter, and gave precise directions by which Damiani found her. Eusapia's phenomena was powerful and diverse: heavy objects moved at her glance and gesture, or floated in the air according to her wish. Facial imprints were made in clay, her body was levitated. Telekinetic movements were accomplished by extra 'limbs' extruded from her body while she was held down. So many famous scientists were convinced of her phenomena, that there is no doubt of her powers. Yet she attempted to cheat in a childish fashion when given the chance. As a person she was illiterate, ignorant, but shrewd. An investigation by the Milan Commission in 1892 brought her before some of the greatest researchers of the day, among whom were, Professor Schiapirelli, Director of the Milan Observatory, Professor Gerosa, Dr G. B. Ermacora, Alexander Aksakov, Dr Charles Du Prel, Professor Charles Richet. A report was issued after seventeen sittings, to quote a part: 'It is impossible to count the number of times that a hand appeared and was touched by one of us. Suffice it to say that doubt was no longer possible. It was indeed a living human hand which we saw and touched, while at the same time the bust and arms of the medium remained visible, and her hands were held by those on either side of her.' Among the many distinguished scientists and researchers who tested Paladino were: Dr Ercole Chiaia, Cesar Lombroso, Professor Tamburini, Camille Flammarion, Professor Morselli, Professor Wagner of the University of St Petersburg, Dr Ochorowitz, Sir Oliver Lodge, F. W. H. Myers, Col. Rochas, Dr J. Maxwell, Professor Sabatier, Baron de Watteville, Professor Flournoy, the astronomer Porro, later Director of Genoa Observatory, Professor Philippe Bottazzi, Director of Naples Physiological Institute, M. and Mme Curie, W. W. Baggally, a conjuror, Dr Hereward Carrington, Hon. Everard Feilding, Howard Thurston, a magician.

Pantheism A doctrine in which the universe is identified with Deity. God as immanent in all things. The philosophy of Spinoza.

Pantomnesia *See* **Paramnesia.**

Pap, Lajos (Born 1883) Non-professional medium of Budapest for apports and telekinesis. Closely studied by Dr Elmer Chergery Pap, retired Chief Chemist to the government, and President of the Budapest Metapsychic Society. A 100-watt green lamp was used at the seances. Under strict control was produced telekinesis of luminous baskets, coloured lights, and hundreds of living apports—beetles, butterflies, small animals and flowers.

Paraesthesia Abnormal prickling or tingling sensations. Mediums are often able to identify a particular control by such physical sensations, which appear to be signals of the entities presence.

Paraffin Moulds *See* **Moulds.**

Parakinesis The movement of objects with contact insufficient by itself to explain the motion observed.

Paramnesia Confusion of the memory; especially a false sensation of a previous experience when in fact, it is being experienced for the first time.

Paranoia Chronic mental derangement, characterized by hallucinations.

Paranormal Supernormal. Not within generally accepted experience of cause and effect.

Parapsychology Termed coined by Boirac, now the science for the study of psi processes in the human or animal mind. 'A division of psychology dealing with the psychical effects which appear not to fall within the scope of what is at present, recognized law.' (*Journal of Parapsychology.*)

Paroptic Sense A faculty of seeing with the etheric body, without use of the eyes.

Parsis Of Persian descent, and following the religion of Zoroaster in India.

Passing Synonymous with 'dying' in Spiritualist terminology. As it is realized that death is not cessation but a passing from one state of existence to another, Spiritualism dissociates itself from the traditional gloomy trappings of funeral lamentations, which are said to distress the departed friend, and have their own simple service for such occasions.

'Patience Worth' Renowned male control of Mrs John Curran of St Louis, automatist. He claimed to have lived in Dorset, England, in the seventeenth century, and was later killed by Indians in America. Some of the statements regarding his early environment were verified. Many books of outstanding literary merit were produced in medieval English. In 1918 'Patience Worth's Magazine' provided an outlet for much of the work of this control.

Peebles, Dr, D.D. Held a pastorate of a large American church, but finding he could give no consolation to the bereaved members, investigated Spiritualism with Judge Edmonds; he then gave up his pastorate and became a travelling spokesman for Spiritualism, went round the world five times in all, and passed to spirit at the ripe age of ninety-nine. He was loved and revered by all who met him.

Pelham, George The pen-name of George Pellew, control of Mrs Piper, friend of Dr Hodgson of the S.P.R., who returned in this way to Hodgson, after a death pact had been made.

Pendulum An instrument used by dowsers and radiesthetists, consisting of a bob suspended by a short cord held in the fingers. According to the amplitude and direction of its gyrations, various deductions are made suitable to the matter in hand. Spiritualists would incline to the view that the results are possibly due to psychic powers of the operator, the pendulum acting merely as a focus of attention.

Pentecost The 'miracles' recorded of Pentecost, have their modern counterparts. 'Tongues of fire'—psychic lights, 'speaking in tongues'—xenoglossis, 'sound of the wind'—psychic breezes and draughts. All these phenomena are well known and attested in the seance room.

Percipient The receiver in telepathic communications.

Percussion   A common feature of the physical seance, usually known as raps, for which a coded communication is possible. The noise is produced by flexible ectoplasmic rods striking various objects in the room.

Perfumes, Psychic   *See* **Smells.**

Perispirit   Allan Kardec's name for the spirit body.

Personality   The sum total of that which constitutes an individual. The characteristics which distinguish one person from another, incorporated in a stream of consciousness. The establishment of the continuance of this stream of consciousness after death, is proof of survival. Secondary personalities intrude when a complete loss of consciousness occurs, cases of this are well known to psychiatrists. Multiple personalities are also recognized of the one person. In mediumship, the control is a different person; a separate entity, and the evidence of this is in the manner of co-operation between medium and spirit, also in the higher level of intelligence manifested. Secondary and Multiple personalities are pathological and degenerative, while mediumship is progressive and non-pathological.

Personation   *See* **Impersonation.**

Personism   Change of personality (Myers).

Peters, Alfred Vout   English trance and clairvoyant medium, widely travelled, repeatedly mentioned in Sir Oliver Lodge's famous book on survival, *Raymond*. In 1927 he succeeded in psychometrizing Joanna Southcott's box at the National Laboratory of Psychical Research, before it was officially opened.

Phantasm   A fanciful image possessing no reality. The substance of hallucination.

Phantasmata Occult term for 'thought forms' capable of communication.

Phantom An apparition or ghostly figure; the evidence for this is overwhelming.

Phenomena Something perceived by observation or experiment.

Phenomena of Spiritualism There have been several attempts to classify these; the categories most generally used today are three: 'Mental', 'Physical' and 'Healing'. By mental phenomena is meant those phenomena where the spirit operators use the medium's *mind* as their instrument of communication. In physical phenomena, the operators use ectoplasm—physical *material* of the medium to form a communicating instrument. Healing may partake of either or both, varying greatly with individual cases. Mental phenomena again may be divided into two classes: (a) where the medium works in the 'normal' by sensory automatism, i.e. clairvoyance, clairaudience, clairsentience, psychometry, (b) where the medium works in trance by muscular automatism, i.e. automatic speaking, writing, painting, ouija, planchette. Physical phenomena are: materialization, transfiguration, levitation, telekinesis, direct and independent voice, apports, lights, raps, psychic photography.

Mental mediumship is fairly common and, at its best, can provide excellent proof of survival for the inquirer. Physical phenomena is comparatively rare, is often fraudulently imitated, and although extraordinary and sensational, even when genuine, it does not always give evidence of survival. Healing does not in itself prove survival, but is a valuable demonstration of spirit power transcending earthly skill.

Phenomenalism A philosophy which holds that phenomena only may be apprehended, not the underlying cause.

'Philosophus'   Control of Rev. Stainton Moses, alleged to be Alexander Achillini, a philosopher of Padua in 1506.

Philosophy   A comprehensive study of all mental and material phenomena. Any particular system of philosophic thought.

Philosophy of Spiritualism   Its *metaphysics* are a legitimate study, as the relationship between the 'real' enduring world and the phenomenal world of the senses can be discovered by paranormal communication between the two. The 'monad' hierarchies of Leibnitz are in accordance with Spiritualist teachings; the monads being equated with spirits inhabiting the 'real' world which underlies the phenomenal world of our senses.

Its *Existents:* from these communications it seems that the enduring reality is an active principle, not the material universe as it appears in any part, but the spiritual relationship of the individual consciousness to the whole, striving for expression at many different levels of conscious experience, manifesting through the senses as matter of various forms.

Its *Theory of Knowledge:* Parapsychology and mediumship have proved that knowledge may be obtained by channels other than the recognized senses. This provides the basis for Spiritualist philosophy.

Its *Ethics:* are the Objectivist order; recognizing the 'real' values of Goodness, Truth, Beauty, Justice, which endure as Good in Themselves. So far as the individual's motives are directed to the propagation of these values, so he is acting in accordance with 'rightness'.

Phone-Voyance   Clairvoyant faculty akin to 'psychic television' over the public telephone system. It was discovered in himself by Vincent N. Turvey in 1905. He was often able to describe accurately conditions at the other end of the line, and give additional information unknown to the listener there.

Photography *See* **Psychic photography.**

Phrenology A scientific study of the shape and contours of the human head, in the belief that there is a correlation between its undulations and the mental faculties and potentialities. Not mediumistic.

Physical Medium One whose ability to produce ectoplasm of suitable substance and quantity, is able to specialize in the production of physical phenomena. Such mediums are usually very sensitive to actinic light, and need to be shielded from it during a seance. Failure to do this may result in serious physical injury to the medium, due to the sudden elastic recoil of the ectoplasm.

Physical Phenomena As distinct from mental phenomena, involves the production of ectoplasm in order that various structures may be used for materialization, telekinesis, etc. The existence of physical phenomena alone, does not prove survival; this can only come through evidence of a recognizable personality. *See* **Phenomena of Spiritualism.**

Physics The sciences which deal with non-chemical changes and properties of matter in energized systems. Formerly known as Natural philosophy.

Pierart, Professor A. T. Died 1878 Of Maubeuge College, France and secretary to Baron du Potet. He founded a rival school to Allan Kardec's. Kardec taught a compulsory scheme of reincarnation, and his followers were described as 'spiritists'. Pierart denied this doctrine and used the word 'Spiritualist' in his journal.

Pink As an auric colour, is associated with affection.

159

Piper, Mrs Leonore E. Of Boston. The most outstanding trance medium in the history of psychical research, responsible for the conversion of such intellects as Sir Oliver Lodge, Dr R. Hodgson, Professor J. Hyslop and many others, to the spirit hypothesis and certainty of human survival. Her daily life for twenty years continuously was under the intensive direct supervision of the A.S.P.R. and the S.P.R. without once giving cause for suspicion by her actions. As an experiment, she was transferred from America to London to see if her mediumship would be affected by new surroundings. Living in Sir Oliver's own household, she supplied astonishing information which confounded a professional inquiry agent engaged by Lodge as a control experiment, to gather information from the same locality.

Pistology A branch of theology concerned with faith.

P.K. Psychokinesis (q.v.).

Plaat, Frau Lotte (Mme von Strahl) Dutch psychometrist, regularly employed by the German police for tracing criminals. Important experiments with her were conducted in 1930 at the Laboratory for Psychical Research, London.

Planchette A small handrest on castors, in which a pencil is fixed. Invented in France in 1853. If a suitable medium places his hand on the apparatus, it may write or draw. This faculty should only be developed in a properly conducted circle.

Planes *See* **Spheres.**

Planetary Information There have been several alleged communications regarding life on other planets, and descriptions from 'astral travels', all of which must remain speculative. Swedenborg was the first who claimed knowledge of the planet Mars. Some cases of supposed Martian language have also been closely studied, but would seem to be sufficiently explained by subconscious dramatization and should not be taken seriously.

Plastics *See* **Moulds.**

Plato (429–348 B.C.) The famous Greek idealist philosopher, admirer of Socrates and author of the dialogues which, with his other writings, formed the first systematic body of philosophic thought. Plato tried for most of his life to formulate a system which would result in the establishment of an ideal state. Of his beliefs we know that (like Spiritualists) he knew that a truer world could be perceived with the intellect. That he guessed at the pre-existence of the soul we deduce from his Theory of Ideas: that knowledge of Universals (values) was a form of recollection of the soul. Love of the Good was to him, the only catalyst which could free the soul from passion. Although his systems never gained ground, he blazed the trail for later philosophers.

Pneumatographers Mediums for the production of direct writing.

Podmore, Frank (1856–1910) Well-known British psychic researcher who first accepted Spiritualism then rejected it and was exhaustive in his attempts to provide alternative explanations of its phenomena. He was the author of many works, including the collaboration with Myers and Gurney for the well-known *Phantasms of the Living*.

Polarian *See* **Root Race.**

Poltergeist A mischievous agency or entity who makes noises, throws objects about, causes fires and breaks domestic crockery. These phenomena are spontaneous and usually occur in the immediate vicinity of some young person around the age of puberty. It is as if this person is haunted or persecuted by the spirit. The presence of others may aggravate the phenomena or cause it to cease. The throwing of small stones is very characteristic of this phenomena all over the world. Peculiarly, the flight of these stones is not a normal trajectory and they are frequently reported as hot to the touch.

Polyglot Mediumship   *See* **Xenoglossis.**

Polytheism   The worship of many gods.

Positive   *See* **Negative.**

Positivism   A materialistic philosophy which denies metaphysics. The Positive philosophy founded by Comte 1798–1857, conceiving science to be an end in itself, evolving through three stages: 1. Theological or mythical; 2. Metaphysical or abstract; 3. Positive or concrete.

Possession   Temporary surrender of a subject's organism to the control of another spirit, usually discarnate, though possession by the living has been known in a few cases. The discernible difference between possession and subconscious personation, is whether new knowledge has been given. An endurance of possession against the subject's will, would be called obsession.

Post-Cognitive Telepathy   Term used in parapsychology. An Extra Sensory correspondence between a present mental pattern of A and a mental pattern of B of which B was conscious in the past, but of which he is not contemporaneously conscious.

Post Mortem Messages   Instances where a deceased person communicates the contents of a sealed letter written prior to his death for the express purpose of proving survival.

'Poughkeepsie Seer', The   *See* **Davis, A. J.**

Powell, Evan J. (1881–1958)   Justice of the Peace, British non-professional trance and physical medium of Paignton, Devon. Was always tied to a chair by his own wish, before the drawn curtains of the cabinet. His chief control, an American Indian named Black Hawk, successfully established his identity by reason of a book he wrote during earth life, in Boston 1834. This was subsequently traced by a book agent, also a memorial in Illinois which was mentioned twenty years before it was finally proved. Powell gave many sittings to the British College of Psychic Science, and the original book is preserved in the museum of the Spiritualist Association of Great Britain.

Power, Psychic A general term descriptive of the various forces employed in the exercise of psychic or mediumistic faculties. In our present state of knowledge it is difficult to differentiate between the various power sources. Some phenomena seems to be entirely mental, while others are due to physical emanations, with many combinations of the two classes. *See* **Emanations.**

Prāna A subtle form of energy permeating the universe, but manifesting in a special form in the human organism. This force is capable of being transmitted from one organism to another, and is the energizing power by which many forms of occult and magic phenomena can be produced (Swami Bhakta Vishita). Yogis believe it can be inspired with the breath.

Pranayama The fourth stage of Yoga. The science of breathing.

Pratya Hara The fifth stage of Yoga. Withdrawal of attention from objects.

Prayer A mental attitude of reaching out to absorb a greater awareness of spirituality (*see* **Awareness**). A communication mental or vocal addressed to a higher or spirit intelligence. Spiritualists would assert that it is not the form, but the sincerity and spiritual value of the motive behind the appeal which makes the prayer, verbal repetition being useless.

'Preceptor'　Control of the 'Imperator' group of Rev. Stainton Moses. Was later revealed as Elijah, a link between Moses and Malachi in a chain of spirit influence from Melchizedek to Jesus.

Precession　*See* **Aquarian age.**

Precognition　Prediction in which the percipient is correctly positive that a particular event is going to happen.

Precognitive Clairvoyance　Term in parapsychology. An Extra Sensory correspondence between a present mental pattern of A and a future object or event in the physical world (Soal and Bateman).

Precognitive Telepathy　(parapsychology)　An Extra Sensory correspondence between a present mental pattern of A and a future mental pattern of B (Soal and Bateman).

Prediction　The foretelling of any kind of future event. There is ample factual evidence of this occurring. When it involves the fate of nations or large units, it is termed prophecy.

Pre-existence　Source of much speculation among Spiritualists. If reincarnation be automatic, an earthly pre-existence must form part of a person's progression. Some spirits say they remember former lives, others do not. According to a communication from F. W. H. Myers, a new soul is born within a group, and has to take an earth pattern already laid down by the thoughts and actions of his group predecessor (*see* **Group Soul theory**). Sir Oliver Lodge was inclined to believe that a spirit had a choice of parentage upon entering its relationship with matter, thus accounting for some of the facts of heredity. It is accepted as a matter of course by Eastern philosophy and was believed by Plato to account for the individual soul's 'recollection' of Universals.

Premonition Prediction where details are not precisely outlined. The lowest degree of prophecy. According to Professor Richet there were two conditions: 1. The fact announced must be absolutely independent of the person to whom the premonition has come. 2. The announcement must be such that it cannot be attributed to chance or sagacity. Premonitions may be received in normal, trance, hypnotic or dream states. The S.P.R. collected 900 premonitions of death, Flammarion, 1,824 cases and Bozzano 260.

Presbyterianism A form of church government by a body of elders, each ruling a court of ministers of equal rank for the churches of a particular district.

Presentiment The prediction of vague future events of a personal nature only. Vague non-personal events are premonitions.

Prevision Presentiment in a visual form.

Price, Harry Founder and Director of the National Laboratory of Psychical Research, London. Former Research Officer of A.S.P.R., Hon. Vice-President of the Magician's Club, London. Investigated Stella C., Eleonore Zügun and Rudi Schneider. Author of many important works on psychic research.

Prince, Dr Walter Franklin Ex-minister of the Episcopal Church, Research Officer of Boston S.P.R. and A.S.P.R. President of S.P.R. 1931–32. Extremely sceptical, remarkable for his studies of the 'Patience Worth' case, the Antigonish Ghost, and his curing of Doris Fischer in a case of multiple personality. Author of many books.

Private Sitting One person only, sitting with a medium. It is usually arranged for a moderate fee in perfect secrecy and anonymity, at reputable Spiritualist organizations. A few well-known mediums work in their own homes and fix their own fees. Evidence can never be guaranteed in either case.

Proceedings Official publications of the various societies for psychical research. The first were those of London S.P.R. in 1882, then the old A.S.P.R. 1885–89, followed by independent A.S.P.R. 1907–27, then the National Laboratory of Psychical Research, which, like the Boston S.P.R., issues books and bulletins but no Proceedings. Details of most of the famous investigations may be found in these volumes, available at many public libararies.

Prodigies Infants who exhibit mature powers of technical or artistic perfection. There is no normal explanation of this, although it is often advanced by the supporters of the theory of reincarnation as evidence of the experiences gained in former lives being carried over to the present consciousness. This theory may be countered by the fact of spirit possession, or mediumship. This view is strengthened by the fact that prodigies have sometimes been suddenly deprived of their powers in later life. *See* **Ariola.**

Prognostication The act of making a forecast.

Progression The pathway of each spirit through the many phases or spheres of experience, constitutes a progression, the ultimate of which we cannot conceive as yet. Spirit communicators and teachings are unanimous on this point. The rate of progression depends on the person's capacity to profit spiritually by his experiences, and in some cases, his deliberate refusal to learn.

Proof Mathematical proof is the only complete form possible. As this proceeds from assumptions, no observed fact can ever form the basis of mathematical proof. The Spiritualist investigator is concerned solely with proofs of identity, and this kind of proof, acceptable in everyday affairs, is called legal proof (*see* **Evidence, Law of**). The current scientific method is to observe a number of facts, then apply various accepted hypotheses to explain them. If one of them fully accounts for *all* the facts, then it is accepted as a working hypothesis. Should no current hypothesis fit the facts, a new one must be formulated. Up to now this method has not consistently been applied to the facts of psychic phenomena, due partly perhaps, to it involving more than one department of science. The spirit hypothesis is the only one which can cover *all* the facts, and therefore demands to be considered at least, as a working hypothesis.

Prophecy An important forecast. A declaration of future events.

Prophet An inspired interpreter. One who foretells the future.

'Prophet, The' Control of Rev. Stainton Moses said to have been a contemporary of Malachi, Haggai by name, of the 'Imperator' group.

Proxy Sittings A device to eliminate the possibility of the sitter's mind being read. The would-be sitter appoints a deputy to sit, who knows nothing of the desired communicator. A record of this sitting is then sent to the inquirer for analysis. Success with this method has been attained, but the one who arranged the proxy must mentally do his best to influence the desired communicator beforehand, and there should be a willing band of co-operative spirits for this work attached to the medium.

Pruden, Mrs Laura of Cincinnati A slatewriting medium who greatly impressed Dr Hereward Carrington when he tested her in 1925.

'Prudens'   Control of Rev. Stainton Moses reputed to be Plotinus.

Pseudopod   The modified tip of an ectoplasmic rod, adapted in the fashion of a rudimentary hand, for grasping objects, thus producing telekinetic phenomena.

Psi   Processes and factors in human personality or in nature, which appear to transcend or deny the accepted limiting principles of science (Thouless and Weisner).

Psyche   Greek word for soul.

Psychiatry   Medical term for mental treatment for mental and some physical disorders.

Psychic   Non-physical. Common term for a medium, metagnome or sensitive. Descriptive of supernormal phenomena. First used in France by Flammarion and in England by Serjeant Cox.

Psychic Art   *See* **Automatic, Clairvoyant, Direct painting.**

Psychic Breezes   *See* **Breezes.**

Psychic Evidence Society   Founded 1931 in London as a psychical research society for clergymen in Great Britain.

Psychic Force   The term was originally suggested in a letter to Sir William Crookes by Serjeant Cox; the persons who employed the force were to be called 'psychics', the science itself as 'psychism' a branch of psychology. The sensations accompanying its emission according to Maxwell are: 1. Sensation of cool breezes over the hands. 2. Slight tingling in palms and tips of fingers. 3. Sensation of a current through the body. 4. 'Spider's web' sensations in contact with the body in various parts. These sensations are now considered due to the emission of ectoplasm.

Psychic Lights   *See* **Luminous phenomena.**

Psychic Music   *See* **Music.**

Psychic Phenomena   *See* **Phenomena.**

Psychic Photography   Falls into two categories: first, photographs produced by normal means for the purpose of psychical research records. These include many excellent pictures of ectoplasm in various forms; rods, figures materialized in whole or part, light sources, telekinetic phenomena, levitations, mostly obtained by flashlight and infra-red techniques. Secondly, pictures produced by supernormal means, psychographs, scotographs, thought projections, various human emanations. Of the appearance of 'extras' (likenesses of a deceased person appearing on an otherwise normally exposed photograph), it may be said that evidence of survival has been given this way, but except in strictly controlled circumstances, it is difficult to eliminate entirely the possibility of faking. (*See* **Society for the study of Supernormal pictures.**)

Psychic Power   *See* **Power, Psychic Force.**

Psychic Rods   Rods and levers built from ectoplasm (q.v.) for the purpose of moving or holding objects, or the production of raps by striking objects. They are extensible, rigid or elastic, according to the spirit operator's requirements.

Psychic Science   A system of knowledge which states: 1. That at the death of the body, man continues to function as a conscious being. 2. That he functions after death in a refined spirit-body or soul which has substance and weight, and which can be seen and photographed. 3. That this soul existed within the physical body during life, and is organic, having brain, nerves, blood-vessels, heart, etc. 4. That the soul can communicate in various ways with persons on earth both before and after death. 5. That the world in which the soul dwells after the death of the body, lies immediately around the physical earth. 6. That a man while alive may leave his physical body, and by the use of his soul, explore spheres of refined physical states, commonly called the spirit world (J. Hewat McKenzie).

Psychic Sounds *See* **Sounds.**

Psychic Touches *See* **Touches.**

Psychic Winds *See* **Breezes.**

Psychical Research Systematic scientific inquiries concerning the nature, facts and causes of mediumistic phenomena. The claimed facts are first tested. If they are established, natural explanations are sought to account for them. If still unknown, the nature of the unknown force has to be investigated. If it shows intelligence, it has to be seen whether it can possibly be due to earthly intelligence. Only after all ordinary sources have thus been eliminated is a supernormal source of intelligence postulated and tested. Most countries have their Society for Psychical Research (S.P.R., in America the A.S.P.R.), or kindred societies who perform much valuable work in testing phenomena and defining the mode of action in many cases. While the existence of phenomena is generally acknowledged, many researchers are still cautious about the 'spirit hypothesis', though many great scientists have openly admitted their belief in it. The early research societies to be formed were first in England, a Ghost Club, founded in Trinity College, Cambridge, in 1851. In 1875 Serjeant Cox founded the Psychological Society of Great Britain. The S.P.R. followed in 1882, and the A.S.P.R. in 1885.

Psychism Psychical research.

Psychist A psychical researcher or a student of psychology.

Psycho-Analysis A study of the interaction between the conscious and the subconscious mental components, for the purpose of treating mental disorders. A method of treatment made famous by Dr Sigmund Freud about 1900.

Psychode A term for ectoplasm (Professor Thury).

Psychogram A spirit message.

Psychograph A scotograph. The supernormal appearance of some text or writing on photographic material.

Psychograph An instrument designed to test psychical phenomena, consisting of a disc with an index rotating over the alphabet. The medium rested his fingertips on the disc.

Psychography Direct writing (q.v.).

Psychokinesis Term of parapsychology (P.K.). An alleged direct influence exerted on a physical system by a person without the use of any known physical instruments or inter-mediating forms of physical energy. The term is usually employed to cover experiments in which certain persons are alleged to have influenced the fall of a die by means unknown to science.

Psychology The scientific study of the phenomena of consciousness.

Psychometry A faculty discovered by Dr J. R. Buchanan in 1842, whereby an object when held by a sensitive person, produces a community of sensation conveying the nature and history of the object. Some mediums possess this faculty, though when demonstrating, it is commonly augmented by other mediumistic faculties, such as clairvoyance, etc.

171

Psychoplasm   Term for ectoplasm.

Psychosis   Mental derangement or disorder.

Psychosomatic   Regarding the mind and the body as a single unit, from the medical point of view.

Public Demonstrations   It is customary to include in Spiritualist services, a demonstration of clairvoyance by a medium. The purpose of this is to give individual proof to newcomers of the continued survival of their deceased friends and relatives. The means by which a medium accomplishes this, is by close rapport with a trusted spirit helper who acts as interpreter and regulator of communications. The actual impression may be visual (clairvoyance) or by hearing (clairaudience) or by sensing the actual physical condition of the deceased before passing. Most platform mediums are developed in more than one faculty and so receive a mixture of these impressions which they interpret according to their own method of working. Public demonstrations of spirit healing are sometimes given, when disabled or incapacitated persons are invited on to the platform where a marked improvement of the affliction is often made obvious to the audience as a demonstration of spirit power. In America, billet-reading sometimes replaces clairvoyance as a public demonstration. This entails the supernormal reading of the contents of folded papers and the giving of answers to them from the spirit world. All these demonstrations take place under normal lighting conditions, and in a friendly atmosphere. There is nothing 'spooky' or hysterical about a Spiritualist meeting.

Purgatory   The Roman Catholic conception of an after death state, where faithful souls are purged of sin through suffering. The Spiritualist's etheric sphere would correspond, although any discomfort would be mental, and the product of the spirit's own desires. In any sphere it is possible for any spirit to advance to a higher state by a mental desire to do so.

Purporting Intending, seeming, signifying at face value.

Pyramidology An occult system of prophecy based on various proportions and measurements of the Great Pyramid, which are held to correlate with important historical events. It is often asserted that the pyramid builders possessed scientific know-ledge superior to that of today, and that the principles of this in symbolic form were imbedded in the pyramid structure. None of this is in accordance with scientific Egyptology.

Qabala *See* **Cabbala.**

Quakers *See* **Friends, Society of.**

Quelle Document One of the earliest references to the life of Jesus, in a Greek translation from an earlier Aramaic writing. It gives a plain, simple teaching, and makes no reference to the miraculous.

Quimby, Phineas Parkhurst The originator of 'mind cure', a system of healing which profoundly influenced Mary Baker Eddy, the founder of Christian Science.

Q'umran Community A Jewish monastic sect which existed from the end of the second century B.C. to A.D. 70. Their head-quarters was a building at Khirbet Q'umran, on the edge of the valley Wady Q'umran. It was here that the famous Dead Sea Scrolls were written. From these writings, we may deduce that they were probably a branch of the Essenes who, like them, were ascetic, ritualistic, practised healing, and community of ownership. Their rules were laid down and strictly observed. Some have found reason to believe that Jesus was an Essene or a member of a similar sect. Lacking direct evidence, from what we do know of his character, this is not consistent. Some of his teachings regarding property are similar, but Jesus, a non-ascetic in eating and drinking, consort of prostitutes and sinners, by teaching that the Sabbath was made for man and vice versa, diametrically opposed monastic ideas of his times.

Qu'ran (Meaning that which is uttered or recited.) The sacred writing of Islam. The work of Mohammed under divine inspiration, the first 'Sura' being revealed to him in fiery letters written on a cloth.

Radiesthesia The theory that dowsing with rod or pendulum, operates by the instrumental detection of subtle radiations from the hidden substance. Dowsing practise on these lines.

Radiations, Human *See* **Emanations.**

Radiographs Dr Ochorowicz's term for supernormal photographs obtained without a camera.

Raja-Yoga The Yoga pathway of philosophy.

Ramakrishna (1834–1886) Well-known modernist reformer of Hinduism. Swami Vivekananda was his disciple.

Raps Sounds produced by physical mediumship. They may simulate almost any known sound, and are said to be produced by beating actions of slender ectoplasmic rods.

Rapport An intimate community of sensation, such as exists between hypnotist and subject, control and medium, object and psychometrist, or in telepathy, sender and recipient.

Rasmussen, Mrs Anna Born 1898 Danish physical medium tested in 1921 at Fritz Grünewald's laboratory in Berlin. According to Professor Winther's account, out of 116 seances, none were negative. Strong electrical conditions in the seance room were recorded, and phenomena took place in daylight or strong artificial light. Automatic scripts in English (unknown language to the medium) were obtained. Harry Price also tested this medium.

Rationalists   Those philosophers who opposed the Empiricists, Descartes, Spinoza and Leibnitz. The rationalists believed that logical reason can arrive at truths independent of sense experience.

Rationalization   Psychologically, the process by which the mind produces a rational argument to justify conduct of which one is ashamed.

Raymond   Son of Sir Oliver Lodge. The famous book of that name, giving evidence for his survival in the spirit world.

Rebutting Evidence   Evidence put forward as refuting the spirit hypothesis, and in 'explanation' of the powers of mediumship. Summarized, it usually falls under one of the following headings: 1. Telepathy, 2. Action of the sub-conscious mind, 3. Split personality, 4. Dramatization, 5. Inaccurate information, 6. Inferences and arguments from physiology and physics.

Receptivity   A mental condition necessary for mediumship. Only by quietude and the stilling of one's thoughts can the first faint beginnings of spirit communication be recognized. It is important to note that the ability to become receptive should be under control of the medium's will. A regulated channel, not an open one, is the ideal.

'Rector'   Control and amanuensis of Rev. Stainton Moses for the 'Imperator' group. He manifested later in the same capacity for Mrs Piper's mediumship.

Reese, Bert   (1851–1926)   American-Polish clairvoyant medium, the subject of experiments by Baron Schrenck Notzing, Edison, Dr Hereward Carrington and Hollaender. Once arrested for disorderly conduct, he proved his powers in court to Judge Rosalsky, by reading sealed messages. He was acquitted.

Red   As an auric colour, red symbolizes passion and anger.

Reflectograph   An instrument for spirit communication invented by George Jobson and J. B. Kirkby. Built like a type-writer with very sensitive keys, it projected the selected letters on a large screen. The presence of a medium (Mrs L. E. Singleton) was necessary for its operation.

Regurgitation   An imitation of physical phenomena produced by swallowing flimsy material before the seance, its subsequent regurgitation purporting to be ectoplasm. This idea was first suggested as an explanation by S.P.R. 1922, in the case of Eva C. in London. It was considered as proved in the Duncan case in 1931. Adequate tests have been devised which makes this deception impossible under controlled conditions.

Reichenbach, Baron   The famous pioneer psychic researcher who discovered and named an emanation of the human body as Odic force 1840. He also experimented with sensitives who could perceive radiations from magnets in the dark. He wrote several important works which have been translated into English.

Reincarnation   The theory that the soul can return to earth many times. A fundamental doctrine widely accepted by Eastern tradition, Hinduism and Buddhism. It was also taught by the Essenes, with whom Jesus may have had some contact. Josephus, the historian, refers to it as a common belief among the Jews at that time. In modern times the Theosophists accepted it as a central doctrine. Allan Kardec of France, based his 'Spiritist' teachings on it, in his *Book of the Spirits* which is still widely read and accepted by South American Spiritualists and many other groups. However, the main body of Spiritualists are divided on this point: there is a general disinclination to accept a rigid law of return; instead they rather favour the idea of a measure of personal free-will. Most would agree on the pre-existence of the soul. The controls when questioned, do not all agree, though it should be remembered that Eastern controls may still be conditioned by their earthly background of knowledge, and no spirit is omniscient. The kind of evidence advanced for reincarnation is: personal memories of former incarnations, prodigies' abilities, hypnotic regression before birth, control's assertions. This evidence, while sometimes impressive, can be explained by the fact of possession or mediumship, with the exception of hypnotic regression, difficult to substantiate and often found to be sub-conscious dramatization. In the case of one musical prodigy of $3\frac{1}{2}$ years (Ariolo Pepito, q.v.), the child's hands *grew* during the performance—a feat explicable in terms of mediumship but certainly not by reincarnation! A way out from the dilemma is promised by Myer's Group Soul theory (q.v.). It is also instructive to note that both D. D. Home and Dr Carl Wickland refer to posthumous recantations of Allan Kardec and Mme Blavatsky.

Religion A system of faith and worship, usually of a God or gods, or of a Higher Power. It implies the binding of man to God.

Religion of Spiritualism Spiritualism is an accepted religion in England and many other countries. It asserts that man is a spirit and part of the Great Spirit; that we therefore honour and serve God by serving our fellow man. The faith of a Spiritualist rests on knowledge; the unshakeable conviction through personal evidence that man's spirit is indestructible and survives death. All religion has its roots in the same psychic phenomena which happen today. Organized Spiritualism has its churches and ministers, but no priesthood. The mouthpieces of the world of spirit, the mediums, are allowed to speak directly to the people, bringing solace and comfort.

177

Repulsion The opposite of attraction, caused by mental disharmony. An inexplicable aversion to a person could be explained by the incompatability of the respective auras.

Rescue Circles *See* **Circle, Rescue.**

Resurrection In Christianity, is based on the physical resurrection of Jesus. Spiritualists would admit 'resurrection' or survival of the spirit body, but not the physical body, and would add that this is really a matter of evidence, not faith.

Retrocognition Knowledge of the past, supernormally acquired.

Retrocognitive Clairvoyance Term in parapsychology for an Extra Sensory correspondence between a present mental pattern of A and a physical event which happened in the past.

Reuter, Professor Florizel von Director of Violin school at Vienna State Academy of Music, was also associated with Baron Schrenck Notzing and the Schneider brothers investigation. His mother was an automatist, receiving communications in seventeen languages containing much evidence and proofs of the communicator's identities. Later, he developed mediumship himself and received direct voice and apport phenomena in his home circle.

Revelation A sudden withdrawing of the veil between the material and the spiritual spheres. Testified by prophets and seers through the ages and the origins of all religions. Spiritualism alone fosters the revelations of today through its mediums.

Reverence Fear, mingled with respect. The conception of a God to be feared is not in accordance with Spiritualist knowledge; the attitude in a Spiritualist church is therefore of respect and lively interest.

178

Revivals Revivalists of religious fervour and enthusiasm have been noted for a variety of psychic phenomena. It is recorded that strange music, healing, prophecy, the gift of tongues (xenoglossy), are characteristic upsurges of exaltation.

Rhabdic Force *See* **Dowsing, rhabdomancy.**

Rhabdomancy Water-divining, dowsing.

Rhine, Professor J. B. Of Duke University, Ohio. Famous researcher in parapsychology. By conducting many thousands of guessing experiments with Zener cards, he has established statistical proof of the existence of Extra Sensory Perception and telepathy. The nature of the results preclude any explanation by the known physical laws of radiation.

Richet, Dr Charles Born 1850 Eminent psychic researcher. Professor of Physiology at the Faculty of Medicine in Paris, Hon. President of the Society of Universal Psychic Studies, President of S.P.R. in 1895, President of Institut Metapsychique Internationale. In 1875 he dealt a death-blow to 'animal magnetism' by proving that hypnotism was psychological, and had nothing to do with magnetic fluids. He took part in the Milan Commission which investigated Eusapia Paladino in 1892. Other notable mediums he tested were: Eglinton, Mme d'Esperance, Martha Beraud, Kluski, Ossowiecki. Although convinced of the existence of genuine phenomena, he believed in a sixth sense, or cryptaesthesia; he doubted survival, but admitted its possibility.

Richmond, Mrs Cora L. V. (Cora Scott, Cora Tappan) (1840–1923) American speaker and healing medium, famous at sixteen years old for inspirational addresses and lectures. Visited England in 1873. Became Pastor of the First Society of Spiritualists in Chicago, and assisted later in founding the National Spiritualist Association. Prolific author and lecturer.

179

Ridley, Miss Hazel American direct voice medium. Her voices were whispers proceeding from the larynx with no movement of mouth, lips or tongue. Dr Wilson G. Bailey, physician of New Jersey, filled her mouth with liquids, but the voice was unaffected. She visited England in 1926 and 1931–32. The testimony of Will Goldston, the famous professional conjurer, was emphatically in her favour.

Rig-Veda (Royal Veda) Earliest Vedic book of sacred Indian Literature, consisting of ten books containing over a thousand hymns in archaic Sanskrit, dated between 1000–800 B.C., but not written down for many centuries.

Rishi Hindu for inspired person or seer.

Robertson, James A great pioneer of Spiritualism from Glasgow. Well known as an author and for his experiments with D. D. Home.

Rochas, Lt. Col. Eugene (1837–1914) Renowned French psychic researcher and author, he studied human emanations, hypnotism, reincarnation and physical phenomena. Founded the well-known theory of 'exteriorization of motricity' during a summing up of his experiments with Eusapia Paladino.

Rochester Rappings *See* **Fox sisters.**

Root Races An esoteric supposition of successive ages of mankind's earthly progression, by the establishment on the continent masses, of 'root races'. There are said to be seven: Polarian (Adamic), Hyperborean, Lemurian, Atlantean, Aryan, and two yet to come.

Rosemary Mediumship An impressive case of xenoglossy. In this instance, ancient Egyptian was spoken fluently by 'Lady Nona' the medium's control, and was translated by Mr Howard Hulme. Dr F. H. Woods believes it is established beyond doubt, that over 140 word-phrases current during the building of the Luxor Temple, have been spoken by this extraordinary means.

Rosicrucianism, A.M.O.R.C. A secret society which flourished in the fifteenth and sixteenth centuries, alleged to have been founded by a German, Rosenkreuz about 1430. They practised healing occultism and alchemy. There is an occult society of this name in existence today, with a metaphysical teaching designed to awaken dormant faculties. Their symbol is a rose in the centre of a cross; they claim a traditional association with the 'Great White Brotherhood' of Egypt, 1500 B.C.

Ruskin, John English author, whose belief in survival was due to Spiritualism.

Sabbath Hebrew, borrowed from the Sumerian 'Shabattu' meaning 'a calming of the heart', observed every seventh day from the full moon festival for Nananar, the moon god, by the Babylonians, as a day of penitential reflection. As these astronomically minded people discovered the lunar month of twenty-eight days, the quarter phases were probably black-listed for astrological reasons: as the moon would be in square aspect to its full position, considered unpropitious for activity. This may provide a reason behind the traditional rest on the Sabbath, and the mystical powers of seven generally. Spiritualists do not regard any day as specially 'holy'.

Sacerdotalism Any religious system based on priestly order, rather than human and spiritual values.

Sacred Writings The most widely distributed forms are the chanted hymns of many religions. Spiritualism does not make distinctions between the merits of various writings to the extent that any are deemed as specially sacred. Inspiration and revelation, it maintains, may be drawn from many literary

181

sources both ancient and modern. Spiritual truth is not confined to one religion, or to any one section of scriptural texts.

S.A.G.B.   The Spiritualist Association of Great Britain (q.v.).

Samādhi   The eighth stage of Yoga; said to be the highest attainable earthly state. A deep trance of higher contemplation, and a complete temporary renunciation of earth life and the body's needs. Some yogis are alleged to have passed their remaining time on earth in this state, ending their days bricked up in a sanctuary by their faithful disciples.

Samsāra   Hindu term for the karmic chain of birth, death and rebirth on earth, according to their reincarnation doctrine. Release from this chain they say, is only to be gained by Yoga practices (identification of the Smaller Self with the Absolute Self).

Sankhya   One of the oldest systems of Hindu philosophy founded by Kapila in 600 B.C. It was dualistic, postulating a positive equilibrium of spirit and substance, eternal without prime cause. Plurality of selves was held to be the consequence of the balance being upset.

Sand Reading   A personal psychic assessment of the imprint of the client's hand in a tray of sand.

Sandwich, The Earl of (1839–1916)   A Spiritual healer in later life, he once testified before a medical committee presided over by the Dean of Westminster in June 1912. His services were always freely given.

Santaliquido, Dr Rocco (1854–1931)   Italian scientist and University Professor, Director General of Public Health in Italy, State Councillor, Technical adviser of the International Red Cross, first president of Institut Metapsychique Internationale, with Jean Meyer and Dr Geley in 1919. By his own experiments he was convinced that messages could not be explained by normal means. Founded a headquarters in Geneva for international psychic congresses and research, now dissolved.

Sarjent, Epes (1813–1880) Early American psychic researcher and editor. Studied mesmerism in 1837 and drew public attention to the Hydesville phenomena. He wrote many works on Spiritualism.

Satori Zen Buddhist term for enlightenment produced by meditation.

Savant A learned person, a scientist.

Scatcherd, Felicity Writer and humanitarian, collaborated with W. T. Stead. Was a keen student of psychical research, especially of psychic photography.

Schermann, Raphael Austrian clairvoyant medium who specialized in graphology. Script, to him, served as a psychometric link to an amazing degree. He was the subject of investigation by Professor Fischer of Prague 1916–18.

Schiller, Professor F. C., M.A., D.Sc., Hon. Ll.D. Professor of Philosophy, South California University, President S.P.R. in 1914. Author of 'The progress of Psychic Research' in *Encyclopaedia Britannica* 1920, and 'Spiritism and telepathy' in Hasting's *Encyclopaedia of Religion and Ethics*.

Schizophrenia A form of insanity associated with a split personality, where the conscious mind alternates with the unconscious. Unlike trance mediumship, there is a steady deterioration of the personality; it is not under control, and new knowledge is not obtained.

Schneider Brothers, Rudi and Willy Two outstanding physical mediums of recent times, tested under the most stringent conditions by Baron Schrenck Notzing. Of Willy's phenomena, between December 1921 and July 1922 over a hundred scientists declared conviction of its reality by demonstration under the most exacting tests. In 1924 he came to London and gave twelve sittings for telekinetic phenomena to the S.P.R. Rudi was tested by Harry Price in the National Laboratory for Psychical Research, using a special 'electric chair' device, which gave instant warning by light signals of the medium's movements. Under these conditions, breezes, levitations, telekinesis, and materialization of hands and arms were produced. Among the scientists who witnessed these phenomena were: Lord Rayleigh, Professor O. A. Rankine, Dr F. C. S. Schiller, Dr C. E. M. Joad, Dr William Brown, Professor Nils von Hoften, Professor A. F. C. Pollard, Mr A. Egerton, Professor A. M. Low, Dr David Efron, Dr Eugen Osty, Dr Jeans. At the end of the experiments, Harry Price presented Rudi with a certificate for authenticity of the phenomena. Rudi also demonstrated satisfactorily for Dr Osty in 1930, at the Institut Métapsychique under fraudproof conditions.

Scholasticism A school of philosophy which stemmed from Thomas Aquinas (1227–74), it attempts to state that faith, reason, religion and science are complementaries. It really presented a fusion of Aristotelian thought with Christianity.

Schrenck Notzing, Baron A. von (1862–1924) Distinguished German pioneer of psychical research. Physician and Psychiatrist of Munich, authority on sexual anomalies and criminal psychopathy. He conducted experiments with every important medium of his time including Eusapia Paladino, Eva C., and Schneider brothers. He was not concerned with the philosophy of Spiritualism, but definitely established the existence of its phenomena for all time.

Schweitzer, Dr Albert Born 1875, in Gunsbach, Alsace. Dr of Philosophy at Strasbourg, accomplished organist, noted for his interpretation of Bach. Author of many important literary works. At twenty-one years of age, he sacrificed a brilliant academic career: he decided to live for music and art until the age of thirty, then devoted his life to the service of suffering humanity in the swamps of Africa. Not an avowed Spiritualist, but an excellent example of the kind of life advocated by Spiritualist religion—the service of God through man.

Scientology 'The science of knowing how to know' according to the Hubbard Association of Scientologists. They employ a technique of 'Dianetics' to uncover memories of previous incarnations.

Scriptograph Messages alleged to have been written by deceased persons, often in their own handwriting, which appears on sensitive photographic materials without any exposure to light.

Scriptures Sacred writings of various religions. The writings comprising the Bible. Spiritualists would consider them all to be of human origin and therefore fallible, while recognizing their inspirational qualities.

Scrolls, Dead Sea *See* **Dead Sea Scrolls.**

Scrying Divination by crystal-gazing.

Seance A sitting for the purpose of obtaining psychic manifestations, or for communications with the spirit world.

Seance-Room This should ideally be a room dedicated for this purpose and used for no other. It should be no larger than necessary, devoid of soft furnishings and draperies as far as

185

possible, with plain wooden chairs and floor, facilities for soft red lighting and window shutters if required for physical phenomena.

Second Death As the soul leaves the earth body for further development in a higher spirit sphere, so it is sometimes said there takes place a similar refinement of personality on passing to the next sphere above. This is a joyful occasion for the spirit people concerned. In occultism, the dissolution of the Kama Rupa (q.v.).

Secondary Personality *See* **Schizophrenia.**

Second Sight Supernormal perception, often symbolic, of the near or distant in space or time.

Seer A natural clairvoyant or prophet.

Seeress of Prevorst Frau Frederica Hauffe, known by the book of Dr J. Kerner of Weinsberg. She was born in 1801, was a chronic invalid, continually surrounded by much curious psychic phenomena.

Sensing Term often used by mediums when describing a community of sensation with a control, deceased person, or psychometry article.

Sensitive A person possessing psychic powers, but who is not necessarily a medium for spirit communication.

Sensitivity, Exteriorization of *See* **Exteriorization of Sensitivity.**

Sensory (Passive) Automatism (Myers) Externalization of perceptions in inner visions and audition, from a source beyond the conscious will. Theory for clairvoyance, clairaudience, crystal gazing.

Sephiroth Kabalistic system, descriptive of ten variously named creative emanations from God, constituting the existence of the world.

Serialism A philosophic system by J. W. Dunne, based on his personal experiments with precognition in the dream state, and a theory of time and causation.

Service, Spiritualist As conducted in most Spiritualist churches it follows an orthodox pattern. The platform is occupied by a chairman, a medium and a speaker. The service opens with a simple spontaneous prayer. Spiritualist hymns are sung, a reading from some inspired work is given and a short address by the speaker follows. The medium then gives a demonstration of spirit return, by relaying messages to various members of the congregation. This is followed by a closing hymn and benediction. The atmosphere is friendly and cheerful.

Seven Principles Spiritualists have no fixed creed; the following principles have, however, been adopted by the Spiritualists' National Union, with the proviso that all members have liberty of interpretation. 1. The Fatherhood of God. 2. The Brotherhood of Man. 3. Communion of Spirits and the Ministry of Angels. 4. The continuous existence of the Human Soul. 5. Personal responsibility. 6. Compensation and Retribution hereafter for all the good and evil deeds done on earth. 7. Eternal progress open to every soul.

Sex Seems to play a mysterious part in psychic phenomena. There are more female mediums than male. According to some S.P.R. reports, some physical mediumship has been accompanied by sexual orgasm. Poltergeist activity usually occurs in the vicinity of boys and girls at the age of puberty, twelve to sixteen years. Yoga teachings emphasize the sublimation of sexual energies into ecstatic states. Freudian thought connects sex and religion. It appears from messages received that sexual characteristics are maintained in the next sphere, although physical relationships are no longer required. The grosser desires would seem to be linked with the earthly body only.

Sextile   An apparent angle of 60 degrees between two celestial bodies, astrologically said to promote harmony between them.

Seybert Commission, The   For the investigation of Spiritualism, instituted by the wish of Henry Seybert, American Spiritualist, who left 60,000 dollars to maintain a chair of Moral and Intellectual Philosophy at the University of Pennsylvania, March 1884, for the purpose of investigation into all systems of morals, religion, philosophy and Spiritualism.

Shakers   Groups of early American religious sects, sympathetic to the Quakers and to refugees from Cevennes. As many as sixty groups existed in 1837. They were often controlled by North American Indians, phenomena which preceded the Hydesville phenomena. The name 'Shakers' was no doubt due to the slight trembling observed as they became inspired. Similarly seen in some mediums prior to speaking under control.

Shaman   Tribal priest, originally of Siberia.

Shamanism   Mediumistic practices of primitive tribes who believed in spirit communication.

Shang-Ti (1200 B.C.)   Ancient supreme god of China. He was not a creator, but was said to be spontaneously evolved by the Yang and Yin interplay.

Shepard, Jesse (Francis Grierson, 1849–1927)   Phenomenal medium for music trance and xenoglossis. His pianistic achievements were acclaimed as supernormal by Prince Adam Wisniewski, a personal friend of Liszt himself. Under the famous name of Grierson, Shepard wrote of his strange life.

Shinto Former monotheistic state religion of Japan (late eighteenth to nineteenth century), which tried to supplant Buddhism. Meaning 'the way of the Gods' it centred around the divine authority of the sovereign Mikado, reminiscent of the older Roman ruler-worship. One of its sects, the Tenri Kyo, bears a remarkable parallel to the modern phenomenon of the founding of Christian Science in the West, through the revelations of Maekawa Miki, a woman who became a faith healer, and also wrote two sacred books published in 1867 and 1875—the same years in which Mrs Eddy's famous books were produced!

Siddhi Superhuman physical powers attained by Yoga experts.

Sidgwick, Professor Henry (1838–1900) Professor of Moral Philosophy at Cambridge. First president of S.P.R. and active for eighteen years in its interests. He took a leading part in testing many famous mediums, including Slade, Eusapia Paladino, Mrs Piper. In 1901 he was purported to have communicated through a Mrs Thompson in a very characteristic manner in the presence of Mr Piddington. Other messages were received through the hand of Mrs Verrall. Mrs Sidgwick also took an active part as president and Hon. Secretary of S.P.R. until 1931, and became convinced of the reality of survival and communication.

Sign A particular 30 degree segment of the tropical zodiac, named after one of the constellations, but not now coincident with it, due to the phenomena of precession.

Silbert, Frau Maria Austrian physical medium known for telekinesis, stigmata, apports and trance phenomena. An interesting feature of her mediumship was the supernormal engraving of cigarette-cases, while her own hands were in full view. She was investigated by British College of Psychic

189

Science, Boston S.P.R., Professor Dr Paul Sünner and Theodore Besterman.

Silence According to the Society of Friends, the basis of worship; when God speaks to the Spirit. Spiritualists know that silence helps one to attune to the spirit world.

'Silver Birch' Greatly loved and admired Red Indian trance control of Maurice Barbanell, and the guide of Hannen Swaffer's home circle. Great orator and teacher from a higher sphere, he has a large following in modern Spiritualism. Many books have been published of this guide's wisdom.

Silver Cord *See* **Astral cord.**

Sin Commonly understood as a transgression of divine laws, or as innate depravity consequent upon the fall of Adam. The Spiritualist view admits divine laws, but does not claim comprehensive knowledge of them, therefore refrains from condemnation of particular *acts* as 'sins'. They hold the personal *motive* as the indicator of wrong or erroneous thinking and doing, and this is hidden by our earthly state (though visible by the aura in the spirit state). Spiritualists would regard the Fall of Adam as a myth.

Sinclair, Upton Famous American novelist who experimented with the possibilities of telepathy, as his wife was gifted with supernormal perception. His method was to make several drawings which were afterwards folded, then his wife in a dark room would select at random and write or draw her impressions of each one.

Sitter A member of a seance or sitting, other than the medium. The mental attitude of the sitter should not be over-emotional or prejudiced. This is most important for the successful production of psychic phenomena, and is due to the spiritual law of 'like minds attracting like'.

Sixth Sense Postulated many times under many names as an alternative to the spirit hypothesis. First used by Tardy de Montravel who considered it the source and sum of all senses. Later, by Professor Richet for telepathy, clairvoyance, psychometry, premonitions, predictions, crystal vision and phantasmal appearances, which he pronounced to be due to a perception of the vibrations of reality. While there may be some truth in these speculations, they cannot account for evidence of the intelligence of a deceased person still manifesting.

Skin Writing *See* **Dermography.**

Skotograph Name devised by Miss Felicity Scatcherd, for spirit writing on an unexposed photographic plate. Also known as 'psychograph'.

Slade, Dr Henry American medium, best known for his slate-writing phenomena. He was the subject of much stormy discussion and alleged trickery, although many famous scientists vouched for his honesty. Fraudulent accusations were made by Professor Ray Lankester and the Seybert Commission. Flammarion gave him specially sealed slates which Slade kept for ten days, but could produce no writing on them.

Slater, John (1861–1932) American clairvoyant medium, for fifty years gave demonstrations of reading sealed letters and remarkable evidence of survival. In 1930 he was arrested in Detroit for making predictions, but he won his case and continued his work.

Slater, Thomas English photographic medium of a mediumistic family, he produced recognizable extras on his photographs. Dr Alfred Russell Wallace declared his work to be genuine.

Slate Writing   Once a popular phenomenon of the seance room, but no doubt owing to the high probability of its fraudulent production, it has now become rare. Two slates were sealed with a fragment of pencil between them, and during the sitting it would be heard writing a message, subsequently disclosed when the slates were opened.

Sleep-State   The normal periodic state of unconsciousness, during which the organism may separate from the spirit body, which can then travel unhampered, though still connected by a vital thread which sustains the physical body. These nocturnal experiences are sometimes remembered in the conscious state on waking (Astral projection). An interesting theory is that communicators themselves have to enter a sleep-state in order to communicate. This may account for their memory difficulties when entering earth conditions.

Sloan, John C.   Of Glasgow. British non-professional medium investigated by the British College for Psychic Science, and for five years by J. Arthur Findlay, author of many authoritative works on Spiritualism.

Smead, Mrs (Mrs Willis M. Cleaveland)   Planchette medium and wife of an American preacher, investigated by Professors Hyslop and Flournoy in 1901. She was responsible for peculiar revelations of life and conditions on planets Mars and Jupiter which were interesting, but not considered convincing.

Smells, Psychic   All kinds from delicate flower perfumes to noxious odours, have been supernormally simulated many times. This phenomena may well have a physical basis, judging by the detailed accounts of Rev. Stainton Moses and others. Some chemical reaction may take place in the body tissues and the scent exuded from the skin. There are many instances of sulphur smells accompanying other phenomena (Ref. Swedenborg, Mirabelli, D. D. Home, Scotto and Mrs Crandon).

Smith, Mlle Helen (1861–1929) Also known as Catherine Elsie Muller, medium of Geneva, who gave revelations of life and conditions on the planet Mars, including a complete language. This was closely investigated by Professor Flournoy, who psycho-analysed the medium and asserted disproval of her supernormal claims. Evidence given of the return of famous historical personages also refuted by Flournoy. Her physical phenomena of telekinesis—much in evidence at the time—he did not attempt to explain. Later she developed a talent for automatic painting, mainly of religious tableaus, of which Professor Deonna ascribed no supernormal powers, although it was beyond any normal effort of her own.

S.N.U. The Spiritualists' National Union (q.v.).

Soal, Dr S. G., M.A., D.Sc., Lond. Noted English E.S.P. investigator and author, and until his retirement, Senior Lecturer in Pure Mathematics at University of London, Perrott student in Psychical Research, Trinity College, Cambridge, 1948, and Fulbright Research Scholar in Para-psychology 1951, past president of S.P.R. He investigated the incidence of telepathy statistically in 1927–32, and repeated the famous J. B. Rhine experiments 1934–36. Automatist and authority on E.S.P. Was awarded the William McDougall Memorial Prize for his book *The Mindreaders*, published 1959.

Society for Psychical Research The British society, proposed by Sir William Barrett and established 20 February 1882. Its objects and aims were summarized: '1. An examination of the nature and extent of any influence which may be exerted by one mind upon another, apart from any recognized mode of per-ception. 2. The study of hypnotism and the forms of so-called mesmeric trance, with its alleged insensibility to pain; clair-voyance and other allied phenomena. 3. A critical revision of Reichenbach's researches with certain organizations called sensitive, and an inquiry whether such organizations possess any power of perception beyond a highly exalted sensibility of the recognized sensory organs. 4. A careful investigation of any reports, resting on strong testimony regarding apparitions at the moment of death, or otherwise, or regarding disturbances in houses reputed to be haunted. 5. An inquiry into the various physical phenomena commonly called spiritualistic: with an attempt to discover their causes and general laws. 6. The collection and collation of existing materials bearing on the history of these subjects.' The results of their investigations are published regularly as 'Proceedings of the Society for Psychical Research'. They have so far established as facts: (a) the possibility of thought-transference, (b) a connexion between death and apparitions, (c) the existence of hypnotic states. On the question of survival they maintain that the constitution of the Society precludes a collective opinion. In its early days, Spiritualists and researchers were equally represented on its council, but a split occurred through various reasons, the main accusation of Spiritualists being a bias against survival.

Socrates Eminent Greek philosopher of 469–399 B.C., who believed it to be his mission to teach his fellows by asking them questions on their fundamental ideas. He never wrote anything so far as we know, but his famous pupil and admirer Plato immortalized him in his *Dialogues*. Socrates claimed a personal guide or daimôn, who advised him unerringly in times of difficulty or emergency. Completely unperturbed by the animosity of his times, he refused offers to escape his judicial death-sentence of the drinking of hemlock poison, and affirmed his belief in immortality to the end.

Society for the Study of Supernormal Pictures, The Established in London 1918. Dr Abraham Wallace was the president: W. G. Mitchell, Sir Arthur Conan Doyle and H. Blackwell were vice-presidents. Members were mostly professional photographers. The report issued in May 1920 after testing thousands of pictures: 'The members here present, desire to place on record the fact that after many tests and examination of thousands of pictures, they are unanimously of opinion that results have been obtained supernormally on sensitive photographic plates under reliable test conditions. At present, the members do not undertake to explain how the results have been obtained, but assert that they have undoubtedly been secured under conditions excluding the possibility of fraud.'

Solar Plexus An important network of nerves situated in the pit of the stomach. It is often associated with one of the psychic centres or 'chakras' of Yoga. Sitters sometimes experience curious 'drawing' sensations in this region, during the production of phenomena.

Solar Plexus Voice Spiritualist medium and writer Maurice Barbanell recounts an experience in full light at the Lily Dale Camp where spirit voices of his wife's dead relatives suddenly broke into an ordinary conversation with Mrs Lily Keiser, a medium from Buffalo. The voice seemed to come from the solar plexus region. Another medium who possessed this faculty was John Kelly, also from Buffalo.

Solipsism A doctrine that the self of the philosopher comprises the whole of reality, therefore denying the external world an independent existence.

Somatic Pertaining to the physical organism.

Somnambules Old term for sensitives who were thrown into mesmeric trances, for the purpose of activating supernormal faculties.

Somnambulism Spontaneous or artificial sleep or semi-trance, where the sub-conscious faculties operate on the body instead of the conscious. It differs from ordinary sleep by reason of the muscular system retaining its waking tension, the eyes are directed upward and inward, and there is insensibility to pain, taste and smell.

Sophistry A spurious type of philosophy which aims to impress and confuse the layman rather than search for truth.

Sordi, Signora Lucia (Born 1871) Italian physical medium investigated in 1911 by Societa di Studi Psichici di Milano, two sittings of which were attended by Baron Schrenck Notzing. An account of an attempted exposure by Professor V. Tummola, tells of the disabling of the medium through a sitter switching on a lamp; this convinced the professor of the genuineness of the phenomena.

Soul In its usual sense it means the indestructible spiritual part of the personality. Spiritualists know that at death the soul leaves the physical body and continues to function in the spirit world. It possesses a finer body, the etheric (astral, double), with which the soul is often identified in Spiritualist terminology, but it is realized that the spirit itself will endure many successions of 'bodies' in different states of being.

Soul Aura That part of the human aura which radiates the intensity of spiritual power attained by the individual. It lies outside of the physical aura, and may extend to some distance in the case of developed souls. It is perceived as a golden light radiating from the entire body, by clairvoyant vision.

Soul, Celestial A being in a highly evolved spirit sphere.

Soule, Mrs Minnie Meserve (Mrs Chenoweth) American trance medium investigated by the A.S.P.R. Professor Hyslop tested obsession cases with her mediumship for many years. Her trance phenomena was outstanding; many famous personalities, including Browning, Mrs Browning, Lord Tennyson and H. W. Longfellow are purported to have communicated, recorded by Professor Hiram Corson of Cornell University in 1914.

Soul Group   *See* **Group soul.**

Soul, Old   *See* **Old soul.**

Sounds, Psychic   *See* **Rappings.**

Space   According to communications, space in the spirit world presents no limitations, the mere wish to travel being sufficient to bring it about. The location of the spirit spheres is usually said to be concentric with the earth's surface, permeating it and extending to a great distance beyond. Others say that space is a condition imposed by earthly consciousness. The inhabitants of the spirit world perceive objects spacially, yet they seem to penetrate the substance of them also; they say they are not dependent on senses as we are. The light by which they perceive seems to proceed from objects themselves, not by external sources, such as the light from our sun is to the earth. The mental states of spirits would seem to condition their surroundings to a considerable degree, to the extent of cutting them off from communication with other spirits, should they be in the habit of self-sufficiency. How far their super-physical state is affected by this mental process, is difficult for us to determine.

Space-Time   The concept of the universe as a four-dimensional continuum of length, breadth, depth and time.

Speaking in Tongues   *See* **Xenoglossis.**

Spectral Flames   Supernormal lights which have been seen around churches and cemeteries (*see* **Luminous phenomena**).

Spectre   An apparition (q.v.).

Speculum   Any light-refracting, shining surface which can be used to focus the attention. The crystal ball is used as such by scryers.

Specularii Name for scryers or crystal-gazers in sixteenth century.

Spheres The several successive states of spirit life following that of earth. They would appear to exist at indeterminate levels above, and concentric with the earth's surface, inter-penetrating, the higher levels invisible to the lower strata. States of consciousness after death would seem to proceed by ascending degrees according to spiritual progress. The environ-ment at first, is similar to that of earth, but of a more refined character. The effects of disease and physical deterioration are absent, the immediate surroundings are directly amenable to constructive thought expression. Those relatives we contact, exist in the next sphere to earth, and know very little more of conditions than we. Owing to communication difficulties, it is hard for them to convey fresh ideas for which no suitable terminology exists. Several controls from more advanced states seem to have made a determined effort to enlighten us on this point (note alleged communications from F. W. H. Myers through Miss G. Cummins and the works of Borgia and Rev. G. Vale Owen). There is a wealth of descriptive literature, but it should be well compared and then accepted only with reserve. Many have tried to define and name different spheres as separate, but confusion has resulted from the differing systems. It seems more logical to suppose an infinite gradation, wherein like minds congregate at different points along the line.

Spheres, Celestial The sphere inhabited by beings far in advance spiritually of earth consciousness. A world said to be of light and harmony.

Spheres, Contemplation Said to be a highly evolved sphere where the main occupation is contemplation of the spiritual universe.

Sphere, Lower   The nearest condition to earth, a transition place through which all must pass at death. If there is an emotionally strong attachment for any particular experience of earth life, it may prolong the stay in this lower state until such time as the spirit wishes to progress.

Spinoza, Benedict (1632–1677)   Dutch rationalist philosopher who aimed to construct, on the knowledge of God, a system of morals by mathematical method. He is known as the father of modern pantheism. Man as a separate being was trivial; by merging with God came understanding; this concept involved a suppression of individuality and freewill, as all finite things are considered as part of a chain of consequences.

Spirit   An entity. In almost every tongue, it is related to 'breath'; the divine afflatus, the indestructible essence of self-conscious life, sensible of all things, limited only by its manifestation or 'body'. The word spirit is often loosely used to describe a discarnate person as distinct from an earthly being. In this sense the spirit possesses a body of material analagous to, but not identical with material elements. An entity is sensible of space and time, but does not appear to be conditioned to it. Spirits are sensitive and communicative to kindred thoughts and emotions which attract mutual spirits in the same and adjacent spheres. It is this fact which makes mediumship possible. When an entity controls a medium, it may perceive our world by means of the medium's sense organs.

Spirit Body   *See* **Bodies.**

Spirit Children   None are born in the spirit world, but children who die before maturity are considered to continue their growing and development in spirit life. Often they help in mediumship, acting in the capacity of controls or helpers. Many earth children are conscious of playmates in spirit, and talk to them freely. This faculty usually disappears as the child becomes more sophisticated and engrossed by earthly considerations.

199

Spirit Communication *See* **Communication.**

Spirit Councils According to many communications, councils are held in the spirit world to determine courses of missionary action in the earth sphere. Everywhere we encounter the idea that God works by delegation.

Spirit Doctors Doctors skilled on this earth, who have passed over but who continue to administer to the sick from the spirit spheres by working through a dedicated medium known as a healer. It is worth noting that not all healers know that they are mediums, or even subscribe to Spiritualist ideas, but the work is affected by intentions, not ideologies, and so far as it is directed to the unselfish alleviation of suffering humanity, it is spiritual work and commands the sympathetic attention of skilled spirit operators (*see* **Healing**).

Spirit Drapery *See* **Drapery.**

Spirit, Great God. Deity. Form of address often used by controls.

Spirit Guide *See* **Control.**

Spirit Hands *See* **Materialization, Moulds.**

Spirit Healing *See* **Healing.**

Spirit Helper *See* **Helper.**

Spirit Hierarchy *See* **Hierarchy of spirit.**

Spirit Hypothesis, The Psychic phenomena covers a huge field of supernormal manifestation. To attempt to explain its varied operations scientifically, all possible physical explanations are tried in turn. In some categories, such as telepathy, there would appear to be no reason to postulate a discarnate spirit as operator. The same could apply to a genuine materialization. It is when an intelligence not of this earth obviously directs the phenomena, that one is logically forced to adopt the simple 'spirit hypothesis'—that the intelligence is what it claims to be—the human mind of an entity who once lived on this earth. The fundamental conditions for its acceptance according to Professor Hyslop are: 1. The information must be supernormal, that is, not explicable by normal perception. 2. The incidents must be verifiable memories of the deceased persons and so representative of their personal identity. 3. The incidents must be trivial and specific—not easily, if at all, duplicated in the common experience of others.

Spiritism An early form of Spiritualism taught by Allan Kardec in France, which embodied the doctrine of compulsory reincarnation. The term is rarely used today, except by a few of Spiritualism's opponents in a vague derogatory sense.

Spirit Lights *See* **Luminous phenomena.**

Spirit Obsession *See* **Obsession.**

Spiritoid Messages which come from the sub-conscious mind, to appear dramatized and personalized (Boirac, Lombroso, Flournoy).

Spirit Operations Cases have been known in spirit healing where portions of diseased tissue have apparently been excised by supernormal means. The explanation usually given, is that the spirit doctor is a surgeon, and has performed an operation on the spirit body; this by sympathy acts on the physical body. The healer, of course, uses no instruments.

Spirit Operators Term for the workers in the spirit band, who are assisting the production of psychic phenomena for any specific purpose.

Spirit Spheres *See* **Spheres.**

Spirit Teachings *See* **Teachings.**

Spiritualism Is the Science, Philosophy and Religion of continuous life, based upon the demonstrated fact of communication, by means of mediumship, with those who live in the Spirit World. Spiritualism is a science because it investigates, analyses and classifies facts and manifestations, demonstrated from the spirit side of life. Spiritualism is a philosophy because it studies the laws of nature both on the seen and unseen sides of life and bases its conclusions drawn therefrom, when sustained by reason and by results of observed facts of the present day. Spiritualism is a religion because it strives to understand and to comply with the Physical, Mental and Spiritual Laws of Nature which are the laws of God. (Definition adopted by the National Spiritualist Association of Churches in America.)

Spiritualist One who has accepted as proven on adequate evidence given through mediumship, the fact that human spirits survive death, that they can communicate with us, that there is a hierarchy of spirit beings, that all spirits are part of a unified consciousness or God.

Spiritualist Association of Great Britain, The Formerly the Marylebone Spiritualist Association, one of the two largest Spiritualist Associations in the world, founded in London 1872 for the study of psychic phenomena and the public dissemination of evidence obtained through mediumship. Among its honorary vice-presidents are many distinguished people. It engages only trustworthy mediums of proved ability, and provides facilities for investigation and discussion without bias under strict anonymous conditions. Its membership is open to all, irrespective of beliefs. An open forum for speakers on all subjects is maintained. It has a magnificent headquarters at 33 Belgrave Square, London.

Spiritualists' National Union, The The other of the two largest Spiritualist organizations in the world, founded in 1890 to promote the advancement and diffusion of the religion and the religious philosophy of Spiritualism on the basis of the Seven Principles (q.v.). It aims to unite Spiritualist churches into a brotherhood, to encourage research and to provide schemes for the certification of lecturers, exponents and healers. Amalgamated with the British Spiritualists Lyceum Union for the spiritual education of children and young people. Has a Government-recognized panel of Ministers serving approximately 500 churches throughout Britain. Its headquarters are 12 Tib Lane, Manchester.

Spirit World A collective term for all the realms of spirit, inclusive of the spheres or planes, but excluding the earth world.

Split Personality *See* **Schizophrenia.**

S.P.R. The Society for Psychical Research (q.v.).

Spriggs, George English non-professional materialization medium, one of the founders of the S.A.G.B. He visited Australia in 1880 where remarkable materialization phenomena were produced, also direct voice and clairvoyant diagnosis. In 1903–5 he gave free healing service at the London Spiritualist Alliance. Helped to found the Psycho-Therapeutic Society.

Square An apparent angle of 90 degrees between two celestial bodies said (astrologically) to be productive of difficulty.

Stead, W. T. (1849–1912) Well-known editor, author, automatist, and a great champion of Spiritualism. He obtained proof of survival through his own hand, by reason of long communications from a Miss Julia Ames, an American editor friend who had died previously. Messages from the living were also obtained by his hand. Through the efforts of his control 'Julia' a Bureau was opened in 1909 giving free sittings to people anxious to establish communication. It cost £1,500 per year to maintain and ran for three years during which time 1,300 sittings were given. Robert King, Vout Peters, Mrs Wesley Adams and J. J. Vargo were the mediums employed. Stead had a very trusting disposition and could never tolerate the attitude of the S.P.R. He once wrote a fiction story about the dangers of icebergs in the Atlantic ocean, a possible omen of his own death when the historic tragedy of the *Titanic* took him with 1,600 others in 1912. Within three days of his passing, he is said to have communicated and established his identity.

Saint Paul The story of St Paul is interesting from the Spiritualist's point of view, as the recorded experiences provide examples of phenomena so familiar to them. He mentioned a natural body and a spirit body, and his listing of 'spiritual gifts' (Ch. XII, 1st Epistle to the Corinthians), is almost a summary of modern mediumship. The vision on the way to Damascus was psychic evidence of survival.

Steiner, Rudolf (1861–1925) Great Austrian psychic and clairvoyant. Founder of Anthroposophy, or 'spiritual science', the son of a stationmaster, known chiefly by his educational influence. His schools number sixty throughout the world; in addition there are thirty alone in Britain for the benefit of handicapped children. He was influenced greatly by Goethe the poet, whose work he once edited. He believed that human history shows an evolution of consciousness, and that new faculties of cognition are still to be developed.

Stella, C. (Mrs Leslie Deacon) English hospital nurse whose mediumship, discovered in 1923 by Harry Price, was investigated by the National Laboratory for Psychical Research.

Telekinetic, levitatory and temperature phenomena were recorded. Price's famous 'trick' table was successfully manipulated besides many genuine effects produced on specially designed apparatus. Dr Eric J. Dingwall witnessed an ectoplasmic formation which crawled across the floor. A paper on these phenomena was read by Harry Price to the Third International Congress for Psychical Research in Paris.

Stevenson, Robert Louis Popular novelist and author who investigated the claims of Spiritualism and as a result of his many experiences with the mediumship of D. D. Home, became one of the first Secretaries for the Scottish Spiritualist Association. He relinquished these duties reluctantly when his health gave way, and retired to Samoa where he passed away with tuberculosis.

Sthenometer An instrument devised by Dr Paul Joire to prove that a kind of nervous force, generated by the medium's body, can be stored for a short time in wood, water and cardboard, in a similar way to light, heat and electricity.

Stigmata Marks on the body spontaneously produced, and usually resembling wounds of the Crucifixion. They may bleed freely and severely incapacitate the person who is often of an hysterical disposition, or under the influence of a strong emotional experience or religious delirium. Authentic cases are legion, St Francis of Assisi, later Therese Neumann of Bavaria. In the case of Eleonore Zügun, the stigmata was recorded in its various stages, by the camera.

Stobart, Mrs A. St Clair Truly remarkable woman, who always acted on her intuition. She was the girlhood friend of Kate Wingfield the medium, though not understanding Spiritualism at that time. Before the 1914 war, she had already distinguished herself by forming the Women's Convoy Corps, a supplementary of the R.A.M.C. which did valuable work in the Balkan War, 1912–13. Active in the Women's War Defence in 1914, she went to Belgium, and narrowly escaped being shot as a spy. A typhus outbreak in Serbia took her to a hospital unit there, where she was given command of a division and eventually led the retreat of the Serbian army successfully in face of incredible hardships. After the war she became convinced of the truth of Spiritualism at the British College of Psychic Science, of which she was later Chairman for two years, then wrote books on her findings relating Biblical events to psychic phenomena. With Rev. Vale Owen she became leader of the Spiritualist Community, its president being Sir A. Conan Doyle, later succeeded by Hannen Swaffer. In 1929 she formed the S.O.S. Society providing a hostel and amenities for the unemployed. Her last great venture was as Chairman of the Confraternity, which sought to unite all religions on a spiritualistic basis.

Stoicism A dour system of philosophy, approaching monotheism, which developed under Zeno and Chrysippus 340–264 B.C., a natural theology of deity as the universe; first as fire, then wind, nature, reason, and destiny. It graduated from a materialistic pantheism to an austere transcendant god, actually called Zeus. It taught universal brotherhood as a duty (not as love or goodwill), and indestructibility of the soul.

Stone Throwing *See* **Poltergeist.**

Subud A mystical movement established in 1947, and stemming from the teachings of Pak Subuh of Indonesia. It does not claim to be a religion, but aims at unity of all peoples in worship of God. They do, however, reserve certain 'divine mysteries' as secrets. Pak Subuh was born in 1901 and claimed revelations in his twenty-fourth year; his coming is supposed to have been foretold by Gurdjieff.

Sub-conscious Colouration In trance communications, the medium's sub-conscious mind is said to be used as an instrument by the unseen operators. The message is therefore liable to colouration by reason of the contents of the medium's mind. So much depends upon the skill of the spirit and the passivity of the medium. No amount of colouration can, however, account for knowledge outside of the medium's range, being brought through.

Sub-conscious Mind That part of the mentality of which one is not immediately aware. It differs from the conscious mind in that it appears to function without awareness of the stimuli, and it has an extensive control over the working details of the bodily organism. Spirit messages have told us that it can be an instrument which they can learn to manipulate in order to control a medium's organs, thus producing automatism phenomena. Under hypnosis, the subconscious mind may be controlled by the hypnotist's suggestion.

Subject A creature of the earth, human or animal, as distinct from a discarnate entity.

Subjective Phenomena That phenomena which arises within the mind, exclusive of external observation. (As distinguished from Objective phenomena.)

Subjectivist Theory of Ethics Theory of philosophy which would ascribe ethics to the results of environments and social conditioning alone, recognizing no influence outside of the natural world, and causation.

Subliminal Psychological term for all mental processes below the 'threshold' of consciousness.

Sudre, Rene Psychic researcher and French scientist, Professor L'Ecole des hautes Etudes Sociales, vice-president of the

National Laboratory for Psychical Research, co-worker with Dr Gustave Geley at the Institut Métapsychique 1921–26. A prolific writer on psychic subjects. Does not accept the spirit hypothesis. Was responsible for the French translation of many important books.

Sufism A mystical development within Islam, mostly of Persian influence. Their doctrines summarized are: 1. God alone exists: He is in all things, and all things are in Him. 2. All things are emanations from Him and have no real existence apart from Him. 3. All religions are indifferent. They serve a purpose, however, as leading to realities. The most profitable in this respect is Islam, of which Sufism is the true philosophy. 4. There is no distinction between good and evil; for God is the author of all. 5. It is God who determines the will of man; therefore man is not free in his actions. 6. The soul existed before the body, in which it is confined as in a cage. Death is not to be desired, for it is then the Sufi returns to the bosom of the Deity. 7. Apart from the grace of God, no man can attain to this spiritual union; it may however be attained by fervent prayer. 8. The principal duty of the Sufi is meditation on the unity of God, the remembrance of the Divine names and progressive advancement in the tariquat, or journey of life so as to attain unity with God.

Suggestion Defined by F. W. H. Myers as a 'successful appeal to the subliminal self'. Hypnotism provides the best examples of its power. As the subliminal or subconscious mind has control over the body far transcending the conscious, a successful suggestion may accomplish seeming miracles; affecting heart beats, circulation, inhibitions, memory, etc. It cannot, however, produce new knowledge, which is the hallmark of mediumship.

Summerland So-called by A. J. Davis. The sphere of the spirit world most often referred to; it corresponds to Myers' 'plane of Illusion' and appears to be a blissful land of rest and harmony, partly a creation of the inhabitant's own desires, but to what extent we cannot determine. We have received many descriptions which seem to suggest the pleasures of earth life minus its drawbacks. They would seem to have trees, animals, houses, lakes, gardens, rivers, recreative activities, halls of learning and infinite leisure.

Superconscious Mind   Term used by F. W. H. Myers to define the higher aspects of the conscious mind, as in intuition.

Supernatural   Phenomena which violate natural laws. There is no reason to suppose that any exist. Psychic phenomena, as all researchers and Spiritualists would agree, is not supernatural; it follows well-defined laws so far as we can discover. Better words are 'supernormal' or 'paranormal'.

Supernormal   Coined by F. W. H. Myers in substitution for supernatural, when describing psychic phenomena. Its modern equivalent is 'paranormal': not as yet within accepted experience of cause and effect.

Supraliminal   Psychological term for the mental content above the 'threshold' of consciousness.

Supreme Spirit   A term often used in Spiritualism signifying God, or Unifying consciousness.

Surgery, Spirit   *See* **Spirit operations.**

Survival   The demonstration of a continuation of personality after death is the cornerstone of Spiritualism. The nature of proof for this most important knowledge must be personal. In practice, it is never sufficient to accept authoritative statements alone on so vital a matter. Each person must test for himself and weigh the resulting evidence in an unprejudiced fashion. It is being demonstrated in hundreds of Spiritualist churches all over the world, through the same means by which the revelations of all religions have come. Certain gifted people, now called mediums, are virtually channels of communication between the earth and the spirit spheres, bringing certainty to those who seek (*see* **Evidence**).

Swaffer, Hannen Born 1879   Popular journalist, author and Spiritualist, succeeded Sir Arthur Conan Doyle as President of the S.N.U. Great propagandist in the press for Spiritualism. Denis Bradley's direct voice phenomena convinced him of survival by the alleged return of Northcliffe in 1924.

Swedenborg, Emanuel (1688–1772)   Founder of the New Church and Swedenborgianism, famous seer of Sweden. Scientist, mining and military engineer, astronomer and physicist of repute, zoologist, financier, economist and prolific author. Son of a bishop, he graduated at Upsala University, studying under such celebrities as Newton, Flamsteed, Halley and Dr Lahire. His famous vision of a fire 300 miles distant is well known. Kant relates several psychic experiences connected with him. Much of his work is in agreement with modern Spiritualism, though bound by theological tradition. He was in a sense, the first 'Spiritualist' who proved that there was no death, and that the next world resembled this one.

Symbolism   The art of representation by different means. Often the easiest and quickest method of conveying information is by a symbolic impression on the medium's mind; i.e. the name 'Penny' could be symbolized by a vision of the appropriate coin. The drawback is the possibility of mis-interpretation. Prophetic visions are often symbolic. Over years of close co-operation between control and medium, it often happens that a symbolic 'code' is built, of extreme reliability.

Synchronicity   A theory of acausal action, relating meaningful coincidences, put forward by Dr C. G. Jung, after a study of the random symbolic methods of various divination practices.

Synoptic Gospels Those of Matthew, Mark and Luke, as giving a general view of the same events.

Table Turning, Rapping Typtology. In the early days of 1850, it became almost a fashionable pastime to hold sittings for this purpose. The sitters would place their fingertips lightly on the table-top, just touching those of their neighbours, then with lowered lights the table would rock slightly, and by an agreed code, spell out messages. A committee of medical men asserted that the movement was due to unconscious muscular action. The 'animal magnetists' welcomed it as a demonstration of odyllic force, whereas the clergy were disposed to attribute it to the Devil! The table is rarely used today. Like automatic writing and planchette methods, it lends itself too readily to subconscious motivation, although it is possible to receive just as good evidence this way as by any other means. It is always the content of the message which counts. Eusapia Paladino asserted that soft pinewood was the most amenable to psychic forces. Maxwell found improvement by covering it with a light textured white material and excluding metal fixtures. We now know that movement of objects (telekinesis) is the result of ectoplasmic material produced by the medium, being used by spirit people for the various phenomena.

Talmud Book of study, A.D. 70–550, containing the fundamental principles of Jewish law. Consisting of a text and commentary (Mishna and Gemara).

Tao Chinese word for Logos, the Absolute, or the course of nature; a conception of an impersonal deity. The Taoist doctrine implies a passive reaction to the world, in sharp contrast to the Confucian system of activity.

Tāpās Yoga exercises designed to free the spirit from the body.

Tappan, Mrs Cora V. *See* **Richmond, Mrs.**

Tarot, The An ancient system of divination by picture cards (the forerunners of our present-day playing cards), showing symbolic figures representing stages in man's destiny. Tarot packs consist of 78 cards divided into two 'arcanas', the major —22 cards—and the minor of 56.

Teachings Among the many communications received through mediumship, there are some which present a code of ethics for human living. They contain many fundamental principles already familiar to us from orthodox scriptures and much fresh material concerning immediate states after death, which is illuminating. Except in a broad sense, they are not wholly consistent; this is due to the varying stages reached by the different communicators. They are, however, unanimous in preaching a gospel of love, personal responsibility for any neglect of one's fellows, denial of vicarious atonement, the removing of fears of death and punishment. These teachers disclaim superiority; they only wish to be known as humble servants who transmit from higher sources, and give in good faith what they honestly believe to be the soundest guidance for humanity.

Telekinesis The movement of objects without normal material connexions to the cause. A common feature of physical phenomena due to ectoplasmic extensions from the medium's body.

Teleology The belief that divine causes can be inferred from a study of means and ends.

Telepathic Control *See* **Book tests.**

Telepathy An extra sensory correspondence between a present mental pattern of A and a present past or future mental pattern of B. The possibility of clairvoyance must have been eliminated. Much statistical work has been done in an effort to learn whether it does occur, and the probable means of its operation. Notably the work of Professor J. B. Rhine of Duke University, Ohio, and Dr S. G. Soal of England. Many thousands of experiments have provided undoubted evidence of its occurrence, but no satisfactory working hypothesis of its action. It appears to be unrestricted by any known laws of radiation and the sequences get mixed in time. The fact of its existence between the minds of the living clears the way for the acceptance of the possibility of telepathy with the minds of the dead.

Teleplasm   From a communication received (*Rock of Truth* by Arthur Findlay), the material of which the voice box is made for the production of direct voice phenomena. Ectoplasm from the medium is mixed by the spirit operators with 'psychoplasm' to produce a palpable substance called 'teleplasm', capable of being moulded into various shapes.

Telescopic Vision   A particular kind of clairvoyant perception, akin to viewing through a long telescope, things not perceivable in the normal way.

Telesthesia   Communication of sensation at a distance (F. W. H. Myers).

Telesomatic   Term descriptive of materialization, coined by Aksakov.

Tellurian   Characteristic of earth. An earthly inhabitant.

Telluric Force   Rhabdic force. Professor Benedict's term for the unknown force which activates the divining rod when dowsing.

Tellurism   A supposed magnetic influence permeating the earth and its creatures, said once to be the cause of animal magnetism.

Temporal Pertaining to earth life, as measured by time. Transient, limited existence.

Testimony Term used by the Society of Friends, for a tenet of their faith.

Tetragrammaton Kabbalistic term for four-letter Hebrew names of God. (J.H.V.H., I.H.V.H.)

Thaumaturgy Miracle working, by superhuman aid.

Theologus, Theophilus Controls of Rev. Stainton Moses.

Theosophy Mme Blavatsky, a founder of the Theosophical Society in 1875, defined it as 'Wisdom Religion or Divine Wisdom, the substance and basis of all the world religions and philosophies, taught and practised by a few elect, since man became a thinking being'. It differs from Spiritualism in ascribing spirit messages to the activities of 'astral shells' or evil spirits. It teaches a doctrine of compulsory reincarnation, and the development of latent psychic powers. According to Dr Carl Wickland, she communicated after death to renounce the reincarnation doctrine.

Therapeutae According to Eusebius, A.D. 265, that what is called Christianity was borrowed from the Therapeutae or Essenes, a healing sect who dwelt in Egypt in 200 B.C.

Third Eye An occult organ of psychic vision situated in the forehead. Attempts have been made to identify this fabulous organ with the pineal gland, at one time considered to be the seat of the soul. This idea is inconsistent with Spiritualist teaching, as the etheric or spirit body is a duplicate of the physical body, and contains only the usual complement of eyes.

Thomas, Rev. C. Drayton   Notable for his book tests; experiments designed to exclude telepathy in mediumistic communications. By this method the communicator quotes a precise passage in a book or newspaper accessible to the experimenter, the appropriateness of which has a direct bearing on the matter under discussion. Excellent results have been obtained by this and similar methods (*see* **cross-correspondence**), and provide some of the best evidence for survival.

Thompson, Mrs R.   English medium who first exhibited physical mediumship, then under persuasion by F. W. H. Myers to give her services to the S.P.R. in 1898 she gave trance sittings only. His belief in survival was mainly due to the many sittings he had with this medium. After his death in 1901, Mrs Thompson on an impulse gave two sittings to Sir Oliver Lodge, who obtained characteristic communications from Myers.

Thought Forms   Apparitions built by thought energy. It is difficult to establish direct evidence for these. It is a fact that thought has been known many times in test cases to produce an image on an unexposed photographic plate; this could explain the appearance of extras if they are known to the sitter. The occult belief in the building up of an objective image by thought concentration is very strong in eastern countries. Some controls when questioned admit their existence, but say they can usually detect the difference between a thought form and a spirit entity. More research is needed.

Thought Photography   Bligh Bond carried out a series of tests on Mrs Deane in co-operation with the British College of Psychic Science. In their charge was deposited a diagram of squares in one of which was marked a cross within a circle. A photograph of the empty diagram taken in the presence of Mrs Deane was successfully marked in the desired place.

215

Thought Power   In spirit messages, the power of thought is constantly stressed as being far more subtle, potent and extensive than is generally realized. Recent tests in Extra Sensory Perception conducted by scientific researchers, would seem to support this assertion.

Thought Reading   Thought transference, or telepathy in reverse. It is often suggested that it may be the remains of a primitive faculty necessary before the time of articulate speech. Critics unacquainted with mediumship from first-hand experience, often offer this as an explanation, but mediums rarely give what is expected of them. A communication is often from some person completely outside of the sitter's conscious thoughts and expectations.

Thought Transference   *See* **Thought reading, Telepathy.**

Thury, Marc (1822–1905)   Professor of Physics and Natural History at the University of Geneva. He was the first to put forward the ectoplasmic theory, naming it 'psychode' as the operating agency of 'Ectenic force'. He believed it to be subject to the will of the medium, though admitted the possibility of wills other than man's being responsible.

Tillyard, Dr R. J., F.R.S.   Chief entomologist to the Commonwealth of Australia. Through the Margery mediumship he became convinced of survival, and published his findings in *Nature* 1928.

Time   Clairvoyant phenomena have a peculiar disregard for the normal time sequence, perception being sometimes of the future or of the past. Similar effects have been noticed in the famous card-guessing experiments by Professor J. B. Rhine. Sometimes the card forecasted has been the next or the next but one to be exposed in the future. Medium's controls are

216

vague and often erroneous in time estimates, saying that they have a different time sense or, 'no time, as you understand it'. Hypnotic experiments, however, reveal an enhanced time sense, the entranced person often being able to register a lapse of time to precise limits when suggested to do so. The faculty of psychometry also gives a sample of past time sequence in the history of the object. The fact of prediction alone, makes one wonder whether our time sense is illusory. J. W. Dunne has some interesting theories based on his own researches wherein he believes that we all travel through a pre-set experience in normal consciousness. When we sleep he says, our point of focus is expanded, and we are then conscious of a little more in advance of the 'now' point, due to the enlarging of the field of focus.

Tomczyk, Mlle Stanislawa (Mrs Fielding) Polish medium, subject of Dr Julian Ochorowicz's investigation in 1908. Her ability was outstanding and several photographs were taken of the phenomena in progress by daylight. Invisible threads were found to extend from her fingers, capable of supporting a pair of scissors. Other tests were made by Professors Flournoy, Clarapède, Cellerier, and Batelli. In 1910 she was tested by the Physical Laboratory in Warsaw, and produced remarkable phenomena. Both Baron Schrenck Notzing and Professor Richet wrote descriptions of her mediumship.

Tongues, Talking in *See* **Xenoglossy.**

Torah Mosaic Law. The Pentateuch.

Touches This phenomena is usually present at seances where objects are moved (telekinesis), and would appear to be caused by a similar agency. They may be soft, hard, warm or cold, and imitate contact with any known substance. It is said that they are produced by spirits operating rods of ectoplasm.

217

Trance   The mediumistic trance is a sleep-like condition which enables the subject's body to be used by a discarnate spirit. It is a state which has usually resulted from a sustained co-operative effort over several years of development, in collaboration with a spirit helper, to fulfil a missionary purpose. The depth of unconsciousness reached, and the degree of control, varies greatly in individual mediums. In the lightest state, the medium is conscious to the extent of hearing any words through her own lips, while in deep trance no memory is retained of anything which transpires. F. W. H. Myers recognized three stages in trance. First, the subliminal self obtains control; secondly, the incarnate spirit whether or not maintaining control of the whole body, makes excursions into, or holds telepathic intercourse with the spirit world. Third stage— the body of the medium is controlled by another discarnate spirit. For hypnotic trance, *see* **Hypnotism.**

Trance Personalities   *See* **Control.**

Transcendental Music   Beautiful, unaccountable sounds of instruments or singing, a phenomenon which has been noticed at deathbeds and funerals.

Transfiguration   A form of physical mediumship whereby a recognizable likeness of a discarnate person is built over the medium's features. It depends on the production of ectoplasm which is fashioned by the spirit operators into a mask. In good subjects the vapoury material can be seen in the process of forming. This phenomena usually takes place in a dim light owing to the sensitive nature of the ectoplasm.

Translation   Ecstatic experience of the higher spheres before death. It sometimes occurs during periods of meditation.

Transmigration of Souls   The doctrine of rebirth of the soul in *any* form.

Transportation   The supernormal conveyance of human bodies through doors and walls, and to great distances is rare, but there are a few cases where evidence is strong. Some mediums are said to have achieved this phenomena before witnesses, notably the Davenport brothers according to Rev. J. B. Ferguson, Mrs Guppy by Dr Abraham Wallace in 1918, Williams by Catherine Berry, Herne by an account by Thomas Blyton 1871–74, Lottie Fowler, Marquis Centurione Scotto in 1928, attested by Ernest Bozzano's report and ten participants, Franek Kluski by Professor Pawlowski, Indride Indridason by Professor Haraldur Nielsson and the Pansini brothers by Dr Joseph Lapponi, medical officer to the Pope in 1906.

Transposition of the Senses   A peculiarity of some trance states, whereby the senses of sight, smell, taste, may be experienced at the fingers, toes, ear lobes or forehead. Observed by Lombroso and others. Yogis also claim this faculty by development.

Transubstantiation   A change of substance, usually referring to the doctrine of the Eucharist sacrament of the Lord's supper, where the bread and wine were declared symbols of the body and blood of Jesus.

Travelling Clairvoyance   *See* **Clairvoyance.**

Travers-Smith, Mrs   *See* **Dowden, Hester.**

Trethewy, Anthony W., B.A., Oxon.   Member of S.P.R. and author of books on psychical research and Spiritualism.

Trine   An observed angle of 120 degrees between two bodies in the ecliptic, said (astrologically) to be helpful for the two principles concerned.

Trollope, Adolphus T. (1810–1892) English author of many works. Investigated the mediumship of D. D. Home and testified against Sir David Brewster's denial in 1855. His testimony on apports via the mediumship of Mrs Guppy, appeared in a report of the Dialectical Society.

Trumpet A megaphone of cardboard or metal, used for direct voice phenomena. It was first used by Jonathan Koons an early American medium. The volume of the voice is amplified by its use. Voice phenomena without the trumpet is termed 'independent voice'.

Tumbler and Letters An improvised method for obtaining spelled communications, on the lines of the ouija board or planchette. The medium and sitter place their fingers lightly on the upended tumbler within a circle of letters. Those letters which are touched by the glass's movements, may spell messages. This method is not a good one, as it is rarely tried by genuine seekers, but rather as an entertainment after a party, when conditions are obviously not conducive to higher contacts. Given the right frame of mind and genuine sitters, however, any form of mediumship can produce good results.

Tummo A method of raising the heat of the body in cold conditions, practised by some Yogis and Tibetan lamas. Ascetics have been known to live in caves in high latitudes without fires and a minimum of clothing.

Tuttle, Hudson (1836–1910) Early medium of Ohio, U.S.A. Possessing no education and of poor parents, under the guidance of his control, he wrote books of great learning and erudition, on natural science and philosophy, some of which were quoted by such men as Büchner and Darwin. He was the author of many books on Spiritualism.

Twain, Mark (1835–1910) The famous American author believed in psychic phenomena and survival. Professor Hyslop of A.S.P.R. was convinced of Mark Twain's return through his experiments in cross-correspondence with Mrs Hutchings, Lola V. Hays and Mrs Chenoweth (Ada Besinnet). Details are to be found in *Journal A.S.P.R.*, July 1917.

Tweedale, Mrs Violet (Born 1862) Novelist and author of many books on Spiritualism. Her experiences were with mediums Williams and Husk, and she attended seances with Lord Haldane, Arthur and James Balfour and W. E. Gladstone.

Twin Soul Occult term for a psychic affinity. Twin souls are said to incarnate together over many lifetimes.

Typtology *See* **Table turning.**

U.F.O. Unidentified Flying Objects.

Ultra Perceptive Faculty A capacity for obtaining information concerning an object or an individual by the employment of a perceptive faculty other than those of the recognized senses of sight, touch and hearing (R. Connell and G. Cummins). This supposes that a psychic 'imprint' can be left on an article after handling, and often is known erroneously as psychometry.

Unfoldment Term descriptive of the development of personal psychic or spiritual powers.

Unidentified Flying Objects *See* **Flying Saucers.**

Union of Spiritualist Mediums Founded by mediums in London 1956, for the purpose of raising the standard of presentation of mediumship and the status of mediums and public speakers presenting Spiritualist philosophy, as well as the training and encouragement of young workers in the movement. An Advice and Information Bureau is maintained.

221

Unitarian   A member of a Christian sect which believe in the unity of the Divine nature, as opposed to the doctrine of the Trinity.

Universalism   A doctrine that all men will eventually be saved.

Universal Mind   Term used by Spiritualist author J. A. Findlay, to describe mind substance as the result of etheric vibration. It is, he says, the creative power in the universe, and its rapidity of vibration makes it plastic. This plasticity of mind leads to image-forming, what we know as thought. Thus the Universal Mind is ever seeking expression. According to this theory, all matter contains this thinking substance.

Universals   Philosophical term for the essential idea of a thing, as against the thing itself. Based on the *Theory of Ideas* by Plato, which was an elaboration of the Socratic method of getting at the essence of something. Plato believed that knowledge of Universals was really a process of re-learning what was known in a pre-existent state.

Upanishads   The second section of sacred Hindu literature, following the Vedas. It centres around the possibility of esoteric teachings to be gained by sitting close to a teacher. Three principal commentaries are by Bādarāyana, Sankara A.D. 800 and Rāmānya A.D. 1017. The study of Yoga had its origins in these.

U.S.M.   Union of Spiritualist Mediums (q.v.).

Vale-Owen, Rev. George (1869–1931)   Vicar of Orford, Warrington, England. He formed a church, and after twenty years' work there, developed automatic writing; receiving by this means, accounts of life after death and spirit teachings. These scripts attracted the attention of Lord Northcliffe who offered £1,000 for the serial rights. Vale-Owen's refusal of the money convinced Northcliffe of his sincerity and the works were advertised extensively in the press. Vale-Owen had to resign as a result of his church's displeasure. He then became pastor of a Spiritualist congregation, toured the U.S.A. and wrote several books which contain detailed descriptions of the spheres of the spirit world.

Valiantine, George American semi-illiterate direct voice medium, about whose powers there was great controversy. He was tested twice in 1925 before the S.P.R., but they were both blank sittings. Yet members of the S.P.R., including their research officer, Dr Woolley, had very good phenomena at Denis Bradley's house. In the presence of Dr Dingwall and Woolley at a later sitting, voices were heard in daylight from the trumpet. The most outstanding event was the alleged return of Confucius in a sitting with Dr Neville Whymant, an authority on Chinese history and ancient literature, who vouched for the accurate pronunciation and recital of standard works in old Chinese. A gramophone record was made of the voice of 'Confucius' in London 1927.

Vandermeulen Spirit Indicator A spirit operated 'doorbell', consisting of two glass prisms, one resin coated, on a board and connected with a battery. Suspended between the prisms was a light wire. The spirit was supposed to generate electricity in the prisms, thus swinging the wire which closed a contact, giving warning of a spirit's wish to communicate.

Vanishing Objects *See* **Asports.**

'Vates' Control of Rev. Stainton Moses, alleged to have been Daniel the prophet.

Veda The oldest section of Hindu sacred literature, the basis of Brahminical faith. The Rig-Veda was the first (1500–1000 B.C.), the later Vedic books including Sama-Veda (sacrificial hymns) Atharva-Veda (charms and incantations), Yajur-Veda (liturgical), followed by the Upanishads.

Vedanta   Hindu philosophy, based on the Vedas.

Vegan   A strict vegetarian who renounces all meat consumption, including animal products (butter, cheese, etc.).

Vegetarianism   The renunciation of flesh-eating for various reasons. One section asserts that meat-eating forms toxins and poisons the body. Ethical objections are raised on the grounds that animals are in the same evolutionary scale as man, and possess a soul. The possibility of cruelty in the killing of animals is another argument used. Some Spiritualists are vegetarians as the result of personal communications, stressing the possibility of a coarsening of the psychical sensibilities as a result of eating meat. There appears to be no body of evidence for this last assertion. Extremists who renounce animal products as well, such as milk, eggs, etc., are termed Vegans.

Ventriloquism   Speech produced without lip movement, has been offered as an explanation of direct voice phenomena, but it has been proved that a ventriloquist can only produce his illusion in daylight, by visual distraction.

Veridical   Possessing the quality of truth (F. W. H. Myers).

Vesme, Count Cesar Baudi De   Noted Italian psychic researcher, and author, born in Turin 1862. He investigated Paladino, Tomczyk, Eva C., and others. He also experimented with prophecy and games of chance. His *History of Experimental Spiritualism* was laureated by the French Academy of Science.

Vibration   A regularly recurring unit of frequency in a given time. A misleading word frequently used by Spiritualists to denote a phase of mental attunement. To reduce the spirit world to time and space concepts, is to make it of the same order of existence as the physical world; different only in degree and still operating in time and space. Yet the spirit people tell us constantly 'we have *no limitations* of time and space'. Therefore their world is of a different order. As we are spirits now, we already know of this non time-space order—the world of ideas. Spirit beings, to contact our environment do not have to do anything mysterious physically, like 'lowering their vibrations', they contact us *as spirit*—'behind' our sense impressions of space and time. The physical order of existence is perhaps erroneous: a part view only of reality, maybe a limitation imposed upon us for our instruction and development.

Vishnu Hindu deity, one of the trinity (with Brahma and Shiva). 'The Preserver', a beneficent god, said to have had a number of subhuman and human incarnations or 'avatars'. Incarnated as Krishna, the charioteer, he is the divine-human spokesman of the Bhagavadgita. Many worthy people of recent times have been considered incarnations of Vishnu by the Hindus.

Vision, Clairvoyant *See* **Clairvoyance.**

Vision, Crystal *See* **Crystal-gazing.**

Vision, Induced *See* **Double.**

Vision, Spontaneous *See* **Apparitions.**

Vision, Telescopic *See* **Telescopic vision.**

Vision May be divided into two classes, objective—perception of material objects in accordance with optical laws, from a definite point in space, and subjective—independent of space, objective existence and optical laws. Clairvoyance or etheric vision should be classed in the latter, although it may yet prove to be 'objective' in a different order of existence.

H

Visionary Existing only in imagination. A person given to daydreaming.

Visitants Spirit communicators. Apparitions.

Vital Body The double or etheric body.

Vital Force *See* **Emanations, Psychic force.**

Vitalism Theories of life, ascribing its phenomena to other than merely physical principles. Non-materialism.

Voice Control Machines Invented by Dr Mark Richardson of Boston, and used for the investigation of the Margery mediumship (Mrs Crandon), to test whether direct voice phenomena was independent of the medium's breathing. The medium had to maintain a column of liquid in a U tube, by blowing through a flexible pipe during the voice production. The height of the liquid was indicated by luminous floats. This experiment was completely successful in proving the independence of 'Walter's' voice. Another invention by B. K. Thorogood, consisted of a microphone completely enclosed in a soundproof box, the wires connected to a loud-speaker in another room. Under this test too 'Walter' was heard distinctly, thus proving the separate existence of the voice.

Voice, The Abbreviated expression for 'the direct voice phenomena'.

Voicebox An instrument fashioned by the spirit operators from ectoplasm, for the purpose of producing the sound of a human voice. It is similar in construction to the human mouth, tongue and larynx, sometimes with a tube leading to the medium's ear or nose. It has often been photographed, and appears as a mass of white substance lying usually on the medium's shoulder. Sometimes it is built inside the trumpet.

Voices, Subjective   *See* **Clairaudience.**

Voices, Supernormal   The direct and independent voice, also voices from materialized forms. Voices heard only by oneself, would be clairaudience.

Vollhardt, Frau Rudolff Maria   German physical medium who produced levitations, apports, stigmata and matter through matter phenomena. She was observed and reported by Dr F. Schwab of Berlin in 1923. Professor Albert Moll accused the medium of fraud, Frau Vollhardt instituted libel proceedings and offered to demonstrate her powers in court. They found Professor Moll guilty of calumny, but acquitted him.

Volometer   An instrument designed by Dr Sydney Alruta of Upsala University, to measure will-power as dynamic energy. It consisted of a board balanced on knife edges affecting a letter balance when one end was depressed. By concerted will, in some cases 40–100 grammes of pressure were registered. These results were vouched for by Professor Flournoy in 1909.

Walker, Miss Nea, B.A.   Secretary for psychical research to Sir Oliver Lodge. Member of the S.P.R. and well-known author on Research.

Walker, William   English spirit photographer of W. T. Stead's Crewe circle. The first man to obtain psychic extras in colour. He received an extra of Stead and a message in his handwriting in the Crewe circle on 6 May 1912, twenty-two days after Stead's dramatic passing in the *Titanic* disaster.

Wallace, Dr Abraham, M.D.   Noted obstetrician. Decided to investigate the phenomena of Spiritualism soon after Sir William Crookes had started his researches. He became convinced of the genuineness of the claims made and from then on, was an ardent supporter of the Spiritualist cause, writing many valuable books on the subject.

Wallace, Dr Alfred Russell (1832–1903)   The famous Naturalist and co-discoverer with Darwin of the principles of evolution, also was a member of the Dialectical Society in 1869. A pronounced materialist before his acquaintance with Spiritualism. Later, concerning its phenomena he said, 'They are proved quite as well as any facts are proved in other sciences.' Among the mediums he tested were: Mrs Marshall, Mrs Guppy, Miss Nicholl, Katie Cook, Haxby, Monck, Eglinton, Slade, Keeler, Fred Evans, Mrs Ross.

Wallis, E. W. (1848–1914)   Outstanding British trance medium, healer, lecturer and author. A great propagandist for Spiritualism. Founder and editor of psychic newspaper *Two Worlds* until 1899, then was editor of *Light*. His wife was also a well-known trance medium, and together they wrote some excellent books on mediumship.

'Walter'   Walter Stinson, the famous control of the Margery mediumship (Mrs Crandon). He was a deceased brother of the medium who had died in a railway accident at the age of twenty-eight. With his medium he was responsible for some of the best attested physical phenomena ever produced. Was also active in Dr Glen Hamilton's circle at Winnipeg.

Water Divining   *See* **Dowsing.**

Water Sprinkling   A phenomena fairly common in physical circles. Small drops of water or perfume are often sprinkled on the sitters, walls and furniture. It has also been noticed in connexion with poltergeist phenomena.

Watseka Wonder, The   The possession of Lurancy Vennum, nineteen years old, in 1865, cured by the spirit of Mary Roff who drove out the obsessing entity and occupied its place herself for a continuous period of sixteen weeks. The girl lived with the Roff family throughout this time, displaying perfect familiarity with all the details of the home life. The story was originally published by Dr E. W. Stevens, afterwards checked by Dr Hodgson of the A.S.P.R. who considered it a correct narrative. It was also verified by Col. J. Bundy, editor of the *Religio-Philosophical Journal* of Chicago.

Wax Moulds   *See* **Moulds.**

Webber, Jack   Powerful Welsh physical medium for apports, direct voice, levitations. He developed his amazing powers in the home circle of the now famous spirit healer, Harry Edwards. Many infra-red photographs were taken of his phenomena in all stages of production, including the supernormal removal of a sewn-up jacket and its replacement without removal of bonds.

Wesley, The Rev. Samuel   *See* **Epworth phenomena.**

White Brotherhood, The Great   Believed by occultists to be the true seat of inner world government by a hierarchy of Masters or Adepts. Not a part of Spiritualist philosophy.

Wheel of Life   Traditional pictorial representation of the eastern doctrine of reincarnation. The wheel symbolizes immortality; the three hub excrescences—ignorance, lust, anger. The six spokes—gods, demi-gods, tortured souls, human beings and animals.

White Spirit, The Great   A spirit's name for Deity.

Whymant, Dr Neville   Expert on ancient China who became convinced that he had heard Confucius speak, through the direct voice mediumship of Valiantine (q.v.).

Wickland, Dr Carl Conducted the Psychopathic Institute of Chicago for the treatment of mental patients. Through the mediumship of his wife he was able, over a period of thirty years, to effect many cures by ridding patients of obsessing spirits. He travelled to California and founded the National Psychological Institute for treatment of obsession. He stated in his book *Thirty years among the dead*, that the spirit of Mme Blavatsky returned and retracted the reincarnation theory.

Will Power Many instruments have been invented in attempts to prove that the human will is capable of exerting dynamic energy (notably Sir William Crookes and Dr Alrutz). Tests with physical mediums tend to demonstrate that all such experiments can be explained by ectoplasmic protrusions from the mediums. Eusapia Paladino could easily move light objects by the exercise of her will. Similar powers were possessed by Mme Tomczyk (q.v., *see also* **Volometer**).

Winds, Psychic *See* **Breezes**.

Wingfield, Miss Kate Died 1927 English non-professional trance and physical medium, childhood friend of Mrs St Clair Stobart, known as 'Miss A.' of Myer's writings and Miss Rawson in Piddington's report in *S.P.R. Proceedings*. Sir Lawrence Jones the S.P.R. President in 1928 had a series of sittings with this medium 1900–1 and observed telekinesis, apports and trance phenomena. This latter convinced him of survival. Her home circle was primarily concerned with rescue work. By automatism she wrote two books of Spiritualist teachings.

Witchcraft It has been estimated that there are about 400 practising witches in England. They claim to follow a nature religion which antedates Christianity. Local groups are called 'covens' and consist of thirteen witches, including a high priestess and six mixed couples. Supernormal powers of healing and thought influence are claimed by the employment of special techniques and ritual.

Witch Doctors Medicine men of primitive tribes who maintained law and order by detecting witches and exorcizing evil spirits.

Wraith An apparition; the etheric double.

Worship In Spiritualism is not abasement of the self, but a realization of man's oneness with the Divine power of the universe. The element of fear, so noticeable in older forms of worship, is completely absent in modern Spiritualist services.

Wriedt, Mrs Etta American direct voice medium of Detroit, did not use a cabinet or go into trance; she even joined in the general conversation during the production of phenomena. Many kinds of languages unknown to the medium were spoken. She visited England five times; 1911–12–13–15–17, and sat many times for W. T. Stead at 'Julia's Bureau' with Admiral Moore. Telekinesis, materialization, apports and luminous phenomena were also produced. The famous control John King manifested through her. Sir W. Barratt believed he contacted Professor Sidgwick through her mediumship.

Wyllie, Edward (1848–1911) Californian spirit photographer, originally a professional photographer, but the repeated spots and lights on his pictures threatened to ruin his business. The Pasadena Society for Psychical Research investigated him in 1900 and accepted the phenomena as genuine, offering a sum to anyone who could duplicate his results under the same conditions. James Coates invited him to England and thoroughly tested Wyllie, to his satisfaction that the pictures produced were genuine.

Xenoglossy   The phenomena of speaking in tongues unknown to the medium. It cannot be accounted for by subconscious memory unless it has actually been heard before. Instances in the scriptures could be quoted. One of the best in modern times was that of the 'Rosemary mediumship' in 1933, when ancient Egyptian was spoken by 'Lady Nona' an entity contemporary with the building of the Temple of Luxor. Mr Howard Hulme was the translator. (*See also* **Valiantine, Marquis Carlo Scotto, Mrs Conant.**)

X-Ray Vision   Some healers have claimed this power, which enables them to see the affected organs within the body. Some sensitives have also possessed this faculty, by which means sealed messages have been read by them.

Yama   The first grade of Yoga consisting of ten rules: non-injury, truthfulness, non-stealing, continence, forgiveness, endurance, compassion, sincerity, sparing diet, cleanliness.

Yesod   Kabbalistic idea of an archetypal world, somewhat akin to the astral sphere.

Yhva   Jehovah, the early tribal god and special protector of the Jews in the Old Testament.

Yi-king   A pre-Confucian writing in ideograms, with a commentary attributed to Confucius 1200 B.C. May have been used for divination purposes, as it contains astrological references.

Yin and Yang   Ancient Chinese cosmic principles of duality, the interplay of which was held to form the background of human experience. Interpretation of any possible Yin-Yang experience is worked out by a divination technique known as the 'I Ching' (q.v.).

Yoga Ancient Hindu system of self-discipline and psychic training (first defined in the Gita, Chap. VI, 10–19), with the object of uniting the Lower with the Higher Self and thus attaining freedom from the otherwise inexorable round of rebirth and Karma. Considerable mastery over the sub-conscious activity and direction over the physical body and its organs can be achieved, and strong psychic powers developed, although these, it is stressed, should not be sought for the sake of power. Many modified systems of Yoga are now popular in the West, using it primarily as a system of physical culture; an objective for which Yoga was never intended.

Yogin One who practises Yoga (q.v.). Loosely applied term for any ascetic. Originally confined to men only.

'Yolande' Control of Mme d'Esperance.

Yomi Japanese term for the spirit world.

Zancig, Mr and Mrs Julius (1857–1929) A couple who performed a professional thought-reading act. They were tested by the S.P.R. in 1907. Although the Zancigs claimed telepathic means, Harry Price professed knowledge of a code they had perfected for their stage work, a view supported by Will Goldston the professional illusionist.

Zarathustra The original Persian prophet of Zoroastrianism, who supplanted an earlier nature religion of Iran, by a spiritual monotheistic conception. It was recognized in 520 B.C. by Darius, but later in 400 B.C. was perverted by Artaxerxes to polytheism. The sacred genuine writings of Zarathustra consist of five Gathas, or songs in early Persian from the Zendavesta. He resembled Moses or Mohammed as a leader, recalling his people to a purer faith. There was no forgiveness for wickedness, but there was belief in a future life and the coming of a saviour. Followers in Bombay are called Parsis. Present-day

Zoroastrianism inclines to dualism—the conflict of good with evil forces.

Zen A sect of Mahayana Buddhism, based on a system introduced in Japan from China by Bodhi-dharma, who taught a technique of meditation on paradoxes (koans). It lays great emphasis upon the doctrine of inaction or 'bending before the storm'. It lies at the basis of the well-known system of self-defence known as Jiu-jitsu.

Zener Cards Used for experiments in telepathy. A pack of twenty-five cards comprising five sets of five diagrams (circle, plus sign, rectangle, star, wavy lines), used by Professor J. B. Rhine and others in Extra Sensory Perception experiments in card-guessing. Later, packs were used which contained random distributions of the five symbols, which simplified statistical evaluation of displacement phenomena.

Zendavesta The sacred writings of the Zorastrians (q.v.).

Zeus The name of God, as accepted by the Stoics (q.v.). Also a supreme deity corresponding to Jupiter of Greek myth.

Zodiac, Sidereal Those particular constellations which lie along the sun's path through the sky (ecliptic).

Zodiac, Tropical The ecliptic (sun's path) extended laterally to seven or eight degrees and divided from the vernal equinox point into twelve equal segments (signs) named after, but not now coincident with the constellations of the same names.

Zohar The oldest known treatise on Hebrew mysticism, the foundation of the Kabbala and the Old Testament.

Zoether Supposed nervous aura, bearing the same relation to spirit that gravitation does to matter.

Zollner, Professor J. C. F. (1834–1882) Professor of physics and astronomy at Leipzig University. Famous for his investigation of the phenomena of Henry Slade, favourable reports which subjected him to the scorn and ridicule of his scientific colleagues. He also tested Mme d'Esperance and Eglinton. Charges of unsound mind were made against him by the Seybert Commission, but were not substantiated. To the moment of his sudden passing, he held his University Chair. Zöllner held a special theory involving the fourth dimension, to explain psychic phenomena as normal happening.

Zombie Haiti term for a corpse, said to be re-animated by black magic.

Zoroaster Latinized form of Zarathustra. 'Zoroaster the Magian' was a fictitious character. The Magian referred to by Herodotus, Strabo, Plato and Plutarch, were not truly followers of the prophet, but clung to older nature religions.

Zuccarini, Amedee Italian medium who was photographed in mid-air during levitations. This phenomena was subjected to detailed study by Dr L. Patrizi, Professor of physiology at the University of Modena and Professor Creste Murani of the Milan Polytechnic.

Zügun, Eleonore Born 1914 A Rumanian peasant, subject to poltergeist persecution and stigmatic phenomena. Harry Price met her in Vienna, pronounced the phenomena as genuine, and invited her to the National Laboratory of Psychical Research in London, which body published a report in *Proceedings* 1927–29. Evidence of telekinesis of coins was also established. She lost her powers at the end of her fourteenth year.

Zwaan Ray An electrical instrument using radio parts and energized from the mains supply, said to assist in development of mediums. Its claims are not generally accepted.

READING GUIDE AND BIBLIOGRAPHY

NOTE: As many of these books will be sought in libraries, for convenience, the authors' names have here been listed in alphabetical order for each category, with the exception of the medium's biography list, which is indexed under the medium's surname.

The books have been divided into four main groups:

> Systems of Belief
> History
> Psychic Phenomena
> Products of Psychic Phenomena

These groups form headings, under which will be found suitable categories, enabling books on any branch of the subject to be quickly noted. The following is a brief selection only, and does not in any sense claim to be exhaustive or final. Omission of any work does not imply inferiority.

SYSTEMS OF BELIEF

GENERAL SURVEY OF SPIRITUALISM

Barbanell, Maurice: *This is Spiritualism* (1959)
Boddington, Harry: *The University of Spiritualism*
Carrington, Hereward: *The Story of Psychic Science* (1931)
Collins, C. Abdy: *Death is not the End* (1946)
Dixon-Smith, Lt. Col.: *New Light on Survival*
Doyle, Sir Arthur Conan: *History of Spiritualism* (1926)
Dowding, Lord: *Many Mansions*

Bibliography

Findlay, J. Arthur: *On the Edge of the Etheric*
                       Rock of Truth
                       The Unfolding Universe
Fodor, Dr Nandor: *Encyclopaedia of Psychic Science* (1935)
Hunt, Ernest: *Spiritualism for the Enquirer*
Leaf, Horace: *What Spiritualism Is* (1957)
              Death Cannot Kill (1958)
Moses, Rev. Stainton: *Spirit Teachings*
White, S. E.: *The Betty Book*

PHILOSOPHY
Bozzano, Ernest: *Animism and Spiritism*
Denis, Leon: *Here and Hereafter*
             Life and Destiny
Dunne, J. W.: *Nothing Dies*
Holms, A. Campbell: *Facts of Psychic Science and Philosophy*
Hyde, Lawrence: *I, who am*
Joad, C. E. M.: *Guide to Philosophy*
Lodge, Sir Oliver: *My Philosophy*
                  Phantom Walls
                  Reason and Belief
Murray, Geoffrey: *Matters of Life and Death*
Shook, Professor Glenn: *Mysticism, Science and Revelation*
Tomlin, E. W. F.: *Great Philosophers of the East* (1952)
              Great Philosophers of the West (1950)
Thompson, Ernest: *Spiritualism in the Evolution of Philosophy and Religion*

RELIGION
Bouquet, A. C.: *Comparative Religion*
Budge, D. (Transl.): *Egyptian Book of the Dead*
Findlay, J. Arthur: *The Psychic Stream*
Hill, J. Arthur: *From Agnosticism to Belief*
Isherwood, C.: *Vedanta for the Western World*
Lodge, Sir Oliver: *The Substance of Faith*

238

May, Rev. George: *Radio Broadcasts*
Schonfield, Dr Hugh: *The Authentic New Testament*

REINCARNATION
Desmond, Shaw: *Reincarnation for Everyman*
Evans, W. H.: *Reincarnation*
Geley, Dr Gustave: *Reincarnation*
Weatherhead, Leslie D.: *The Case for Reincarnation*

OCCULT SCIENCES
Anthroposophy
Shephard, A. P.: *Scientist of the Invisible*
Steiner, R.: *An Outline of Occult Science*

Astrology
Hone, M. E.: *Modern Textbook of Astrology* (1950)
Rodgers, J.: *The Art of Astrology* (1960)

Atlantis
Bellamy, H. S.: *Atlantis Myth*

Fourth Dimension
Gurdjieff, G. I.: *All and Everything*
Ouspensky, P. O.: *In Search of the Miraculous*
                 Tertium Organum
                 Fourth Dimension (1909)
                 New Model of the Universe
Walker, Kenneth: *A Study of Gurdjieff's Teachings*

Huna
Long, Max Freedom: *Recovering the Ancient Magic*

Numerology
Matthews, S. L. Macgregor: *The Kabbalah Unveiled*

Pyramidology
Spencer Lewis: *Symbolic Prophecies of the Great Pyramid*

Rosicrucianism
A.M.O.R.C.: *Rosicrucian Manual*
Heindel, Mac: *Rosicrucian Cosmo-Conception*

Subud
Rofé Husein: *The Path of Subud*

Theosophy
Blavatsky, H. P.: *The Secret Doctrine*

Yoga
Coster, G.: *Yoga and Western Psychology* (1934)

HISTORY

PSYCHICAL RESEARCH GENERAL
Brath, Stanley de: *The Physical Phenomena of Spiritualism*
Carrington, Hereward: *The Invisible World*
Crookes, Sir William: *Researches into the Phenomena of Spiritualism*
Dreisch, Dr Hans: *Psychical Research*
Hyslop, Dr James: *Psychical Research and Survival Science and the Future Life*
Johnson, Dr Raynor C.: *The Imprisoned Splendour*
Lodge, Sir Oliver: *The Reality of a Spiritual World Raymond Phantom Walls*
Richet, Professor C.: *30 Years of Psychical Research*
Vesme, Count Cesar B. de: *A History of Experimental Spiritualism*
Wallace, Dr. A. Russell: *On Miracles and Modern Spiritualism*

Also publications of the various Societies for Psychical Research, as *Proceedings*, *Journals*, and *Bulletins*.

MEDIUMS, THEIR LIVES AND PHENOMENA

Bailey, Lilian, O.B.E.: *Death is her Life*, W. F. Neech

Bangs Sisters: *Annals of Psychic Science* (July–September 1910), H. Carrington

Beraud, Martha: *see* Eva C.

Bessinet, Ada: *Glimpses of the Next State*, Admiral Moore

Blake, Mrs Elizabeth: *Proc. A.S.P.R.*, Vol. 7, Professor Hyslop

Blavatsky, Mme H. P.: *Proc. S.P.R.* Vol. 3, 1885, Dr Hodgson
Old Diary Leaves, Col H. S. Olcott, 1895
Mme Blavatsky, John Symonds, 1959

Britten, Emily Hardinge: *Biography*, Margaret Wilkinson

Cayce, Edgar: *Many Mansions*, Dr Gina Cerminara

Chenoweth, Mrs: *see* Soule

Collen-Smith: *Miracle Healing*, L. Mayhew

Compton, Elizabeth: *People from the other World*, Col. H. S. Olcott

Cook, Florence: *Reports*, Sir William Crookes, 1874

Cooper, Mrs Blanche: *Proc. S.P.R.* Vol. 35, 1921–22, Dr S. G. Soal

Crandon, Margery: *Margery the Medium*, Malcolm Bird

Curran, Mrs John H.: *The Case of Patience Worth*, Dr W. Franklin Prince

Davenport brothers: *Biography of the Brothers Davenport*, T. L. Nichols, 1864

Davis, A. J.: *The Magic Staff*, Autob. Twelve Lectures of the Harmonial Philosophy of A.J.D., W. H. Evans, 1925

Deane, Mrs Ada E.: *Journal A.S.P.R.* May 1925, Dr H. Carrington

Dowden, Hester: *Far Horizon*, Edmund Bentley, 1951

Eddy Brothers: *Modern Spiritualism*, Frank Podmore

Edwards, Harry: *Born to Heal*, Paul Miller, 1948

Eglinton, William: *Twixt Two Worlds*, John S. Farmer

d'Esperance, Mme E.: *Shadow Land*, Autob.
Angelic Revelations, William Oxley

Eva C. (Martha Beraud): *30 Years of Psychical Research*, Professor C. Richet

Fox, Kate and Margaret: *The Missing Link*, Leah Fox, 1885
Footfalls on the Boundary of Another World, R. Dale Owen, Autob.

Garrett, Eileen J.: *My Life as a Search for the meaning of Mediumship*, Autob.

Goligher, Kathleen: *Psychic Structures*, Dr W. J. Crawford

Guppy, Mrs.: *Experiences in Spiritualism*, Catherine Berry

Haxby: *My Life*, Dr Abraham Russell Wallace

Home, Daniel Douglas: *D. D. Home, His Life and Mission*, Mme Home
The Gift of D. D. Home, Mme Home
Experiments in Spiritualism with D. D. Home, Lord Adare

Hope, William: *The Case for Spirit Photography*, Sir A. Conan Doyle

Husk, Cecil: *Glimpses of the Next State*, Admiral Moore
Ghosts I Have Seen, Mrs V. Tweedale
Psychic Force, Gambier Bolton

Indridason, Indride: *Light, Oct.–Nov. 1919*, H. Nielsson
Journal, A.S.P.R., 1924, Professor Gudmundar Hanneson

Ingeborg, Mrs: *We are Here*, Judge Dahl, 1931
Psychic Science, April 1931, Dr T. Wereide

Judd, Pearl: *The Blue Room*, Clive Chapman, 1927

Kahn, Ludwig: *Journal S.P.R.*, Vol. 23, Dr E. J. Dingwall, 1926

Kluski, Franek: *Wspomnienie Z. Seansow Z.*, Col Norbert Ocholowitz, 1926

Leonard, Gladys Osborne: *My Life in Two Worlds*, Autob.

'Margery': *see* Crandon

Marshall, Mrs Mary: *Outlines of 10 years investigation into the Phenomena of Modern Spiritualism*, P. Barkas, 1862

Miller, C. V.: *Occult Experiences*, Willie Reichel
    Annales des Sciences Psychique, Sept., Oct. 1908,
    Cesar de Vesme

Mirabelli, Carlo: *Psychic Research*, Nov. 1930—Professor
    Hans Dreisch
    Psychic Research, July 1930—Dr E. J.
    Dingwall

Morris, Mrs Meurig: *Past Years*, Sir Oliver Lodge

Morse, J. J.: *What am I?* Serjeant Cox

Moses, Rev. Stainton: *The Controls of Stainton Moses*, A. W.
    Trethewy
    Proceedings S.P.R., Vols. 9 and 11,
    F. W. H. Myers

Neumann, Therese: *Therese Neumann*, Dr Fritz Gerrlich
    Impression des Stigmates, Rev. Frederic
    V. Lamah

Nielsen, Einar: *Physicalische Phenomene des Mediumismus*,
    Baron Schrenck-Notzing
    Solid Proofs of Survival, Autob.

Ossowiecki, Stephan: *From Unconscious to the Conscious*, Dr
    Geley

Paladino, Eusapia: *Eusapia Paladino and her Phenomena*, Dr
    Hereward Carrington
    l'Exteriorisation de la Motricité, Albert des
    Rochas
    After Death, What? Cesar Lombroso
    Mysterious Psychic Forces, Camille Flam-
    marion
    Psicologia e Spiritismo, Professor Morselli,
    1908

Pansini Brothers: *After Death, What?* Cesar Lombroso
    Hypnotism and Spiritualism, Lapponi

Piper, Mrs Leonore E.: *The Life and Work of Mrs Piper*, Alta
    L. Piper
    Mrs Piper and the S.P.R., M. Sage

Both Sides of the Veil, Anna Manning Roberts

Pruden, Mrs Laura: *Journal A.S.P.R.*, 1926–7

Richmond, Mrs Cora V. (Cora Scott-Tappan):
Life and Work of Cora Richmond, H. B. Barrett
My Experiments Out of the Body, Autob.

Roberts, Estelle: *The Trumpet Shall Sound*, M. Barbanell
40 Years a Medium, Autob.

Rosemary mediumship: *This Egyptian Miracle*, F. H. Woods
Ancient Egypt Speaks, F. H. Woods and Hulme

Shermann, Raphael: *Psycho-graphology*, Baggar, 1924

Schneider, Rudi and Willy: *Rudi Schneider*, Harry Price
Les Pouvoirs inconnus de l'esprit sur le Matiere, Osty

Shepard, Jesse: *The Valley of Shadows*, Francis Grierson
Modern Mysticism, Francis Grierson (Autob.)

Silbert, Frau Maria: *Psychic Science*, Jan. 1931, Dr Paul Sunner

Sloan, John C.: *On the Edge of the Etheric*, A. J. Findlay
Looking Back, A. J. Findlay

Smead, Mrs: *Spiritism and Psychology*, Professor Flournoy

Smith, Mlle Helen: *From India to the planet Mars*, Flournoy, 1899
Planete Mars en Terre Sainte, Professor W. Deonna, 1932

Soule, Mrs M. M. (Mrs Chenoweth): *Leonards and Soule Experiments in Psychical Research*, Dr W. F. Prince, 1929

Stead, W. T.: *Stead, the Man*, Edith K. Harper
Has W. T. Stead Returned? James Coates

Stella C. (Mrs Leslie Deacon): *Paper to 3rd International Congress for Psychical Research*, Paris, Harry Price

Stobart, Mrs A. St Clair: *Miracles and Adventures*, Autob.

Thompson, Mrs R.: *Proceedings S.P.R.*, Vol. 17, 1901–03
Tomczyk, Mlle Stanislawa: *30 Years of Psychical Research*, Professor C. Richet
Physikalische Phenomene des Mediumismus, Schrenck-Notzing, 1920
Travers-Smith, Mrs: *see* Dowden
Tuttle, Hudson: *Arcana of Spiritualism*, Hudson Tuttle
Vale Owen: *Life Beyond the Veil*, Vale Owen (5 Vols.)
Valiantine, George: *Towards the Stars*, Dennis Bradley
Vollhardt, Frau Maria: *Teleplasm and Telekinesis*, Dr F. Schwab, 1923
Webber, Jack: *The Mediumship of Jack Webber*, Harry Edwards
Wyllie, Edward: *Photographing the Invisible*, James Coates
Zuccarini, Amedee: *Annales des Sciences Psychiques*, Vol. 17, Dr L. Patrizi and Professor C. Morani
Zügun, Eleonore: *Proceedings, National Laboratory for Psychical Research*, Vol. 1, 1927–9
'Some account of the Poltergeist Phenomena of E. Zügun,' *Journal A.S.P.R.*, Aug. 1926, Harry Price

PSYCHIC PHENOMENA
Healing

SPIRIT HEALING
Barbanell, Maurice: *The Saga of Spirit Healing*
Beard, Rebecca: *Everyman's Search*
Chapman, George: *The Return of Dr Lang*
Edwards, Harry: *Guide to Spirit Healing*
The Evidence for Spirit Healing
Miller, Paul: *Born to Heal*
Roberts, Ursula: *Health, Healing and You*
Salmon, Elsie H.: *New Key to Healing*

Bibliography

Winn, Godfrey: *The Quest for Healing*
Woodard, Dr C.: *A Doctor Heals by Faith*

OCCULT HEALING
Connell and Cummins: *Healing the Mind*
                    Perceptive Healing
Eeman, L.: *Co-operative Healing*
Macmillan, W. J.: *Reluctant Healer*

YOGA HEALING
Johnson, Rev. Youlden: *Healing Fingers*
Ramacharaka, Yogi: *The Science of Psychic Healing*

AUTOMATIC WRITING
Bentley, Edmund: *Far Horizon*
Blake, William: *Jerusalem* (*Poem*)
Cummins, Geraldine: *Scripts of Cleophas*
                   Road to Immortality
                   Beyond Human Personality
Doten, L.: *Poems from the Inner Life*
          Resurrexi
Moses, Rev. Stainton: *Spirit Identity*
Newbrough, Dr J. B.: *Oahspe. Kosmon Bible*
R.M.T.: *Letters from Christopher*
       Letters from Lancelot
Scott, John: *As one Ghost to another*
Tuttle, Hudson: *Arcana of Nature*

CLAIRVOYANCE
Bazett, L. M.: *Beyond the Five Senses*
Leaf, Horace: *What mediumship is*
Leonard, Gladys Osborne: *My Life in Two Worlds*
Peters, Alfred Vout: '*Light*' Oct. 11, 1913
Roberts, Estelle: *Forty Years a Medium*

DOWSING
Beasse, P.: *Dowsing*
Maby and Franklin: *Physics of the Divining Rod* (1939)
Maury, Margaret: *How to Dowse*
Trinder, W. X.: *Dowsing*

OUIJA, TUMBLER AND LETTERS
Bentley, Edmund: *Far Horizon*
Dowden, Hester: *Voices from the Void*
Palmstierna, Erik: *Horizons of Immortality*

PLANCHETTE
Flournoy, Professor: *Spiritism and Psychology*

PSYCHOMETRY
Baggar: *Psycho-graphology* (1924)
Buchanan, Dr J. R.: *Manual of Psychometry*

RADIESTHESIA see Dowsing

SPEAKING IN TONGUES (XENOGLOSSY)
Bozzano, Ernest: *Polyglot Mediumship*
Wood and A. J. H. Hulme: *Ancient Egypt Speaks*
                         This Egyptian Miracle

STIGMATA
Gehrlich, Dr Fritz: *Therese Neumann*
Lamah, Rev. Frederic V.: *Impression des Stigmates*
Price, Harry: *Journal A.S.P.R. 1926*

TRANCE SPEAKING
Curran, Mrs: *Telka (Poem)*
Davis, A. J.: *Nature's Divine Revelation*
Duguid, David: *Hafed, Prince of Persia*
               Hermes, Disciple of Jesus

Harris, Thomas Lake: *Epic of the Starry Heavens*
            Lyric of the Starry Heavens
Richmond, Cora: *Discourses through the Mediumship of
      C. L. V. Tappan*

WATER DIVINING see Dowsing

Physical

APPORTS
Brath, Stanley de: *The Physical Phenomena of Spiritualism*
Dixon-Smith, Lt Col: *New Light on Survival*
Edwards, Harry: *The Mediumship of Jack Webber*
Holms, Campbell: *The Facts of Psychic Science and Philosophy*

ASTRAL PROJECTION
Muldoon and Carrington: *The Projection of the Astral Body*
            The Phenomena of Astral Projection
Richmond, Cora: *My Experiments Out of the Body*
Yram: *Practical Astral Projection*

AURA
Buchanan, Dr J. R.: *Manual of Psychometry*
Kilner, Dr W. J.: *The Human Atmosphere*
Ouseley, S. A. J.: *Science of the Aura*
Roberts, Ursula: *Mystery of the Human Aura*

BREEZES
Crookes, Sir William: *Researches into the Phenomena of
            Spiritualism*

DEMATERIALIZATION
Aksakov: *A Case of Partial Dematerialisation* (1898)
Button, William H.: *Journal A.S.P.R. Aug. Sept. 1932* (*Margery*)
Edwards, Harry: *The Mediumship of Jack Webber*

248

DIRECT VOICE
Barbanell, Maurice: *The Trumpet Shall Sound*

Bradley, Dennis: *Towards the Stars*
Findlay, J. A.: *On the Edge of the Etheric*
                Where Two Worlds Meet

DIRECT WRITING
M.A. Oxon (Stainton Moses): *Psychography* (1882)
Owen, J. J.: *Psychography*

ECTOPLASM
Crawford, Dr W. J.: *Psychic Structures*
                    The Reality of Psychic Phenomena
Geley, Dr Gustave: *Clairvoyance and Materialisation*
                   From the Unconscious to the Conscious

ELONGATION
  Refer to Mediumship of: Florence Cook, Frank Herne,
D. D. Home, J. J. Morse, Eusapia Paladino, R. Thompson.

EMANATIONS
Bienedal, Dr J.: *Zeitschrift für Parapsychologie, Jan. 1930*
Bolton, Gambier: *Psychic Force*
Bue, A.: *Le Magnetisme Curatif*
Reichenbach (Trans. by Gregory): *Researches on Magnetism*
Kilner, Dr W. J.: *The Human Atmosphere*

EXTRAS see Photography

FIRE IMMUNITY
Adare, Lord: *Experiences in Spiritualism with D. D. Home*
Crookes, Sir William: *Proceedings S.P.R. Vol. 6*
Leroy, Oliver: *Les Hommes Salamanders* (1932)

INDEPENDENT VOICE see Direct Voice

LEVITATION
Adare, Lord: *Experiences in Spiritualism with D. D. Home*
Berry, Catherine: *Experiments in Spiritualism*
David-Neill, Alexandra: *With Mystics and Magicians in Tibet*
Edwards, Harry: *The Mediumship of Jack Webber*
Lombroso, Cesar: *After Death, What?*
Sudre, Rene: *Introduction a la Metapsychique*

LIGHTS, PSYCHIC
Adare, Lord: *Experiences in Spiritualism with D. D. Home*
Schrenck-Notzing: *Materialisation Phenomena*

MATERIALIZATION
Bolton, Gambier: *Ghosts in Solid Form*
Bath, Stanley de: *The Physical Phenomena of Spiritualism*
Carrington, Dr H.: *Behind the Scenes with Mediums*
Geley, Dr Gustave: *Clairvoyance and Materialisation*
Phenomena of Materialisation
From the Unconscious to the Conscious
Leaf, Horace: *Materialisations*
Neilsson, Einar: *Solid Proofs of Survival*
Schrenck-Notzing: *Phenomena of Materialisation*

MATTER THROUGH MATTER
Button, William H.: *Journal A.S.P.R. Aug. Sept. 1932 (Margery)*

MOULDS
Refer to mediumship of: A. Blanchard, Margery Crandon, Mme d'Esperance, Kathleen Goligher, Mary M. Hardy, Kluski, Paladino, Frau Silbert, Slade, Valiantine.

PHOTOGRAPHY, SPIRIT
Coates, James: *Photographing the Invisible*
Doyle, Sir A. Conan: *Budgets of the Society for Supernormal Pictures*
The Case for Spirit Photography

Fukurai, T.: *Clairvoyance and Thoughtography*
Lockwood, Professor: *Scientific Analysis of Spirit Photography*

SKOTOGRAPHS (*Scriptographs*)
Henslow, Rev. J. H.: *The Proofs and Truths of Spiritualism*

TELEKINESIS
Carrington, Dr H.: *Eusapia Paladino and her Phenomena*
Schwab, Dr F.: *Teleplasm and Telekinese* (1923)

TRANSFIGURATION
Bradley, Dennis: *The Wisdom of the Gods*
Erwood, Rev. W. J.: '*The National Spiritualist*' Chicago 1931

Spontaneous

ANIMALS, PSYCHIC SENSE OF
Geley, Dr Gustave: *From the Unconscious to the Conscious*

APPARITIONS
Gurney, Myers and Podmore: *Phantasms of the Living*

ASTRAL PROJECTION
Muldoon and Carrington: *The Projection of the Astral Body*

DREAMS
Carrington, Dr H.: *Higher Psychical Development* (Van Edeen
        experiments)
Dunne, J. W.: *An experiment with Time*
Flammarion, Camille: *Death and its Mystery*
Joire, Dr Paul: *Psychical and Supernormal Phenomena*

HAUNTING
Collins, C. Abdy: *The Cheltenham Ghost*
Dingwall, Goldney and Hall: *The Haunting of Borley Rectory*
Price, Harry: *The End of Borley Rectory*

NATURE SPIRITS
Charters, Daphne: *A True Fairy Tale*
Desmond, Shaw: *Tales of the Little Sisters of St Francis*
Gardener, E.: *Fairies*
Hodson, G.: *Fairies at Work and Play*

POLTERGEIST
Carrington and Fodor: *The Story of Poltergeist down the Centuries*

PREMONITION
Bozzano records 260 cases; Flammarion 1,824; S.P.R. 900.

THOUGHT FORMS
David-Neill, Alexandra: *Mystics and Magicians in Tibet*
Gurney, Myers and Podmore: *Phantasms of the Living*
Moberley and Jourdain: *An Adventure*

PRODUCTS OF PSYCHIC PHENOMENA

BODIES
Cummins, Geraldine: *Beyond Human Personality*

CROSS CORRESPONDENCES, BOOK TESTS AND PROXY SITTINGS
Bird, Malcolm: *Margery the Medium*
Glencower, Lady: *The Earthen Vessel*
Hyslop, Professor: *Contacts with the Other World*
Moses, Rev. Stainton: *More Spirit Teachings*
Saltmarsh, H. E.: *Evidence for Personal Survival from cross-correspondence*
Thomas, Rev. Drayton: *Some New Evidence for Human Survival* (1927)
Life beyond Death, with Evidence (1928)
Walker and Richmond: *Through a Stranger's Hands*

EVIDENCE OF SURVIVAL
Baird, A. T.: *A Casebook for Survival*
Dowden, Hester: *Psychic Messages from Oscar Wilde*
Hill, J. Arthur: *From Agnosticism to Belief*
Lodge, Sir Oliver: *Raymond*

EVIDENCE OF ANIMAL SURVIVAL
Barbanell, Sylvia: *When your Animal Dies*
Bradley, Dennis: *Towards the Stars*
Buchner, E. D.: *Immortality of Animals*

GROUP SOUL THEORY
Austin, Paulette: *The Philosophy of White Ray*
Cummins, Geraldine: *Beyond Human Personality*
　　　　　　　　　The Road to Immortality

HISTORICAL DATA
Bond, Bligh: *The Gate of Remembrance*
　　　　　　The Company of Avalon
　　　　　　The Hill of Vision
Cummins, Geraldine: *Scripts of Cleophas*
　　　　　　　　　Paul in Athens
　　　　　　　　　The Great Days of Ephesus
　　　　　　　　　When Nero was Dictator
　　　　　　　　　After Pentecost
　　　　　　　　　The Childhood of Jesus
Levi: *Aquarian Gospel*
Wood, Frederick and A. J. H. Hulme: *This Egyptian Miracle*
　　　　　　　　　　　　　　　Ancient Egypt Speaks

PHILOSOPHY AND TEACHING
Austin: *Teachings of Silver Birch*
Austin, Paulette: *Philosophy of White Ray*
Cummins, Geraldine: *Beyond Human Personality*
　　　　　　　　　The Road to Immortality

253

Bibliography

Kardec, Allan: *Book of the Spirits*
Levi: *Aquarian Gospel*
Moses, Rev. Stainton: *Spirit Teachings*
Newbrough: *Oahspe. Kosmon Bible*
Palmsti erna, Erik: *Horizons of Immortality*
Stead, W. T.: *Letters from Julia*
White, S. E.: *The Betty Book*
　　　　　　Unobstructed Universe
Wingfield, Kate: *Guidance from Beyond*
　　　　　　More Guidance from Beyond

PLANETS

Deonna, Professor W.: *Planete Mars en Terra Sainte* (1932)
Evans, W. H.: *Lectures on Harmonial Philosophy of A. J. Davis*
Flournoy, Professor: *From India to the Planet Mars*
　　　　　　Spiritism and Psychology

REINCARNATION

Cummins, Geraldine: *Beyond Human Personality*
Kardec, Allan: *Book of the Spirits*
Palmstierna, Erik: *Horizons of Immortality*
Wickland, Dr Carl: *30 Years among the Dead*
Wingfield, Kate: *More Guidance from Beyond*

SPIRIT WORLD, DETAILS OF

Barker, Elsa: *Letters from a Living Dead Man*
Borgia: *Life in the World Unseen*
Cummins, Geraldine: *Beyond Human Personality*
　　　　　　The Road to Immortality
Findlay, J. A.: *The Way of Life*
Owen, Rev. G. Vale: *Life Beyond the Veil*
Tuttle, Hudson: *Arcana of Spiritualism*
Wingfield, Kate: *Guidance from Beyond*
Wood, Dr F. H.: *Through the Psychic Door*

THEORIES OF PSYCHIC PHENOMENA

Animal Magnetism
Abrams, A: *New Concepts in Diagnosis and Treatment* (1916)
Binet, A. and Fere: *Animal Magnetism* (1887)
Bozzano, Ernest: *Animism and Spiritism*
Reichenbach, (Trans. Byrne): *Letters on Od and Magnetism*
(1926)

Cryptaesthesia (Sixth Sense)
Richet, Professor: *30 Years of Psychical Research* (1923)

Cryptomnesia (Unconscious memory)
Lombroso, Cesar: *After Death, What?*

E.S.P. see Telepathy

Fourth Dimensional Physics
Dixon-Smith, Lt Col: *New Light on Survival*
Smith, W. Whately: *A Theory of the Mechanism of Survival*
Zöllner, Professor J. C. F.: *Transcendental Physics*

Hypersensitivity
Myers, F. W. H.: *Human Personality*

Hypnotic Regression
Bernstein, Morey: *The Search for Bridy Murphy*

Psychology
Prince, Dr Morton: *The Dissociation of a Personality*

Telepathy and E.S.P.
Crenshaw, James: *Telephone between Two Worlds*
Greenwood, J. A.: *E.S.P. after 60 Years* (1940)
Hettinger, Dr J.: *Exploring the Ultra-perceptive Faculty*
Telepathy and Spiritualism
Heywood, Rosalind: *Telepathy and Allied Phenomena*
Prince, Dr Franklin: *The Sinclair Experiments demonstrating*
Telepathy

Bibliography

Rhine, Professor J. B.: *Extra Sensory Perception*
                      The Reach of the Mind
Sinclair, Upton: *Mental Radio*
Soal, Dr S. G. and F. Bateman: *Modern Experiments in Telepathy*

DEVELOPMENT OF PSYCHIC TECHNIQUES

Hypnotic states
Cannon, Dr A.: *The Science of Hypnotism*
Cuddon, Dr Eric: *Hypnosis, its Meaning and Practice*
Pelt, Dr S. J. van: *Hypnotism and the Power Within*
                  Hypnotism and Waking Hypnosis

MEDIUMSHIP AND DEVELOPMENT CIRCLES
Bull, Dr Titus: *Analysis of Unusual Experiments in Healing, etc.*
Carrington, Dr H.: *Higher Psychic Development*
Carson, Professor H.: *Spirit Messages* (1914)
Edwards, Harry: *Guide to Mediumship*
Leaf, Horace: *Psychology and the development of Mediumship* (1926)
                  What Mediumship Is (1938)
Macgregor and Underhill: *Psychic Faculties and their Development*
Morse, J. J.: *Practical Occultism*
Prince, Dr W. Franklin: *Leonards and Soule Experiments* (1929)
Roberts, Ursula: *Hints on Mediumistic Development*
Wallis, E. W. and M. H.: *Guide to Mediumship*
Zerdin, Noah: *The Modern Home Circle*

YOGA
Day, Harvey: *Study and Practice of Yoga*
Ramacharaka: *14 Lessons in Yoga Philosophy*
Ramayandas, S. D.: *First Steps in Yoga Philosophy*
Wood, Ernest E.: *Practical Yoga*